SACRED CALLING, SECULAR ACCOUNTABILITY

SACRED CALLING, SECULAR ACCOUNTABILITY

Law and Ethics in Complementary and Spiritual Counseling

Ronald K. Bullis, Ph.D., J.D., M.Div., L.P.C.

USA	Publishing Office:	BRUNNER-ROUTLEDGE *A member of the Taylor & Francis Group* 325 Chestnut Street Philadelphia, PA 19106 Tel: (215) 625-8900 Fax: (215) 625-2940
	Distribution Center:	BRUNNER-ROUTLEDGE *A member of the Taylor & Francis Group* 1900 Frost Road, Suite 101 Bristol, PA 19007-1998 Tel: (215) 785-5800 Fax: (215) 785-5515
UK		BRUNNER-ROUTLEDGE *A member of the Taylor & Francis Group* 27 Church Road Hove E. Sussex, BN3 2FA Tel: +44 (0) 1273 207411 Fax: +44 (0) 1273 205612

SACRED CALLING, SECULAR ACCOUNTABILITY: Law and Ethics in Complementary and Spiritual Counseling

1 2 3 4 5 6 7 8 9 0

Printed by Sheridan Books, Ann Arbor, MI, 2001.

A CIP catalog record for this book is available from the British Library.
⊗ The paper in this publication meets the requirements of the ANSI Standard Z39.48-1984 (Permanence of Paper).

Library of Congress Cataloging-in-Publication Data

Bullis, Ronald K.
    Sacred calling, secular accountability : law and ethics in complementary and spiritual counseling / Ronald K. Bullis.
      p. cm.
    Includes bibliographical references and index.
    ISBN 1-58391-061-1 (alk. paper)—ISBN 1-58391-062-X (pbk. : alk. paper)
    1. Pastoral counseling—Law and legislation—United States.   2. Pastoral counseling—Moral and ethical aspects.   3. Counseling—Law and legislation—United States.   4. Counseling—Moral and ethical aspects.   I. Title.

KF4868.C44 B853   2001
342.73′0852—dc21

                                                           00-054516

ISBN 1-58391-061-1 (case)
ISBN 1-58391-062-X (paper)

DEDICATION

This work is dedicated first to my siblings: Mike, Pat, Gary, and Gregory, whose presence in my life becomes even more precious as time passes.

Second, I wish to express my gratitude to my undergraduate school, Hartwick College, in Oneonta, New York, where I learned not just how to think for myself, but how to acquire the intellectual and spiritual tools to do so.

CONTENTS

ACKNOWLEDGEMENTS

This book is both fruit and root. It is the fruit of my earlier works particularly *Spirituality and Social Work Practice* and *Clinical Social Worker Misconduct and the Ethics of Dual Relationships* and *Legal Issues and Religious Counseling*, written with co-author Rev. Cynthia Mazur, Esq. I am also grateful for the legal work of Michael Cohen, the author of *Complementary & Alternative Medicine: Legal Boundaries and Regulatory Perspectives*.

PREFACE

There are three central objectives for this Preface: 1) to state assumptions inherent in this book, 2) to distinguish between key definitions in this book, and 3) to note the purposes of this book.

The definitions compared here include: religion and spirituality; legal and ethical distinctions in the laws pertaining to medical practice and the law pertaining to counselors; distinctions between alternative, complementary, and spiritual counseling; and the differences (and similarities) between law and ethics.

These distinctions make a difference. Law tends to turn on subtle distinctions. For example, as we will see, the constitution protects "religion" not "spirituality." If a person's beliefs are idiosyncratic, without some tradition of belief and practice or without a moral or ethical system, courts may not protect those beliefs from compromise by the state. A counselor should be precise in determining if his or her alternative therapy with clients might or might not be constitutionally protected. Likewise, it is necessary for a counselor to be precise in determining whether or not his or her client's behavior might be similarly protected.

There was a time when many counselors, particularly those working in government agencies, were loath to discuss religion or spirituality with clients for fear of illegally interfering with their beliefs. This book makes clear when and under what circumstances such discussions are within the law and outside the law. The short answer is: Freedom to practice religion does not mean freedom from any discussion of religion.

Another key distinction is between law and ethics. Behavior on the part of a counselor may either be illegal, unethical, or neither. A counselor needs to know whether his or her behavior might offend the ethics committee of their profession, their state licensure requirements, or the civil law. It is ethically and legally hazardous to confuse what will be criminalized, what might give rise to liability and what is deemed unethical by licensing boards. In short, **criminal law** is strictly construed. That is, what is not specifically prohibited, is acceptable. On the other hand, the civil tends to be more fluid. Continual pulse-taking is a must in keeping current with legal trends that impact the counseling professions.

The third purpose is to note the goals of the book as a whole. This purpose is not to strike the fear of law into the heart of counselors. It is, rather, to illustrate the ways in which counselors who use complementary therapies or interventions may face legal challenges—with a view to *prevent* them from arising.

Law and ethics are like the twin-headed, Roman, god Janus. Sometimes they look behind to belatedly address social trends. Sometimes they look ahead to anticipate social movements. The premise of this book is simple: Because counselors are increasingly practicing spiritual or complementary interventions, the law is increasingly examining how counselors use such interventions.

This legal scrutiny is not done because the law and ethics is "picking" on practitioners who use such interventions. It is only true because as the frequency of such interventions rise, so will the frequency of legal issues. It is not a matter of discrimination, just mathematics. The law seeks to protect clients from incompetent or harmful practice and as the numbers of clients increases so will the legal and ethical dilemmas. Thus, the increased use of and popular support for these interventions compel increased awareness of the legal and ethical issues these same interventions generate.

Legal and ethical obligations particular to spiritual and alternative treatments, are embedded in ethical and legal principles (Bullis, 1996; Cohen, 1996, 1998; Sale, 1999). While a few authors are exploring these issues with the medical profession, almost none, if any, have addressed these issues with mental health counselors.

Toward that end, reciting cases and statutes applicable to spiritual and complementary interventions is necessary and useful. However, understanding the legal and ethical *context* of the law is better still. Without understanding the legal authority and **precedence**-value of a case, the ruling may be misinterpreted, misconstrued, and misapplied. Thus, the Preface and first chapter spend valuable time outlining how influential a given case may be or its limitations. As we will see, "all law is equal, but some law is more equal than others."

For starters, twelve key assumptions must be established. Briefly stated, these twelve, organically related assumptions are:

1. *Fear can be useful in preventing a successful lawsuit against a counselor.* The nature and content of this book may cause consternation, even fear, among some counselors and counseling students. Lawsuits *are* scary things. Even the prospect of being sued is scary. The author is sympathetic to this concern; however, there is no way to ease the fear. We are a litigious society and there is no basis to expect any less suits against counselors any time soon. It is a disservice to offer a false sense of security in this regard. Nor is the denial tactic of "It can't happen to me" of any value.

   Fear may propel counselors to more legally aware and sophisticated. Not understanding the legal risks involved in counseling is like playing "Russian roulette" with your career, reputation, and money. Ignorance of the law is only a false sense of security. Knowledge is the first and best defense against lawsuits. Reading books like this, taking classes and seminars, and engaging in continuing education classes are good ways of preventing lawsuits in the first place. Prevention is the best medicine because once a complaint or suit is lodged against a counselor, it is costly (in terms of money, anxiety, and reputation) to defend against even a groundless suit. It may take years just to recover from an unsuccessful suit.

   If a counselor is to fear anything, he or she should fear legal ignorance, misinformation, or half-truth. There are many legal "urban legends" among counselors. A half-truth about the law and liability can be very harmful. Such illusion tends to anesthetize awareness and motivation for prevention.
2. *Buying insurance does not buy vindication.* **Malpractice** insurance pays off the judgment awarded in a lawsuit—up to the limit of coverage. Sometime counselors also purchase insurance to cover the costs of defending the suit. Insurance cannot repay the embarrassment, loss of reputation, lost earnings, and self-respect that is often lost when one is a **defendant** in a lawsuit. It goes without saying that excellent malpractice should always be part of any professional expense, but paying premiums neither ensures against getting sued in the first place or successfully defending against them in the second place.

3. *Using spiritual and complementary interventions is no longer "cutting edge."* For years now, counselors, social workers, psychologists, and psychiatrists have used a variety of client interventions referencing non-material aspects of the human psyche, sometimes referred to as the "soul" or "spirit," and have both studied and utilized interventions related to prayer, prophetic dreams, meditation, and clarifying spiritual and religious values and meaning. Additionally, many counselors have used cross-cultural spiritual interventions as well.

   When a Business Week article (Jackson, 1997) proclaims "Alternative Medicine: Not So Alternative Anymore," the edge is off the blade when it comes to the "cutting edge" of spiritual and alternative interventions. The article recites current research in both usage and in insurance coverage. Current research indicates that nearly 60% of managed care companies will offer some sort of coverage for alternative medical therapies including chiropractic, acupuncture, and massage.

4. *Counselors using spiritual and complementary interventions must now move on to a next phase of maturity: ethics and law.* Now that these kinds of interventions have enjoyed such popular support, it is necessary to address the many legal and ethical issues pressed by such widespread use by clinicians.

5. *What clinicians do not know can hurt them.* It is well settled that law and ethics are significant partners in competent clinical practice. It is equally well settled that new interventions present new ethical and legal concepts and considerations to bear.

6. *What clinicians **think** they know can hurt them worse.* While knowledge of law is necessary for competent clinical practice, the law is often either unknown or misunderstood. Clinicians who *think* they know the law, can endanger themselves and their clients more than those clinicians who know they don't know the law. Such clinicians tend to be wisely cautious. Thus, the first chapter is devoted to explaining major legal concepts which will put the rest of the legal material into a proper context.

7. *There are two distinct ways in which the law impacts counselors who use complementary and spiritual interventions:* 1) those which arise out of the counselor's own practice, and 2) those legal issues which the clients themselves may bring to the sessions. Generally, the first category are legal issues caused when the counselor's own interventions or practice places the client at risk. These risks can arise from either the content or the procedure of the interventions themselves. The first three chapters offer an assortment of lawsuits arising from a wide variety of practice settings, including private practice, prisons, and schools.

   The second category of legal issues arises from issues of a spiritual or religious nature which the client brings. For example, Chapters 6 and 7 discuss religious affiliation or "cult" behavior, ritual abuse, and the "cultural defense" for criminal actions. As the explanation for this defense unfolds, we will see how religious and spiritual attitudes from other countries and cultures impress themselves upon American jurisprudence and upon the continuing jurisprudence of counselors who use spiritual and complementary interventions.

8. *The law provides no separate, discrete category for mental health professionals using spiritual or complementary interventions.* The law influencing such interventions must be culled from a number of different species and categories of law. Thus, while Chapters 2 and 3 discuss the major areas of criminal and civil law, each chapter discusses a wide variety of categories within these types of law. This book refers to this process as "making law by analogy." Additionally, when the law discusses cases involving spirituality, it must often employ a First Amendment freedom of religion analysis.

9. *There is a legal difference between using complementary or spiritual interventions in therapy and in using such interventions as part of a religious or spiritual practice.* Religious

practice, not the practice interventions of counselors, is constitutionally protected. The next chapter will describe how the First Amendment protects religious practices and also describes the limits of that protection. Additionally, the religious world view or cosmology is also described in Chapter 5. Counselors must recognize the difference between using complementary and spiritual interventions for religious purposes and using such interventions strictly as counseling techniques.

10. *Counselors using spiritual and complementary interventions are likely to employ a wide range of "holistic" interventions.* While employing a holistic repertoire of interventions is in some ways laudable, there are legal consequences such as in issues of advertising, licensure, and in some criminal actions. Thus, while a holistic or eclectic approach brings disparate interventions to bear on issues, it can raise important ethical and legal concerns.

11. *The law is a moving target.* The law is constantly changing. Judge Oliver Wendell Holmes once said, "The law should be stable, not stagnant." In order to help the reader understand the law, this book explains both traditional legal principles and current cases. Moreover, this book reasonably extrapolates what the future might hold for clinicians using spiritual or complementary interventions.

It is no secret that many counselors, across every discipline or category of licensure, are using spiritual, alternative, or complementary interventions with their clients. The empirical evidence is clear in that respect. What is unclear are the legal and ethical obligations of counselors who use such techniques. Yet, counselors legally and ethically obligate themselves to conform to new legal doctrines when they use these interventions.

12. *Alternative and spiritual interventions compel new legal and ethical awareness and responses.* As the saying goes, new wine should not be put in old wineskins. The cutting edge is no longer what specific spiritual or alternative interventions are employed. That issue is the province of methodology. The current cutting edge issue is how counselors can best protect their clients, themselves, their employers, and the public when using such interventions. This is the province of law and ethics and is the focus of this book.

In a nutshell, law and ethics seek to outline duties and responsibilities. Law, of course, employs the coercive power of the civil and criminal justice systems. Ethics employs the social controls of morality and social norms. In either case, both law and ethics reflect social, religious, spiritual, and economic policy. Law and ethics are, if not twins, at least siblings.

Thus, each chapter combines insights of case law and statutory law to demonstrate both law and ethics. Each chapter seeks to recognize trends in public policy, embodied in legal and ethical principles, that apply to counseling by spiritual or alternative means.

This chapter, and the remaining chapters of this book, will use "case studies" to illustrate points of law and ethics. The first case study follows.

☐ The Case of the Social Worker using "Treatment by Spiritual Means"

The following law case illustrates the premises of this book. We will revisit this case again in Chapter 3 on "civil liabilities." Social worker Robert Spratt was fired from his counseling job at the Kent County (Michigan) Honor Camp where he conducted therapy sessions for inmates. He was fired because he "admixed religious counseling with psychological counseling." He appealed his termination to the federal district court on the grounds that his dismissal violated the Title VII of the 1964 Civil Rights Act, the "free exercise" clause of the First Amendment, and the equal protection clause. His appeal failed and the court **affirmed** his dismissal (*Spratt v. County of Kent*, 1985).

While working at the Honor Camp, Spratt admitted that he employed a counseling technique he described as "treatment by spiritual means." This treatment intervention included such things as Bible reading, prayer, addressing spiritual issues, and "casting out of demons." Spratt spent the first sessions diagnosing his clients, then presented them with treatment options. Spratt conducted such counseling only if the clients requested his religious counseling.

Spratt had warning that his counseling interventions were causing a stir both with inmates and with his supervisors. One supervisor warned him not to combine his religious counseling with his psychological duties. He was later warned about his "spiritual" counseling methods and he was even transferred between facilities because inmates objected to Spratt "evangelizing" them.

Spratt's dilemma anticipated the issues faced by many counselors today. The bio-psycho-social spiritual model was asserted in my earlier book *Spirituality in Social Work Practice* (Bullis, 1996).

These assertions, however, did not assist Spratt in court. He testified that while his religious faith does not require Bible reading or praying with co-workers and that "treatment by spiritual means" was not the practice of his religion, "but that it was the practice of mental health counseling." Spratt seemed to be saying that his religious interventions were part and parcel to his mental health counseling.

The federal district court in 1985 rejected Spratt's claims and upheld his termination. This case illuminates how courts can limit spiritual counseling practices in public settings. This case puts counselors who use spiritual and alternative interventions on notice that the First Amendment does not offer unlimited protection with such interventions. Limits of First Amendment protections for such counseling practices are discussed in Chapter 1.

☐ The Joy of Defining Terms of Art

How someone frames a question helps determine how it will be answered. In counseling and in psychotherapy, definitions are the heart and soul of the inner work. Definitions are not just "semantics." They are not just hair-splitting or "distinctions without a difference," as the lawyers say. As we shall see often, law and ethics often turns on subtle nuance of language.

Definitions describe and discern among crucial distinctions. For example, the DSM-IV (American Psychiatric Association, 1994) makes distinctions between eleven different personality disorders, eleven different anxiety disorders, and five different gender identity disorders.

Such a distinction is appropriately and necessarily made between "spirituality" and "religion." The necessity arises for two reasons. First, spirituality is the operative term used with alternative or complementary medicine and counseling. Religious healing is one thing and spiritual healing is something else. Religious healing is a kind of healing that this book will discuss, particularly in the legal chapters.

Second, without these distinctions, the two kinds of healings cannot be properly understood. Because religion and spirituality have different purposes, they yield different results based upon different ideologies.

☐ Religion versus Spirituality

"Spirituality" refers to the experience with ultimate reality (Underhill, 1915). This definition is admittedly, and necessarily, general. Spirituality can also be described as life "lived from the inside, not the outside."

"Religion," conversely, refers to organized, expressed systems of belief and rituals of practice. As such, creeds, liturgies, and symbols are some badges of religion. In some respects, religion is the expression of the spiritual life.

Of course, religion and spirituality are connected, even intimately connected. People who are spiritual often express that spirituality through religious means. By the same token, people who attend religious services or adhere to a religious creed often have vital spiritual lives. However, other people might have spiritual lives largely unconnected with religion.

The DSM-IV (American Psychiatric Association, 1994) recognizes this distinction in its sole entry for a "religious-spiritual" diagnosis. In a new and unique diagnosis, the DSM-IV describes in the only condition specifically related to spirituality. V62.89 "Religious or Spiritual Problem" reads:

> This category can be used when the focus of clinical attention is a religious or spiritual problem. Examples include distressing experiences that involve loss or questioning of faith, problems associated with conversion to a new faith, or questioning of spiritual values that may not necessarily be related to an organized church or religious institution.

This diagnosis is very helpful for three reasons: 1) it distinguishes between spirituality and religion, 2) it offers some specific instances of such problem areas, and 3) this diagnosis marks a shift of psychiatric cosmology by allowing for a view of spirituality that is neither infantile or neurotic. This shift in paradigm or "cosmology" is discussed in the following chapters, particularly Chapter 5.

The DSM-IV "religious-spiritual" diagnosis would be even more helpful if it offered, as it does with other diagnoses, data and information on the nature, the causes, and the duration of this diagnosis. This additional information would be helpful to "map the crises." For example, the very murky area of "cults" or "cultic activity" would be enhanced with such information. This book struggles with these issues in Chapter 6.

☐ The Legal Definition of "Religion"

The previous section uses "religion" in the theological sense, not the legal sense. The legal definition of "religion" is not so easy. As usual, different courts can define it somewhat differently. As a matter of law, the threshold for determining whether ideas are "religious" is low. That is, the parameters courts use to define "religion" must be broad. But "broad" does not mean "boundless." The protections of the First Amendment hinge upon defining a set of beliefs as "religion" and not "philosophy," "a way of life," "ideology" or some other term.

For example, in a case we will revisit in Chapter 2 (*U.S. v. Meyers*, 1996), cited federal district's ruling (U.S. v. Meyers, 1995) where the defendant was convicted of marijuana use and **intent** to distribute. During trial and on **appeal,** defendant Meyers raised the issue that his use and distribution of marijuana was protected by his First Amendment freedom of religion. Meyers claimed that his using and distributing of marijuana was prompted by a religious impulse. The court had to determine whether or not Meyers' opinions rose to the level of a religious belief protectable by the First Amendment.

In the process of making its decision, the federal district court considered the following five factors:

1. Ultimate ideas
2. Metaphysical beliefs
3. Moral or ethical system
4. Comprehensiveness of beliefs
5. Accoutrements of religion, including
   a. founder, prophet, or teacher
   b. important writings
   c. gathering places
   d. keepers of knowledge
   e. ceremonies and rituals

These factors are important because they offer a legal analysis of under what circumstances courts will treat a constellation of ideologies and practices as a religion. Once courts determine that ideas and practices are a religion, it will receive constitutional analysis. If it does not, then the analysis will not even begin.

These factors are helpful for two primary sets of counselors. Of course, they are helpful for counselors who use spiritual or alternative interventions. These interventions *may* receive constitutional protection because of the religious or spiritual nature of the intervention.

The second class of counselors who should know the above criteria are school counselors. Schools have been battlegrounds for both religious and spiritual beliefs in recent years. Unfortunately, sometimes they have become live battlefields as well. As school counselors try to maintain student safety, they must also not violate students' religious rights. We will discuss cases of students who wear pentagrams and other spiritual insignia and how schools may view these as gang badges.

☐ Ethical and Legal Analogies Between Medical Practice and Counseling

The following is a description of terms associated with spiritual healing. These terms have been most clearly, specifically, and organizationally defined in the medical profession. However, these definitions are employed here for three significant reasons. The first is that these are the most commonly and universally used definitions to describe the concepts in question. The medical profession's terminology is often used by the counseling professions. The second reason is that these terms are often used by the courts. The law requires clear, precise definitions. It makes all the difference in the world whether one is charged with "manslaughter" or "reckless endangerment" or whether one defends actions under the "establishment clause" or the "freedom clause" of the First Amendment. The law turns upon seeming fine distinctions.

The third reason is that as the medical profession goes, so goes the counseling profession. However, it is often the case that the first suits in professional **negligence** cases (malpractice) arise against medical doctors. Then, often, the "causes of action" and "standard of care" are established. These terms are defined in Chapter 5. The following section describes three seminal terms: *alternative*, *complementary*, and *spiritual counseling*.

Alternative, Complementary, and Spiritual Counseling

Often, the terms "alternative" and "complementary" have been used interchangeably in medicine and counseling. Recently, however, they are used in tandem and distinctively. Alternative counseling refers to interventions and models of treatment that are outside the normal purview; alternative medicine refers to those medical treatments that are unaccepted by the majority of orthodox practitioners (Feasby, 1997). "Holistic" medicine is often associated with alternative or complementary medicine. Holistic refers to the combination of two human elements: the physical and the psychic. Attention to both are deemed necessary for true and lasting health. As we shall see in Chapter 2, holistic health practices assert alternative paradigms as well as alternative interventions.

"Complementary" interventions are those interventions that are used in conjunction with traditionally used interventions. Today, "alternative" medicine is quickly and steadily gaining acceptance, as we will note in the next chapter. In fact, in the near future the term "alternative" medicine may be as anachronistic as the "new" math.

"Spiritual" interventions could be part either of alternative or complementary counseling, or both. By definition, spiritual interventions are also holistic interventions. These interventions address the psychic or spiritual core of our humanity. This book will use the term "complementary." As "alternative" and "spiritual" interventions get less "alternative," the term "complementary" makes more sense.

It is evidence of how far complementary medicine has come, both in popularity and being at least studied (if not accepted) by the medical establishment, that the National Institute of Health (NIH) has developed a Committee on Alternative Medicine (CAM). The NIH has also classified many alternative interventions into categories. Two categories, "Alternative Systems of Medical Practice" and "Mind/Body Control" are of most immediate concern to most counselors.

Following is the NIH Classification of Alternative Medicines, developed by the Advisory Panel to the National Center for Complementary and Alternative Medicine (NCCAM). These are:

Alternative Systems of Medical Practice
- Acupuncture
- Anthroposophically-extended medicine
- Ayurveda
- Community-based health care practices
- Environmental medicine
- Homeopathic medicine
- Latin American rural practices
- Native American practices
- Natural products
- Past life therapy
- Shamanism
- Tibetan medicine
- Traditional Oriental medicine

Mind/Body Control
- Art Therapy
- Biofeedback

- Counseling
- Dance therapy
- Guided imagery
- Humor therapy
- Hypnotherapy
- Meditation
- Music therapy
- Prayer therapy
- Psychotherapy
- Relaxation techniques
- Support groups
- Yoga

With such a broad and inclusive menu, it is clear that many counselors practice at least some interventions that can be considered "alternative" if not spiritual. However, counselors should always be aware of how using new interventions may compel new challenges in either law or ethics.

☐ Law and Ethics

This book addresses both law and ethics. In a perfect world, maybe law, ethics, morality, and justice would all be the same. In our world, they are not. While morality and justice may have high principles and lofty sources, law is the fruit of very human activity— passing statutes and making judicial decisions. In fact, the adage that one should not see either sausage or laws being made is true enough! The specific sources of law will be discussed more fully in Chapter 1.

The legal distinction between ethics and law is pointedly made in *Hester v. Barnett* (1987). In that case a husband and wife (the Hesters) sued their minister with a smorgasbord of causes of action including: spousal alienation of affections, **tortious** interference with contract, defamation, and ministerial malpractice. In declining the ministerial malpractice **cause of action**, the court said, "The tradition that a spiritual advisor does not divulge communications received in that capacity, moreover, even if a tenet of "ministerial ethics" . . . describes a moral, not a legal **duty**. In the absence of a legal duty, a breach of a moral duty does not suffice to invest tort **liability**" (p. 554). The court was loathe to extrapolate a legal duty from moral or ethical expectations. Thus, the court refused to countenance that particular claim.

Ethics, for the purpose of this book, is defined simply as what right and is wrong. Chapter 5 will specifically discuss characteristics and concepts relative to analyzing and interpreting ethical issues.

Five appendices round out the legal/ethical and other supplemental material of this book. Appendix A contains a short course on finding the law; Appendix B is a legal glossary and abbreviation explanation, Appendix C, empirical data on spirituality, counseling and ethics, Appendix D a mediatherapy bibliography, and Appendix E, which is comprised of chapter-by-chapter test questions.

☐ Purposes for this Book

Before speaking about what this book *is* about, let us discuss what this book is *not* about. This book is *not* about assessing the merits of complementary, alternative, or spiritual healing. There are many books and many articles debating this issue. Neither is this book a description of how to use spiritual or alternative interventions. This book has an altogether different focus. It is a book that describes the ethical and legal use of those interventions.

Neither ethics nor the law of professional liability nor regulation require an inquiry into the efficiency of the treatments under question. The reason "why" is simple. Both the law and ethics are, except in certain circumstances, unconcerned with the state of mind of the counselor or the client. The law sanctions behaviors, not thoughts. While intentions are legally relevant, mere intentions, without actions, are private affairs.

An example may help to clarify the difference in sanctioning behaviors as opposed to examining the state of mind. Suppose a counselor did not believe in past life regression, but practiced it with clients because they requested it. The counselor, however, read up on it, maybe even taking seminars on the technique. So the counselor practiced it in a manner causing no harm to his or her clients. Should such a counselor be considered fraudulent? Professional ethical standards and the law concentrate upon the counselor's ability to diagnose; to effectively communicate the risks of treatments; to articulate risks and opportunities of interventions; and to skillfully execute the interventions themselves. By the same token, a counselor need not believe all of Jung's theories in order to practice Jungian interventions without harming clients.

The state of mind or the consciousness of the counselor is described in Chapter 5, but only to the extent that such cosmologies are significant in understanding the nature of complementary or spiritual interventions.

Neither is this book legal counsel. Nothing here should be taken as legal advice. This book addresses potential legal problems, but cannot and does not offer advice for particular legal dilemmas. If particular situations arise, as they say, "get yourself a lawyer!"

What this book *does* address are three purposes and three audiences. The purposes and audiences are connected. First, this book is designed for those counselors who are now using or are intending to use complementary or spiritual interventions in their practices. This book provides the practitioner, or potential practitioner, with the conceptual background necessary to use such interventions legally and ethically.

Chapter 1 provides major legal principles. Without at least a passing knowledge of these principles, the rest of the chapters may be misconstrued. Legal doctrine is the subtext of any legal decision. Knowing a case's *decision* is only half the knowledge required. The other half is to know the legal context of the case. It matters a great deal whether the case was decided by the federal **court of appeals** sitting in Richmond or a Virginia Supreme Court decision also sitting in Richmond. The wise counselor will know the power and reach of any court decision. Chapter 1 also offers a historical overview of some earlier cases where spiritual counselors were prosecuted.

Chapter 2 gets right to the point. It reviews how the criminal law may impact upon spiritual and alternative interventions. Chapter 3 discusses the other principle prong of the legal environment—**civil law**. Civil law is where counselors get sued. Legal and ethical issues arising from licensing and insurance are addressed in Chapter 4. Ethics issues and methods of how they can be understood and addressed are the topics of Chapter 5. Chapter 6 provides insights and guidance with "cults" and religious groups, particularly in the context of school counselors.

Chapter 7 explores two important legal developments, 1) the cross-cultural legal issues surrounding the controversial "cultural defense," and 2) the vicarious liability of counseling education and training schools for the bad acts of their field education students. This book also includes a glossary of legal terms and abbreviations and a note on how readers may find legal materials for themselves.

The second purpose, and audience, for this book is to provide a resource for counselors who do not use such interventions themselves, but who have clients who wish to explore them. Given the extent and intensity of the interest in complementary and spiritual interventions, it is likely that counselors will be asked about such interventions, to suggest a referral to a clinician who uses such interventions, or will be asked by clients to use such interventions with them.

The third audience and purpose of this book is as a guide for school (or other institutional) counselors, counselor supervisors, employers, and school administrators who have interns or field education students deployed. This book offers insights on how spiritual or complementary interventions can give rise to vicarious liability in the case of employers, supervisors, or school and First Amendment issues that arise when students, inmates, or psychiatric residents claim constitutional protections for otherwise contraband material, clothing, badges, or practices. All told, these interventions offer a rich legal and ethical soil.

In whatever scenario, clinicians need to know the ethics, law, and underlying cosmology of spiritual interventions. This knowledge is necessary so that clinicians who do not use such interventions can refer clients to those who can continue with such clients responsibly.

In *Spirituality in Social Work Practice* (Bullis, 1996), the author noted that social workers who practice spiritual interventions are *de facto* theologians. This assertion is even more significant when addressing ethical and legal issues. Theologians discern and analyze the purposes, utility, effectiveness, and efficiency of religious and spiritually oriented techniques as to their spiritual and religious function. It would be wise for counselors to use their clinical and analytical skills to determine similar traits in their clinical functions.

Complementary and spiritual counseling, while certainly not demanding their own idiosyncratic ethics, do constitute challenges to established models of applying ethical and legal principles. Newly applied interventions require newly applied ethics and law.

☐ Conclusion

This Preface has set the stage for a professional discussion of legal issues facing counselors, and counselors using complementary therapies in particular. This book is intended to be a legal prophylactic against lawsuits, criminal actions, and ethical inquiries against counselors. Fear of the law is justified only if you rely upon ignorance, the advice of the unknowing, or legal legend. The legally responsible counselor need only be aware that most counseling actions can have legal consequences and that the cures for fear are good books, good training, and vigilance.

This book might seem dense and hard to digest. In many respects, the law itself is dense and hard to digest. To dilute or to "dumb down" law does a disservice to the law, to counselors, and to clients. The author suggests only to read slowly, carefully, and to use the glossary, case studies, and discussion questions to illuminate the concepts. Finally, the author has sought to illustrate the legal concepts with facts taken directly from law cases. Any value this book might serve, I attribute to the excellent sources cited. Only the mistakes are mine.

PROLOGUE

To rephrase a passage from the Gospels, the law is an apartment building with many rooms. In U.S. **jurisprudence**, the apartment is built by the law, governed by the law, and changes tenants by the force of the law. Counselors, licensure, and disciplinary actions, and school authorities and policy are tenants in this apartment.

The law can be an uneasy landlord, however. The tenants can change the rules, petition for redress or for more heat, fine a noisy neighbor or request to change rooms. But everybody has to have a room and everyone needs to pay the rent.

Jurisprudence and Spiritual or Complementary Interventions

☐ Objectives

1. To explain key concepts in law—jurisdiction, levels of courts, precedence, and *stare decisis,* the differences between the civil and criminal law, and First Amendment protection and limitations.

Without such foundations, reading law cases and decisions cannot be either properly interpreted or applied. This entire chapter introduces the broad outlines of legal issues inherent using complementary therapies.

2. To note the "religious" exemption to state counseling laws.

Did you ever wonder why clergy and other religious professionals can offer counseling without benefit of state licensure? The short answer is the First Amendment. A longer answer enables the counselor to more fully understand the ethical and legal dynamics inherent in such diverse legal matters as what the difference is between a client suing a counselor in civil court and when a district attorney issues an arrest warrant when both offenses stem from the same facts? Or what does it mean to appeal a decision against you? Under what circumstances can spiritual or complementary counselors claim First Amendment rights? When they meditate with a client? When they engage in prayer or discuss religious or spiritual values with a client? Can school counselors be accused of infringing First Amendment rights when they discuss values or morals with a student?

3. To begin to understand how the First Amendment law applies to school counselors.

As government organizations, the law applies to schools differently than it does to private counselors. This chapter acquaints the reader with some legal issues posed by public counselors and complementary and spiritual interventions.

4. To offer a historical context of early legal actions addressing alternative and spiritual counseling.

Specific examples include the criminalization of fortune telling and practicing astrology, as well as negligence (civil) suits for practicing exorcism. This chapter outlines the four primary elements of a malpractice action. Counselors might take offense at these elements of malpractice being applied to them. The fact remains that there is no longer any bright line of distinction between traditional counseling methods and complementary therapies. For example, my own empirical research reveals that some counselors use exorcism in their practice. Counselors who use guided imagery, past-life regression, or the enhancement of psychic, shamanic, telepathic, or prophetic abilities, in fact, might well fall into the criminal sanctions imposed from the more strict statutes. Where one state licensing board may not blink at a counselor using past-life regression or induced trance techniques, another licensing board may raise ethical issues. Prudent counselors have their fingers on the pulse of their state and private licensing boards and are prepared to defend their prudent practices both legally and ethically.

For being a rather litigious society, many know little about the mechanics of law. Misunderstandings abound about the sources and implications of law and legal decisions. Counselors cannot afford such misinformation. This chapter begins with an overview of the sources and key principles of law.

This chapter is extremely important because it outlines crucial legal concepts, without which many may misconstrue the nature and impact of legal decisions. Without such an introduction, the later descriptions of law cases and statutes may be misleading or misunderstood. It is a truism that "what you don't know about the law is bad, but what you *think* you know about the law is worse."

☐ Case Study: The Counselor Without Consent

A hypnotherapist and counselor appealed his conviction on four rape charges (*State v. Speed*, 1998). He was convicted under a statute many states have enacted that specifies a charge of 2nd degree rape when the alleged perpetrator is a health care provider, when the victim is a client, and when the intercourse occurs during an interview or treatment session. The counselor had a statutory right to assert the affirmative defense that the clients consented, with the knowledge that the sex was not therapeutic. These "therapeutic exploitation" statutes are treated with some depth in Chapter 2. Such statutes have been enacted in several states and can be considered a trend in the law about which counselors need take notice and action (Bullis, 1995).

Five former clients testified at the defendant's trial. Three were complaining witnesses. They testified that the defendant suggested sex in the context of therapy, usually in connection with Tantric sex. Tantric sex—a technique of sexual yoga or sexual philosophy—has sometimes been the source of spiritual energy or development, and the source of some law cases (Bullis, 1996). The defendant claimed that he used his office for both Tantric sex and counseling, but that he never mixed the two. He admitted that he had sex with three of his clients in his office and he admitted that he made therapeutic tapes for them. One witness testified that her sexual relations were separate from Tantric exercises and that the defendant never charged the client when they had sexual intercourse. Given this evidence, the appellate court ruled that a reasonable trier of fact (judge or jury) could find him guilty. The counselor lost his appeal and his conviction stood.

This case illustrates points we will discuss later in this chapter. First, this case is a criminal case, not a civil case. The statute under which he was convicted has been noted. So, his penalty, a felony, may well be jail, probation, or at least a hefty fine. In a civil case, the penalty can only be money damages.

Second, while this is a criminal case, the defendant may also be civilly liable and subject to disciplinary action by his state licensing board and/or his professional association. One penalty does not immunize someone from other penalties.

Third, this case was taken on appeal. That means that the counselor, found guilty at the lower, trial court, asked the judges to review his conviction. They agreed but did not retry the case. The appeal just heard lawyers reargue some of the legal points before a panel of judges from a higher court. Had the appellate court ruled in his favor, they may have thrown out his conviction and ordered him a new trial.

Fourth, this case was decided by a court of appeals in the state of Washington. This decision has no effect on other state courts. Federal courts, whose jurisdiction (authority) lies within that state can use it to interpret Washington State law. This case has limited jurisdiction. Thus, it is unwise to think that a counselor practicing in California is bound by this decision. The next sections address principles of law in greater depth.

☐ Sources of Law

How many times has someone asserted, "That's against the law!" or claimed, "That's perfectly legal!"? The proper retort from a professional is, "What is the statute or case?" Further, the more sophisticated questioner will ask, "What is the jurisdiction of the court?"

These are no idle questions. They go directly to the validity of assertions about what the law is and how widely the law applies.

There are principally two sources of law: statutes or case law. Statutes are the ordinances passed by governments. Whether passed by municipalities, states, or the federal government, such rules are the statutes controlling only that level of government. Of course, a statute passed by the Iowa state legislature has little or no effect in New York State. We will discuss more about the concept of **jurisdiction** in the next section.

Regulations, including executive orders, are a form of statute. For example, the state legislature may empower an organ of state government to promulgate the rules for licensing psychologists, social workers, or other counselors. While the full legislature may not have voted upon the specific regulations, they have empowered a department or commission to enact regulations on its behalf. Regulations, thus, have the force of statutes. The Code of Federal Regulations (C.F.R.) is an example of federal law promulgated by, say, the Departments of Energy or Education. State and local governments enact similar law.

Judicial decisions are law by another route. Case law are the legal decisions judges make from the bench. In American jurisprudence, the branch of the government called the judiciary (judges) have the authority to *interpret* statutes and to hold statutes unconstitutional. This is part of the American concept of "checks and balances."

The U.S. Supreme Court has overturned many state and federal laws. By the same token, they have interpreted the constitution and other statutes to, in effect, make law. A prime example of where the U.S. Supreme Court made its own law was in the case of *Loving v. Virginia* (1967). In this case, the Court held that a Virginia Statute, prohibiting blacks and whites from marrying, was unconstitutional. Upon the date of this decision, the Virginia statute, and those of the other 16 states with similar statues, became null and void. Thus, the Court became a legislature by eliminating states' law.

Courts can create law as well as overturn it. In *Miranda v. Arizona* (1966), the court required that those detained in "custodial surroundings" be advised of constitutional safeguards. Known by heart by every crime drama buff, this warning includes the right "to remain silent but if you do speak, anything you do say can be used against you in a court of law." A right to an attorney is also included. This ruling, of course, applied to all U.S. jurisdictions.

Certainly, the U.S. Supreme Court is in a privileged position. All other courts and legislatures are under its power–that is to say, jurisdiction. This is not true for all courts or legislatures.

☐ The Jurisprudence of Jurisdiction

Jurisdiction means "power." State legislatures have the jurisdiction over their own states. They cannot legislate beyond their own borders.

The same is true for courts. The jurisdiction of courts is often thought of in terms of "levels." Each state, and the federal government, has distinctive levels of courts which have separate levels of jurisdiction. Grasping these levels is often confusing, however, doing so is extremely important to understand how significant or how far-reaching the decision is. A trial court decision, while it may receive considerable notoriety, may have limited legal significance. Thus, every legal decision must be viewed in the context of jurisdiction.

Jurisdiction information is important for counselors to know because a case of a lower jurisdiction may not apply to the counselor's practice—even if the counselor is practicing in the same state where the decision was made. For example, a New York Supreme Court sitting in Albany does not have jurisdiction over a Supreme Court sitting in Manhattan. A counselor may read that a New York Supreme Court's decision from Albany may now be *the law*—when this is not so, unless courts apply the same rule in Manhattan or an Appellate Court says so.

The following chart illustrates both the similar and varying names for these court "levels." These levels are depicted from the highest (top) to the lowest (bottom).

Federal	Virginia	New York
Supreme Court	Supreme Court	Court of Appeals
Court of Appeals	Court of Appeals	Supreme Court, Appellate Division
	Circuit Court	
District Court	District Court	Supreme Court

Four points need to be made in reference to this chart. First, note that some states have different names for similar court jurisdictions. For example, New York State calls their lowest or trial court the "Supreme Court" while Virginia and the federal systems reserve that title for their highest court.

Second, the lowest courts are called "trial" courts. The trial courts are the courts where innocence or guilt is tried by a judge or jury. While high drama, the O.J. Simpson trial was held in California's court of least jurisdiction—their trial court. If an appeal were taken, there would be no jury, just lawyers arguing their cases before a judge or a panel of judges.

Third, each court level has both a *subject* and a *geographical* jurisdiction. Most court levels, listed above, will hear most legal issues, including those dealing with counselors and mental health professionals and their legal problems arising from practice.

However, most states have some specialized courts such as military courts or bankruptcy courts.

Geographical jurisdiction is of more immediate importance. Generally, the lower the court, the less the geography of its power. For example, there are two **federal district courts** in Virginia. The Eastern District Court sits (hears cases) in Richmond. The Western District Court sits in Roanoke. The Eastern District Court and the Western District Court divide their power between the eastern and western that areas of the state.

Should an appeal be taken from one of these federal courts, that appeal would be addressed by the U.S. Court of Appeals for the Fourth Circuit which also sits in Richmond. If an appeal were taken from the Circuit Court, it would be go to the U.S. Supreme Court.

A state case also could end up in the Supreme Court, but by a different route. For example, if a case decided in the Henrico County District Court in Virginia is appealed, it would be heard in the Virginia Circuit Court of Appeals. From there it may be appealed to the Virginia Supreme Court. Finally, should an appeal be taken from there, it would go to the U.S. Supreme Court. It is not a good bet that the U.S. Supreme Court would grant **certiorari** (take the appeal) from any one of the thousands of cases sent to it for review.

The U.S. Supreme Court did, however, grant cert. for the *Loving* (1967) case. As the Virginia Supreme Court upheld its state law prohibiting interracial marriages, the plaintiffs appealed to the U.S. Supreme Court.

In this book, every effort has deliberately been made to include only those cases decided on appeal and to note the name of the deciding court and name its jurisdiction. Why this is so should be clear from the preceding discussion. A case decided by the trial court has only limited jurisdiction; thus, the case has limited applicability. So, a state judicial ruling in a trial court in Northern Virginia may not apply to someone in the Virginian Shenandoah Valley.

Fourth, some states have special courts that sometimes are not listed among the regular court levels. For example, juvenile and domestic courts, bankruptcy courts, military courts, and special drug courts have special jurisdictions as their various names imply.

The Importance of Precedence and Stare Decisis

Jurisdiction is connected to another key legal concept: **precedence**. Precedence means to what extent courts of "inferior" jurisdiction must comply with the rulings by courts of "superior" jurisdiction.

Precedence is the operational definition of *stare decisis*—a Latin term meaning "stable decision." For a society to conduct its affairs consistently, its laws must not be arbitrary or capricious. Laws may change, but legal principles must remain consistent. The speed limit on Route 66 might change, but speed limits must be preserved for everyone's safety. To the end of *stare decisis*, precedence might mean that a higher court could affirm a lower court's ruling or overturn the previous ruling, among other things.

Precedence allows the law to address new issues, alternative and spiritual interventions included, while at the same time maintaining coherence with earlier decisions. Judge Oliver Wendell Holmes expressed it better when he wrote, "The law should be stable, not stagnant."

One particular set of cases that best illustrates both precedence and jurisdiction. In 1890 a Louisiana statute required "separate, but equal accommodations for the white and colored races." Mr. Plessy, claiming he was "seven-eights Caucasian and one-eighth

African blood," refused to vacate his seat in the White compartments. He was arrested in violation of that law. He found no relief in Louisiana state court and appealed his case right up the U.S. Supreme Court. In 1896 he was to be disappointed there, too. In *Plessy v. Ferguson*, the Supreme Court held that the state ruling was constitutional.

A different U.S. Supreme Court reversed itself fifty-eight years later. *Brown v. Board of Education* (1954) specifically declared the doctrine of "separate, but equal" in *Plessy v. Ferguson* unconstitutional and held that the segregated Topeka, Kansas, schools must be racially integrated.

This set of cases illustrates how the Supreme Court can, and does, reverse its own earlier cases as well as those of other state and federal courts. As social conditions and legal attitudes change, so does the law. Of course, because of the jurisdiction of the U.S. Supreme Court, every other similar law in every other state was also held unconstitutional. Due to the operation of precedent every other court in the country had to rule similar desegregation cases in the same way.

☐ Civil versus Criminal Law

Two principal kinds of law are available in American jurisprudence: the civil and the criminal law. As we shall see, counselors who use alternative and spiritual interventions can be subject to both. These different kinds of law possess disparate characteristics. These characteristics can be summarized as follows:

Distinguishing characteristics between civil and criminal law

	Civil	Criminal
Terms for Fault	Causes of action	Offenses
Penalties	Money only	Fines and jail
Term for Disposition	Liable/negligent or not	Guilty/acquitted
Who Prosecutes	Private attorneys	Government lawyers
Role of Person Harmed	Party to proceedings	Witness only
Standard of Proof	Preponderance of Evidence or clear and convincing evidence	Beyond a reasonable doubt

Some points in this chart need further explanation. First, the **"standard of proof"** is the term for the degree of guilt or innocence needed to find guilt or to acquit, or in civil cases, to find liability or not. Significantly, the standard of proof is higher for a criminal conviction than for civil liability. That criminal standard, "beyond a reasonable doubt" is high, because the loss of liberty is so noxious to U.S. citizens. The criminal standard is so high that any reasonable doubt in a juror's mind requires acquittal. The standards for civil liability are much less onerous, with "clear and convincing" being higher than "preponderance of the evidence".

The two O.J. Simpson trials served to illustrate several aspects of civil versus criminal trials. First, the differences between civil and criminal standards of proof can yield very different results—even based on the same facts. Mr. Simpson was acquitted in the criminal trial, yet held liable in the civil trial. Many say that at least part of the reason was that the criminal jury had enough of a reasonable doubt to acquit, while the civil jury could find liability.

Second, Simpson was arrested and tried by Los Angeles County under a murder statute. The costs of that prosecution were borne entirely by the citizens of that County. In the civil trial, the Goldman family paid a private attorney to sue Mr. Simpson.

Third, the harmed party plays different roles in criminal and civil actions. In a criminal action the victim of the crime is not a party to the trial. It is the government who prosecutes the criminal case. The victims are relegated to the role of witnesses, if that. In fact, a government prosecutor may indict a criminal defendant over the objections of a victim. This can happen in some domestic disputes, where the victim does not wish to file charges. In a civil trial, however, the "victims" are the plaintiffs. They take an active role in filing and pursuing the lawsuit. Without them, there would be no lawsuit.

Fourth, civil and criminal law are empowered by different kinds of statutes. The criminal law code, federal or state, is different from civil statutes. Criminal defendants are charged under specific criminal statutes—whether they be jaywalking or drug smuggling. Similarly, civil defendants must be sued under a specific statute authorizing a specific "cause of action." A cause of action is the legal "peg" upon which a civil action is hung. Without a recognized cause of action, the suit will be dismissed.

For example, in the late 1980s, a family brought suit against a pastor and church when their son committed suicide after going to the pastor for counseling. The family sued under a cause of action for "clergy" malpractice in the state of California. After a prolonged appeal process, the California Supreme Court held that California would recognize no such type of suit (*Nally v. Grace Community Church* (1988). Thus, that part of the suit was dismissed.

Fourth, if Mr. Simpson were to have been found guilty in the criminal suit, he could have faced many years in jail. As it was, the civil **verdict** of liability in the wrongful death suit meant that he had to pay millions to the Goldman family.

☐ The First Amendment's Religious Protections

No discussion of spiritual or complementary counseling is possible, or even adequate, without a discussion of the First Amendment. The First Amendment to the U.S. Constitution can directly and significantly impact any legal discussion of these issues. The First Amendment, ratified in 1791, reads:

> Congress shall make no law respecting an establishment of religion, or prohibiting the free exercise thereof; or abridging freedom of speech, or of the press; or the right of the people to peacefully assemble, and to petition the government for a redress of grievances.

Four points, pressed by the First Amendment, bear further discussion. First, this amendment consists of a constellation of rights. These include assembling, speaking, reporting, and petitioning, as well as practicing religion. Second, each of these rights has limitations, discussed in the next paragraphs. Third, the First Amendment really encompasses two separate freedoms: 1) to be free of government *establishing* a religion and 2) to be free from government *prohibiting* the free exercise of religion. The legal analysis of each of these freedoms is also different and distinct.

Fourth, the much vaunted "wall" separating church and state is as overrated as it is misleading. If there is any wall at all, it is a porous one, if not downright leaky. As we shall see in the following case of *In re Bartha* (1976), the state can, and does, regularly impinge upon religious behavior. The First Amendment is no panacea for those who wish to practice their religion or spirituality in a way that contradicts other statutes. As one court succinctly put it, "Freedom to believe may be said to be absolute, freedom of conduct is not and conduct under religious guise remains subject to regulation for the protection of society" (*Tilton v. Marshall*, 1996). We shall see the same result in peyote cases.

The First Amendment can act as a shield to government interference with some kinds of spiritual or complementary counseling. An interesting and relevant example is the religious and spiritual use of peyote and marijuana (Bullis, 1990b, 1996). This issue pits the government prohibition of controlled substances against the religious freedom clauses of the First Amendment. This issue is especially significant for Native American healers and counselors (who enjoy some legal protection in the use of peyote) and for spiritual and complementary counselors who may have clients who use or who may wish to use such substances in their spiritual quests or counseling.

A significant case involving the 1st amendment's religious protections and the use of prescribed drugs is *Employment Division, Department of Human Resources v. Smith* (1990). The defendants, Native American substance abuse counselors, were denied state (Oregon) unemployment compensation claims when they were fired for participating in a Native American Church peyote ceremony. The U.S. Supreme Court upheld the firing. This case, decided by the U.S. Supreme Court, held that the free exercise of religion does not relieve someone from complying with a valid law. The court also held that a criminal law that substantially burdens religious liberty does not have to be justified by a "compelling state interest." Such a "compelling" interest means that governments have a diminished legal burden in proving their laws interfere with religious freedom. Many viewed this decision as seriously undermining personal religious freedom, in strengthening the power of the state in general and in disallowing the sacramental use of peyote in particular.

Congress acted relatively swiftly in blunting the legal impact of the Smith case and passed the Religious Freedom Restoration Act (hereinafter, the RFRA). The RFRA (U.S.C. §2000bb-1(a)) states: Government may substantially burden a person's exercise of religion only if it demonstrates that application of the burden to the person

1. is in furtherance of a compelling governmental interest; and
2. is the least restrictive means of furthering that compelling governmental interest.

Basically, the RFRA "restores" the necessity for a government to prove that its laws have a "compelling state interest" in order to justify when its laws burden religious freedom. The RFRA, basically, was enacted to make it harder to the government to prosecute a case where someone is practicing a *bona fide* religious act.

☐ Religious Exemptions from State Licensure

Additionally, to the RFRA's provisions upon governmental activity, spiritual and complementary counseling alternatives may fall into other categories protected by the First Amendment. When they do, the legal equation changes. One clear example is that many states, under First Amendment protection, exempt "religious" counselors from state licensure requirements.

Bullis and Mazur (1993) outline the general characteristics of when religious counselors may be excused from such state requirements: 1) the counselor is already ordained, licensed, or otherwise recognized by their denomination; 2) the counselor is under the supervision or control of the denomination; 3) counseling activities are an integral part of the counselor's denominational activities; and 4) the counselor does not use or imply that he or she is a state licensed counselor. Thus, the state may not interfere, by licensing schemes, with religious counseling.

We have already seen how a religious counselor can be excused from at least one cause of action. In the *Nally* case the "clergy malpractice" causes of action were dismissed against the minister and church. This dismissal was due, in part, to the fact that no legally recognizable "standard of care" is uniform throughout all religions. That is to say, the level of competency for the care of depressed or suicidal clients has not been legally established—and courts, with deference to the First Amendment, are unlikely to do so.

How different the same facts may be for the secular counselor! There are relatively objective standards of competency in secular counseling licensure. Tests, examinations, interviews, supervision, and reference checks all help licensing boards determine an applicant's "fitness" for licensure. When a counselor is subjected to a suit for negligence, expert testimony may advise a judge or jury as to the standard of practice under certain circumstances and with a certain client.

Courts are loath to establish such a criteria for "religious" counselors for First Amendment reasons. It seems likely that if a secular counselor was accused under the same facts as *Nally*, the suit would at least go to trial. The First Amendment also affords disparity in the treatment of secular and religious counselors. Further impacts of the First Amendment upon spiritual and complementary counseling alternatives are discussed in the following chapter. This disparity between secular and religious counselors may not be fair, but it's constitutional. This is one reason why some counselors, for perfectly legitimate reasons, want to be designated as "spiritual" or "religious" counselors.

The previous section explained significant legal concepts which have a direct bearing upon spiritual or complementary counseling. With this background, the following cases will become more clear. The following section begins the explicit discussion of spiritual and alternative counseling cases.

☐ Schools: Battlegrounds for Spiritual and Complementary Counseling

The Case of the Magic Rock

Both public and private schools can be seen a fertile legal soil for First Amendment and counseling disputes. School and other institutional counselors must be aware of the limits imposed and freedoms allowed under First Amendment. Such a situation is offered in an appeal from the U.S. District Court for the Western District of Missouri. In *Cowan v. Strafford School District*, 1998) a elementary school teacher, teaching on a probationary period for the past two years, sent a letter home to her students on the last day of school. It read in full:

> You have completed second grade. Because you have worked so hard, you deserve something special and unique; just like you! That something is your very own magic rock.
>   The magic rock you have will always let you know that you can do anything that you set your mind to. To make your rock work, close your eyes, rub it and say to yourself three times, "I am a special and terrific person, with talents of my own!" Before you put your rock away, think of three good things about yourself. After you have put your rock away, you will know that the magic has worked.
>   **HAVE FUN IN THE THIRD GRADE!!!!**

That summer, the teacher's principal informed her that two families had withdrawn their kids from her public school and placed them in private Christian schools because of the "magic rock" letter. The principal also told the teacher to avoid "magic ideas" in the classroom and that some community members were concerned about the magic rock letter. That fall, the principal admonished the teaching staff to avoid "magic" ideas in class and informed them that a local pastor would be leading a seminar on New Age infiltration into the community.

In the Spring of the next year, the school board failed to renew the teacher's contract and the teacher sued under a Title VII religious discrimination claim, a First Amendment claim under the constitution, and for reinstatement of her job. The federal district court found for the teacher and awarded her $18,000 under the Title VII claim, no damages under the constitutional claim, but did not reinstate her in her teaching post. Both parties appealed—the school district because they lost, and the teacher because the lower court did not reinstate her.

American jurisprudence weighs a jury verdict heavily. It is hard to overturn. In legalese, an appeals court must view the evidence (as the appeals court did in the Cowen case) in a "light most favorable" to the jury verdict. This being the case, the Cowen court found that the lower court did not abuse its discretion in accepting the jury verdict.

Public schools are not the only institutions sued in regard to religious or spiritual issues. A Roman Catholic elementary school was sued by an unmarried teacher for being dismissed because she was pregnant. The trial court upheld the dismissal, but the Sixth U.S. Court of Appeals reversed the lower court's decision saying that although the school may insist that the teacher's contract may reflect the church's morality and prohibit premarital sex, it cannot single out only women in its sanctions. As of this writing, the school's attorneys are "evaluating its options" (Wall Street Journal, 2000).

These cases can easily be applied to the school counselor—either because they may offer interventions analogous to the "magic rock" or because they face an environment rich in religious diversity and must walk a fine line between recognizing religious or spiritual traditions and not seeming to make one "more equal" than the rest. First, school counselors need to be aware of what others in the community may take for the "establishment" of a religion. In the "magic rock" case, some in the community felt that the teacher was promoting or "establishing" a religious activity. Keep in mind that "establishing" is the constitutional term for governmental promotion of a faith. The second-grade teacher probably had little notion that she would raise a constitutional question by her letter or that members of the community would be so offended.

School counselors need never to be blind-sided by their actions. They need to be scrupulously aware of the religious and spiritual sentiments of the communities in which they serve. The author's suggestion of an **"ethical ecology,"** explained and discussed in Chapter 5, is designed to review the environment for such ethical/legal decisions. If counselors chooses to take a risk, such as by sending a "magic rock" letter, at least the counselor does so with his or her legal and ethical eyes wide open.

Second, school counselors can decide to rely upon the *Cowen* case for support of similar interventions or encouragement of students. This too, should be a decision that ought be made fully aware of the consequences. but such a scenario is educative in how the law works. For example, this case was decided by the 8th U.S. Circuit Court of Appeals. This circuit has federal jurisdiction over seven midwestern and northern plains states. (Please see the glossary for a description of the states in all the federal circuits). The 8th circuit's jurisdiction is plenty big, but not unlimited. As noted earlier, other circuits will decide a similar case under their own sense of precedence unless, of course, the U.S. Supreme Court decides first or **overrules.**

☐ Early Civil and Criminal Actions Analogous to Complementary and Spiritual Counseling

"If we don't know where we've been, we don't know where we're going." This section is designed to introduce the topic of law and spiritual and alternative counseling from a historical perspective. Modern-day counseling professionals are not the first to practice such counseling approaches. The "New Age," as it is now called, did not begin with contemporary practitioners. Earlier generations practiced many similar interventions and developed similar ideas. "New Age" ideas about health and healing are very ancient. The cases chosen for discussion are previous to 1980.

These cases are important for four reasons. First, they offer insights into the precedent for subsequent cases. Second, they illustrate many of the concepts previously discussed in this chapter. Third, they illustrate how, in some cases, the law will later change. Fourth, while earlier cases do not expressly involve today's classes of counselors, they do involve current issues of contemporary spiritual or complementary counseling. Some counselors may today vigorously disclaim any connection with, for example, astrologers and "fortune tellers." However, many of today's spiritual techniques involve "energy fields" or "chakras," or contacts with spirit or angels. These cosmologies and anthropologies, as did their counterparts in an earlier age, pressed the edges of the legal envelope.

What the law considered suspicious some years ago is now gaining wider legal credence. If we don't appreciate legal precedent, we cannot respond to legal antecedent.

Criminal Actions of Fortune Telling and Astrology

Earlier cases involving fortune telling were not good news for the criminal defendant. In 1917, Alice Ashley of Brooklyn, N.Y., had a client who asked for some personal advice. The appellate decision records some of their conversation:

Q: Will I get the position for which I am looking? Will I marry soon?
A: The spirit of your mother comes to me and says that you are to do as you are prompted yourself.

Ms. Ashley hesitated and said, "You will get the position and you will marry the man and you will have a small family of two or three children"(*People v. Ashley,* 1918).

The client asked how much Ms. Ashley charged and Ashley replied, "A dollar." That's not all she got from this client.

The client turned out to be an informant and Alice Ashley was charged with a New York City disorderly conduct **misdemeanor** for "pretending to tell fortunes."

She appealed on First Amendment grounds. Ashley claimed that she was the President and a minister of the "Brooklyn Spiritist Society" and that she was simply offering "advice," albeit with the help from some departed spirits. Her arguments were in vain.

With a rationale we shall hear again and again, the court rehearsed the policy of the New York statute. The statute, modeling those in early England, were designed to protect "ignorant" persons from being "deluded and defrauded". Next the court scoffed at any defense related to the different methods of prophesy. "One method of prophesy is as bad as the next," they might just as well have said. Finally, the court determined that Ashley went beyond deducing her clients' character and offered them general advice. Instead, the court found that she gave them specific marriage and family advice. The appeals court affirmed the trial court's decision.

Fifty-eight years later and on the opposite side of the country, the result was pretty much the same. Actually, the facts are similar as well. An undercover police officer attended a tarot card reading by Zsuzsanna Bartha, a well known practitioner of Wicca ("white" witchcraft). She is also known as Z. Budapest, the author of *The Holy Book of Women's Mysteries* (1979).

The officer asked three questions after drawing eight cards each time. Budapest answered each question in turn. Then the officer asked how much the reading was. Budapest answered, "ten dollars". The officer put the money on the table and left. Another officer entered the building and arrested her under a California statute prohibiting advertizing fortune telling, restoring lost love, uniting lovers, husbands, and wives by means of occult or psychic powers, clairvoyance, psychology, spirits, prophesy, astrology, or other means (Los Angeles Municipal Code §43.30).

Budapest based her appeal upon a claim that her activity fell with in an exemption for "the exercise of any religious or spiritual function of any priest, minister, rector or an accredited representative of any *bona fide* church or religion" (Los Angeles Municipal Code §43.31). Her defense was that she was a high priestess of Wicca. She also claimed that being paid for her services is perfectly consistent with her professional status. She said, "I've read for 75 cents. I have read for a single rose. I read for nothing. And I've read for a kiss."

The California court was as unimpressed with these arguments as was the New York court. First, the court concluded that the defendant's religion did not require her to perform tarot readings so she neither met the statutory exemption nor unduly interferes with her free exercise of religion. Second, the court almost summarily dismissed the assertion that the ordinance was unconstitutionally vague. The court held it clearly and unambiguously described the offending behaviors.

In the following case, we see how these ordinances are interpreted in different times and circumstances. The thawing of this cool reception by legal authorities began in the 1980s in a big way. In **Marks v. City of Roseburg** (1984), the city ordinance prohibiting the practice of the occult arts including astrology, clairvoyance, spiritualism or any other practice or practices generally considered to be unsound and unscientific whereby an attempt or pretense is made: 1) to reveal or analyze past incidents, 2) to analyze or to define the character or personality, 3) to foretell or reveal the future, 4) to locate by such means lost or stolen property, or 5) to give advice or information concerning any matter or event (Roseburg Municipal Code §10.04).

This statute may approach the work of many spiritual or complementary counselors. It may even seem relevant to many orthodox counselors. Even the courts recognize this connection, as we shall see.

The defendants challenged the ordinance on constitutional grounds. The Oregon constitution (Article I, §8) reads: "No law shall be passed restraining the free expression of opinion, or restricting the right to speak, write, or print freely on any subject whatever, but every person shall be responsible for the abuse of this right."

The court found that defendants do not violate the statute by practicing "unsound or unscientific" practice. The court reasoned that defendants violate the statute by communicating those ideas or information to clients. If someone considers their methodology "unsound or unscientific," the court concluded social, political, or economic history might be prohibited under this statute as well as psychology or psychiatry. Thus, the court held this statute is over broad and, therefore, unconstitutional.

A year later, the California Supreme Court dealt the same fate to Azusa Municipal statute. This time the defendants, the Spiritual Psychic Science Church, challenged the statute on commercial free speech grounds. Commercial free speech is like First Amendment free speech applied to business.

Remembering the political adage that, "all politics is local," it is important not to assume these cases constitute a mass and universal renunciation of municipal ordinances against "astrologers," "fortune tellers," "palm readers" or anyone else who uses psychic methodologies. While it appears to this writer that a "critical mass" of courts striking down such statutes, a national trend may mean nothing in the local community of any one counselor. These prohibitions, depending on how they are written, may be construed against counselors who use clairvoyance, spiritual guides, angels, visions, or other like media as interventions.

Civil Actions for Exorcism: Negligence and Malpractice

Exorcism, the dispossession of malicious spirits, might seem an unlikely venue for spiritual or complementary counseling. Of course, it is too close for comfort. The modern science of psychotherapy wants, in some ways, to distance itself from its ancient antecedents. "If mental healers were to be summoned to the patient's bedside in the order of their appearance in history, the magician or medicine man would be the first to answer the call" (Ehrenwald, 1991, p. 37). The exorcist may have been the first psychiatrist.

Exorcism is a standard item in the history of many religions. The New Testament has several references to Jesus as an exorcist. One story goes that when Jesus came down from the Mount of Transfiguration, a man begged Jesus to heal his son. The father described his son's symptoms as follows: "Suddenly a spirit seizes him, and all at once he shrieks. It convulses him until he foams at the mouth; it mauls him and will scarcely leave him" (Luke 9:39 New Revised Standard Version). Jesus becomes annoyed that, while his disciples try to heal the boy, they cannot. In the end, Jesus "rebuked the unclean spirit" (Luke 9:42 NRSV).

Nor was Jesus the only exorcist practicing at that time. Luke also records another exorcist who not only is "casting out demons," but is casting out demons in Jesus' name. At first the disciples are outraged, and try to stop the interloper. Then Jesus, rebuking his disciples, says, "Do not stop him; for whoever is not against you is for you" (Luke 9:50 NRSV).

Demons described dysfunctions in a pre-scientific cosmology. Reality has not changed since the time of Jesus, *our notions of reality* have changed. Exorcism was just as real to the ancients as the DSM-IV is for the modern psychotherapist.

Nor is exorcism a relic of the dim, pre-scientific past. It is still very real today, particularly in a crosscultural context. Bullis' (1996) empirical research of a random sample of clinical social workers in Virginia revealed that a couple of clinicians performed exorcisms (M = .14; SD = 1.8). The manual of exorcism is now in paperback and popularly available (Karpel, 1975).

Exorcisms tend to hit the newspapers, especially if a professional is involved. A psychiatrist agreed to pay a former female client $2.4 million in an out-of-court **settlement** after she accused him of malpractice in diagnosing her with 120 different personalities (one of which was Satan himself) and in performing an exorcism on her (Associated Press, 1997). As usual, in an out-of-court settlement, no admission of guilt was tendered. The former patient accused the doctor, who treated her from 1986 to 1992, of leaving her with suicidal thoughts and false memories. The **plaintiff**-patient claimed that, although she did not believe in the devil, the psychiatrist strapped her to a bed and conducted the Roman Catholic rite of exorcism. When she became frightened and asked him to stop, he said that it was only the Satan inside of her telling him to "stop."

From the parties' point of view, an out-of-court settlement may be good. But from a legal discussion point of view, it leaves the pertinent issues unresolved. Would the former patient have a cause of action? Would the case be dismissed? Would there be enough evidence for liability to attach or would a jury refuse to impose liability?

The following case is also significant and relevant. It is an excellent example of civil law applied to a form of complementary counseling. Additionally, this case affords the opportunity to introduce the four elements of a "tort" or negligence suit. A negligence suit is a form of civil action. Against a professional like a counselor, a negligence case is termed "malpractice."

Briefly put, these four elements are:

1. Duty
2. Breach of Duty
3. Proximate Cause
4. Damages

Duty is the legal obligation on the part of the defendant. For a counselor, duties may be found in the professional code of ethics or the duties promulgated by the state licensing board. The breach of the duty means that the counselor's behavior fell below that of the accepted **standard of care**. Proximate cause is the "causal link" between the breach of duty and the damages. Damages is the harm to the plaintiff done by the defendant. Damages now can include emotional or psychological harm so long as it can be verified. *In re Pleasant Glade Assembly of God, Rev. Lloyd McCuchen, Rod Linzay, and Holly Linzay* (1998) illustrates these points.

In the summer of 1996, 17-year-old Laura Schubert attended an "all-nighter" at her church with other teens to prepare for a church-sponsored garage sale the following day. One of the other youth exclaimed that he saw a demon in the another part of the church. The youth minister, Rod Linzay, and his wife, Holly, gathered the other youth together and said that demons were trying to get into the church. Rev. Linzay had the young people anoint the church with holy oil. Through the night the leaders and the young people prayed to cast the demons out of the church. The all-night experience was frightening to Laura and her stomach hurt.

Later that week Laura "balled up" in a youth meeting in some kind of distress. Rod told Laura to lie "spread eagle" and to pray that the devil would come out of her. The church pastor also prayed over her, telling her to "Just say the word 'Jesus.'" Laura was later taken home by her parents.

Laura's father, Tom, an ordained Assembly of God minister, and her mother were both members of this same church. This church believes that demons, as the New Testament relates, but subsequent events brought Tom to write his concerns to the Church's pastor, Rev. Lloyd McCutchen. The Schuberts also withdrew their membership from the church and wrote to the District Council—the church's supervisory authority.

They also sued the church, the pastor and the two youth pastors. The "causes of action" were a menu of civil claims: false imprisonment, assault, battery, negligence, gross negligence, professional negligence, and intentional infliction of emotional distress. Put differently, causes of action are legal terms to describe the exact claims against the defendant.

The Schuberts, asserted that their injuries arose from the defendant's entire course of conduct surrounding Laura's "exorcism.". Those "causes of action" are various legal "pegs" upon which to hang Laura's harm. These are the plaintiff's swords. But the defendant also has a shield.

As we have already said, one of the principal shields of those who employ religious counseling is the First Amendment. Those who employ *spiritual* counseling may also try to use this defense as well. While we will discuss this defense in a subsequent chapter, the effect of such a defense is illustrated in this case. The impact upon the case was total and unequivocal. The court didn't even allow the plaintiffs to proceed with **discovery**— the fact-gathering process prior to trial. The court concluded "that the Schuberts' claims would involve a searching inquiry into Assembly of God beliefs and the validity of such beliefs, an inquiry that is barred by the 1st amendment (at 3)." The ruling may not be fair to the plaintiffs, but it is constitutional.

The Ethics Related to the Four Elements of a Legal Duty

As mentioned earlier in this chapter, law and ethics are connected. They are not clones, but they are chromosomally related. The four elements of a negligence action have their basis in ethical principles. These principles are permeated by two ethical norms: individuality and personal responsibility.

Individuality is as old as American law itself. The American constitution speaks in terms of personal rights and freedoms. The first ten amendments, the "Bill of Rights," is concerned with protecting personal rights. Personal responsibility is also a long-standing legal tradition. This sense of responsibility may have at lease some of its origins in the Western origins of the church with its emphasis upon personal confession. After all, it is a person who enters the confessional and an individual who pays the penance. While religious groups often offer corporate confessions and pardons as part of the religious service, whole families and whole towns are not known to crowd into the confessional booth.

American jurisprudence holds individuals personally guilty or personally liable for mistakes, misjudgments, and misdeeds. The criminal law is a prime example of the long arm of statutes holding individuals accountable for their personal actions. In the next chapter, we examine how law hold counselors who use spiritual and complementary interventions personally responsible for their actions. In the next chapter, we examine the how the criminal law holds counselors, who use spiritual and complementary interventions, responsible for their actions or inactions.

☐ Conclusion

This chapter builds the foundation upon which the later chapters will depend. Without a clear and well-grounded understanding of jurisdiction, precedence, *stare decisis*, the differences between the civil and criminal law, and the levels of courts, interpreting legal decisions and applying them to specific counseling situations is a house of cards.

This chapter has offered significant principles of U.S. jurisprudence. With so much misunderstanding about the law, it is easy to misinterpret or to misapply the law. These principles provide a sound underpinning for properly understanding cases and statutes. Without such a foundation, it would be easy assume an over- or under-importance or significance of the case or to misapply a statute. With such an understanding, statutes and case law decisions can be understood in their proper context.

☐ Legal Exercises and Audits

1. a. Are you practicing as a member of the clergy or as a secular counselor? If clergy, are you going to avail yourself of the clergy privilege in your state for your practice? Are you practicing *with* a state license or are you exempt from such license due to your clergy status?
   b. If you are a clergy and practicing under a state license, are you practicing as a clerical or as a secular counselor? Even more to the legal point, if your client confesses child abuse, will they insist that you claim the clergy status and privilege of confidentiality, thus probably avoiding abuse-reporting requirements?
   c. Are you practicing in a secular or ecclesiastical setting? If you are a secular counselor, yet practice in a religious or spiritual setting, might some of your clients *think* that you are entitled of the clergy privileges? How are you disabusing them of that notion?
2. a. Are your clients students, residents of a psychiatric facility, inmates, or otherwise institutionalized? If so, what are the policies and procedures regarding the use of spiritual or complementary interventions? Can you use them, if you choose, or are there institutional prohibitions? Are you disclosing the content and process of your interventions to your supervisors? Why or why not?
   b. Conversely, does your employer desire or demand that you use spiritual or complementary interventions? Does this violate your spiritual or religious traditions? Are you discussing these issues with your supervisors? Coming to agreements?
3. a. Practice analyzing the four elements of a "tort" or negligence action from personal experience. Have you ever been in counseling before? Can you think of some intervention or process of your counselor that could, conceivably, have given rise to a negligence action? Think through the four elements, particularly the duty of the counselor that may or may not have been breached. (If you've never been in counseling or you can't think of anything your counselor may have done wrong, then think of something in your practice that may have or possibly could have gone wrong.)
   b. What was the duty that was possibly breached? Remember, this must be a specific duty—arising from a legal duty or an ethical mandate from the profession. Does this duty translate into a "cause of action?" Was that duty breached? How was it breached? Keep your answer brief and focused.
   c. Try thinking like a lawyer. Where would you place this case—in civil or criminal court? Would this be an easy or hard case to prove? Why or why not?
   d. Finally, how might this situation have been avoided in the first place?

2

Criminal Charges

Objectives

1. To provide illustrations of how the criminal law can apply to spiritual or complementary counselors.
2. To offer examples of how specific criminal statutes (i.e., therapeutic deception or exploitation, fraud, criminal sexual conduct, informed consent, practicing without a license, the use of peyote, marijuana, or other hallucinogens, and child abuse) might apply to counselors using spiritual or complementary therapies.
3. To acquaint counselors with defenses to criminal actions against them.
4. To understand the role and function of "**expert witnesses**" in criminal prosecutions against counselors using complementary therapies.

Criminal charges are violations against society. Such charges are distinguished by two levels of seriousness: misdemeanors and felonies. Misdemeanors are the lesser of the two. If charged with a misdemeanor, the defendant is often simply fined. Felonies are the more serious charges of the two. If charged with a **felony**, chances are that any fine imposed will be considerable and the defendant may be punished with jail time and/or probation. It bears repeating that a criminal conviction usually makes it easier to impose civil liability as well.

Additionally, criminal convictions require two types of guilt. Conviction usually requires a **guilty** mind (**mens rea**) and a guilty act (**mens actus**). Without both, there may be no conviction.

This chapter begins where the discussion of criminal law in Chapter 1 ended. This chapter concludes the previous discussion of "fortune-telling." I have styled this discussion under the general legal rubric of "fraud." The chapter continues with a discussion of sexual assault or sexual misconduct, peyote, tantra practice, and child abuse. The final section of this chapter describes the defenses applicable to counselor defendants.

The following case study begins the legal discussion of criminal charges. The case was chosen both to illustrate principles of the criminal law and to examine behaviors linked to spiritual or complementary practices.

☐ Case Study: The Criminal "Curandero"

Juan Espinosa Cardenas was convicted in the Superior Court of Los Angeles County for six counts of grand theft, seventy counts of sexual misconduct, and (significantly) findings that he occupied a position of special trust. Cardenas held himself out to be a "curandero"—a faith healer. He appealed his convictions on the grounds that there was insufficient evidence to support the findings that his criminal behaviors were accomplished by "force, violence, duress, menace, or fear of immediate and unlawful bodily injury to the victim or another person" (California Criminal Code, **section** 288 (b) and 289 (a)).

The California Appeals Court focused a fair portion of its decision on the history and function of the curandero. An expert witness, knowledgeable in folklore and mythology, testified that "Curanderismo" is a religion based partly upon the belief in spirits, the healing power of plants, and the role of human intermediaries between the spiritual powers and followers of the religion. The curandero fills such a role.

The court found that the curandero has the status of a holy man. He is the confidante to those following Curanderismo. Believers will talk to the curandero about things they will not reveal to anyone else. Believers will visit a curandero for a variety of purposes, for physical cures, resolutions to love problems, to resolve marital problems, or business issues. Additionally, believers may find that the curandero can have access to divine powers, can see the future, and perform exorcisms.

Interestingly and significantly, the court also opined on sexual proscriptions associated with curandero healings. The court noted that healings are sometimes conducted upon naked believers; however, such healings are conducted in a way obviating sexual arousal. In fact, followers believe that sexual activity reduces the curandero's spiritual potency and desecrates his or her work. The court then applied this background material to the crimes alleged.

The central issue in this case was whether or not Cardenas used his position to coerce or to otherwise undermine his patient's ability to consent to his sexual activity with them. "Consent" is a legal term of art requiring knowledge and freedom. A person needs both to know exactly what he or she is consenting to and have a true choice about whether or not to give consent in the first place. It goes without saying, then, that those under the influence of drugs or alcohol, those underage, or those with mental impairment cannot give their consent, even if they "choose" to. As we shall see, there are other ways, specific to spiritual or complementary interventions, which mitigate a client's ability to consent.

The court used the terms "psychological coercion" and "physical deprivation" to denote this process. That he *had* sex with his patient-followers was not at issue on appeal. Cardenas argued that all his patient-followers give their consent to his sexual activities with them. The court disposed of all the appellant's arguments. The court quickly dispatched one part of the consent issue. One of Cardenas' patient-followers was a 13-year-old girl, and given her age, she was not legally competent to give consent to anything. The court then found that even if the women and girls consented to being treated in general for their concerns and difficulties, this specific consent cannot be expanded into a general consent to the defendant's sexually-oriented "treatments."

Finally, the court was persuaded that physical and psychological deprivations undermined the patient-followers' ability to give their consent. Basically, the court found that Cardenas used his purported role as a curandero to hold power over the women. For example, the court recorded that he deprived the women of outside activities and held them psychologically captive. He gathered all his "patients" into a single apartment in order to control their behavior. He told the women not to go near the windows or demons would push them out. Cardenas ordered the women not to leave the apartment or demons would kill them. He convinced them that spirits would also harm them if they watched t.v. or used the telephone. He changed the phone number twice. He even gave the rent to the landlord so that she would not ever see the landlord in an effort to cut off outside influences.

Nor was this the end of the control. The court noted that Cardenas deprived the women of sleep, controlled their diet, and coerced them into drinking alcohol. He saw to it that one of the women never became fully dressed. In a word, he wanted to dominate them. The court rejected Cardenas' appeal and upheld his conviction (*People v. Cardenas*, 1994).

☐ Consent, Coercion, and Spiritual or Complementary Counseling

The above case illustrates the legal issue of the circumstances that differentiate mere persuasion from coercion. Persuasion is well known as a legitimate healing agent (Frank, 1973). Persuasion—from the subtle confidence of hanging diplomas on office walls, to more overt advertisements of statistics regarding results gained or experience in one's field—can encompass benign forms of raising positive expectations for treatment.

The beneficial, persuasive characteristics of the curanderismo, tribal and indigenous healing practices, shamanism, as well as other similar interventions, have received remarkable academic and lay attention in recent years (Doore, 1988; Halifax, 1979; Kakar, 1982; Kalweit, 1988). These ancient practices have often been translated and reinterpreted into contemporary psychological or therapeutic interventions (Nicholson, 1987; Villoldo & Krippner, 1987). "Shamanism," "Native American practices," and "Latin American practices" are specifically enumerated by the National Institute of Health's National Center for Complementary and Alternative Medicine. Such practices are specifically applied in the context of counselors and other mental health practitioners (Krajewski-Jaime, 1991; Krassner, 1986; Laird, 1984; Sanville, 1975; Voss et al., 1999).

While the ethics of abusive spiritual or complementary counselors is addressed in Chapter 5, this chapter identifies principle areas where the criminal law addresses such behavior. The criminal law, by its very nature, addresses the darker side of human experience. While taking nothing from the positive role of shamans or curanderos, the criminal law makes inquiries into such practices based upon forensic principles, not social, cultural, or even therapeutic principles. To date, law and the social sciences are uneasy allies.

The law looks to behaviors that prove or strongly imply (via "circumstantial evidence") the elements of the crime. For example, the court did not recite the history and function of the curandero (and take evidence on it) as an idle exercise.

States have come to recognize that counselors enjoy a specific and special relationship of trust and confidence. This special relationship can induce clients and others to lower their normal defenses and to allow the counselor to suggest and to persuade their clients to do things they normally could not or would not. This persuasive power can have enormous and beneficial therapeutic effects. Such persuasive power can encourage the fearful to successfully face challenges or enable the grieving to live fully again; in fact, it can well be argued that is why clients attend counselors in the first place. Counselors, in fact, are paid to use their persuasive gifts on behalf of the client.

However, persuasion can become perverted into an abuse of power toward those who place religious or spiritual leaders in positions of trust. Trust, and its abuse, is a legal link between "therapeutic deception" and spiritual and complementary counseling. Those who practice counseling with an expertise in spiritual or complementary practices sometimes enjoy the aura of a spiritual leader or even the status of one who has secret or special "mystical" knowledge. States increasingly recognize the special relationship, therapeutic persuasiveness, and sometimes even the control that counselors enjoy.

Traditionally, the criminal law has shifted abuses of power and authority to the civil law. Increasingly, however, states will criminally sanction offenses which abuse professional power. These new laws are often titled under the description of "therapeutic deception." The title pretty well expresses the law's intent. These laws should be of particular relevance to spiritual and complementary counselors. Such counselors, as we have seen in the *Cardenas* case, are often placed on pedestals by clients, even more so than other mental health practitioners. Those who enjoy spiritual prestige often also enjoy heightened power over clients as well. The next chapter explores these causes of action. More recently, the criminal law has begun to specifically sanction counselors who abuse their clients under the guise of treatment.

☐ Aggravated Sexual Assault: Therapeutic Deception or Exploitation

An increasing number of states have passed a form of aggravated sexual assault charge with specific reference to the legal terms "therapeutic deception" or "therapeutic exploitation." For example, a Colorado statute (C.R.S. 18-3-405.5) makes such sexual contact a felony. The statute reads:

> (1) (a) Any actor who knowingly inflicts sexual penetration . . . on a victim commits aggravated sexual assault on a client if:
> (1) The actor is a psychotherapist and the victim is a client of the psychotherapist; or
> (2) The actor is a psychotherapist and the victim is a client and the sexual penetration occurred by means of therapeutic deception.
> (3) For the purposes [of the above statute] consent by the client to the sexual penetration . . . shall not constitute a defense to such offense.

Three aspects of this, and similar, statutes need emphasis and explanation. First, for the purposes of the statute, who are therapists? The answer, as we have noted in the Preface, is found only in the statute itself or case law. As it happens, Colorado defines who psychotherapists are with some particularity—and broadly. The statute (C.R.S. 18-3-405.5(4)(b)) defines "psychotherapist" as: "any person who performs *or purports to perform* [author's emphasis] psychotherapy, whether or not such person is licensed or certified by the state . . . ." "Purports" is an important term. This term puts on notice those who *claim* to be psychotherapists and, in fact, are not. Because this statute talks about "psychotherapists," those who seek to escape this statute by not really being psychotherapists will fail.

The statute defines psychotherapy as "to assist individuals or groups to alleviate mental disorders, understand unconscious or conscious motivation, resolve emotional, social, or attitudinal conflicts, or modify behaviors which interfere with effective emotional, social, or intellectual functioning." This is an inclusive definition, pulling into the purview a wide range of persons who offer therapies, with or without counseling credentials—quite likely those offering alternative, complementary, or spiritual interventions.

Second, the statute defines "therapeutic deception" as "a representation by a psychotherapist that sexual . . . penetration . . . by a therapist is consistent with or part of the client's treatment" (C.R.S. 18-3-405.5(4)(d)). Luckily, or unluckily, Colorado has a case, under this statute, which helps develop this definition. In *Ferguson v. People* (1992) a psychotherapist appealed his conviction, in part, by claiming that the state should have to prove that the *client* did not consent to sexual activity. In dismissing this part of the appeal, the court said: "The special character of psychotherapeutic treatment involving as it frequently does a person who is in a vulnerable emotional state and likely to develop an *extreme dependency* [author's emphasis] relationship with the therapist, provides a reasonable basis in fact for the legislative decision [to disallow the defense of consent by the client].

Further, the court also noted how the trust and confidences necessary for effective therapy may add to this emotional dependence saying that "effective psychotherapeutic treatment often may require the client to disclose . . . highly intimate and personal details which the client reasonably expects will be treated as confidential. We also recognize that the client, during the course of treatment, may develop a deep emotional dependence on the psychotherapist" (*Ferguson v. People*, 1992, p. 5). The court correctly assessed the vulnerability–dependency cycle in the therapeutic relationship and affirmed the state legislature's constitutional right to deny the accused that defense. The *People v. Cardenas* case is an illustration of how dependency can be exploited or encouraged. Such dependency can be exploited even by well-meaning counselors. We shall explore the ethical implications of the therapeutic vulnerability–dependency cycle in Chapter 5.

Third, what exactly is the nature of "therapeutic deception"? What makes such "deception" different from, say, other forms of sexual assault? As noted in the previous paragraph, the client often develops a strong emotional bond with the counselor. The *Ferguson* court noted, that "transference, for example, can well account for some of the privacy and associational expectations that might be generated by the psychotherapist–client relationship" (p. 5). This is the court's way of saying that the powerful psychological phenomenon of "transference" is a powerful emotional experience that a counselor can use to the client's benefit. Or not.

When a counselor misuses transference, he or she uses powerful feelings "transferred" to the counselor to take advantage of the client. The counselor, in this fashion, does not properly encourage the client to take this power for the client's own benefit, but uses that power for the counselor's own ends: sexual, financial, social, or *spiritual*. Given the extraordinary power, authority, and control spiritual and complementary counselors can exert over their clients, such counselors need to be particularly sensitive toward and knowledgeable of the policy behind these kinds of statutes. The precise pattern of statutes may change, but the policy is likely to endure.

It would not be uncommon, for example, if projected feelings transferred by the client upon the counselor were of a religious nature. These feelings might reflect those toward a religious figure in the client's past, an idealized spiritual figure, or a hoped-for figure of exceptional kindness or compassion. When this happens, the counselor's power and control grows to, if you will, celestial proportions. The client will do almost anything to get into the counselor's good graces. When the counselor speaks, it is almost, literally, the voice of divinity. The client will move heaven and earth to satisfy the counselor.

The lawful and ethical counselor will explain this phenomenon to the client and declare that such affection or power bestowed upon the counselor, while complementary, must be channeled only in appropriate ways. The legal and ethical counselor may even go out of his or her way to demonstrate that, far from being divine or even semidivine, he or she seeks to have no more power over or favor from anyone (except maybe a pet or grandchildren!).

☐ Fraud

Fraud is the deliberate misrepresentation of material facts. Fraud is an increasingly popular and potent peg upon which prosecutors hang prosecutions for misleading and self-promotional information.

For example, a physician who injected aloe vera into terminally-ill cancer patients was convicted in Virginia of fraud. The doctor pleaded guilty to charges of obtaining money, and attempting to obtain money, through false pretenses in using the aloe vera and cesium treatments though they have not been approved by the Food and Drug Administration (FDA).

According to state police, the physician and his assistant represented that the treatments were approved by the FDA and that they would get rid of the tumors. Patients paid up to $15,000 for the treatments (Associated Press, 1999f). Three months after his conviction, he was sentenced to two years in prison. His license to practice medicine was revoked as well (Associated Press, 1999g).

Months later, the feds took their turn in bringing charges against the doctor. The doctor pled guilty to mail fraud and conspiracy to produce an unapproved drug. He could receive, on top of state sentences, 46 to 57 months in jail (Associated Press, 2000a). This development not only illustrates medical fraud and attendant charges. But it also illustrates how one set of deeds can result in both state and federal charges. These additional charges do not constitute "double jeopardy," as they are completely different charges—even though they arise out of the same acts. To take a hypothetical situation, a counselor who defrauds clients with a scheme of healing all their problems by communicating with their past lives or astral bodies and who uses the phones or mail across state lines to perpetrate that fraud could face federal charges simply for using interstate commerce in doing so. These federal charges might be in addition to state charges.

Prudent counselors need to be certain that there is a "fire wall" between their spiritual or complementary interventions and the kinds of fraud noted in the above case. Of course, there are huge differences between alternative counseling interventions and injecting unapproved substances. There are, however, examples of distressingly close connections to some alternative interventions as well.

In *Farley v. Henderson* (1989), Gary Magno, a professed "psychic surgeon" was arrested by Phoenix, Arizona, police and convicted for medical fraud. He appealed his conviction on the grounds that his arrest violated his First Amendment rights of religious freedom. The court defined "psychic surgeons" or "psychic healers" as those who "use psychic powers to remove tumors and other diseased tissues from patients without making any surgical incision or using any surgical equipment" (p. 2). The defendant, and others involved with the suit, were members of the Holy Spirit of God Church, whose religious beliefs included this practice.

The court considered the evidence submitted by the defendants. Such evidence included two newspaper articles and an affidavit from a clinical psychologist. The articles discuss the positive aspects of psychic surgery. The psychologist stated that he had studied "psychic surgeons" and that he had personally witnessed over 8,000 such surgeries. He stated that only 2% to 5% of the operations are fraudulent. The psychologist affirmed that psychic surgery is a "real valid phenomena" that has "helped thousands..from chronic illness."

However, the law required Magno to offer proofs **"beyond the pleadings"** (see Glossary) to overcome the district court's conviction. Going beyond the pleadings means that defendants must have evidence beyond their own affidavits, **depositions**, or answers to interrogatories. The appeals court ruled that those offers of proof did not succeed. Thus, Magno's conviction stood.

Fraud can be found among counselors' printed promotional materials as well. Counselors need to be clear, accurate, and truthful in the kinds of advertising and promotional materials they distribute. A California court held that the publisher of the "Beardstown Ladies' Investment Club" book jackets does not enjoy First Amendment protection and can be sued if the dustcover information untruthfully played up the investment returns (Book-jacket returns, 1999). Counselors have ample opportunity to advertise or promulgate their practices in writing, in lectures, and on the Internet. Counselors should scrutinize these communications to make sure that no information is distorted, misrepresented, or inaccurate. Unverifiable claims for therapies should also be avoided.

Counselors who misrepresent the effectiveness or efficacy of treatments may be tending to fraud. How, then, might the legitimate raising of expectations of health and healing be misinterpreted, misapplied, or misconstrued as the illegitimate misrepresentation of facts? Some of the factors counselors need to consider are:

1. *To what extent are the interventions professionally acknowledged in professional journals, articles, and papers?* While absolute "proven" effectiveness is probably not required, at least no negative or spurious results should be shown. Largely "ineffective" results from treatments may also give rise to allegations of fraud or misrepresentation.
2. *To what extent are the interventions being promulgated among the seminars and training opportunities offered or sponsored by professional associations?* It is usually easier to establish the credibility of an intervention if it is being taught or at least discussed by professional groups.
3. *To what extent do the interventions appear in the history, literature, disciplines, or sacred literature of a religious or spiritual group?* Even if an intervention is not discussed in professional counseling associations, this does not mean that the intervention is questionable. The credibility of an intervention can be established as a spiritual or religious intervention. For example, the "Jesus Prayer" is a method of prayer and meditation often associated with the Christian Eastern Orthodox Church. While not the subject of a multitude of psychological studies and not even well known (or practiced) outside the Orthodox Churches, it is widely known, discussed, and practiced within those denominations. The counselor should have no trouble in verifying that method of prayer's (and associated breathing techniques) use, tradition, and utility.
4. *To what extent do side effects accompany the procedure?* Disclosure of any such effects is an element of an informed consent. Informed consent is a hallmark of an ethical practice. Informed consent is what makes a client's assent to engage in any intervention voluntary and legally cognizable. Without consent there is no assent. Information is the element that makes the consent an "informed" consent. Without an "informed" consent, the consent is "ignorant" consent. Ignorant consent is no consent. An informed consent "form" for meditation practice is included in Chapter 5.
5. *To what extent is the case determined by expert opinion?* Expert witnesses play an increasingly informative and important role in helping triers of fact to adjudicate cases. It is to the advantage of every spiritual and complementary counselor to cultivate sufficient knowledge among their professions so that spiritual and complementary methods

and interventions are increasingly accepted and understood in the forensic setting. This will be critical to the profession in the coming years. A detailed discussion of expert witnesses appears in Chapter 3.

Informing your clients, additionally, is a good way to establish credibility with clients. Clients respect the counselor who respects them—and their safety. So, for a legally sound and ethically responsible practice (so to steal a real estate phrase) the key to success is "disclose, disclose, disclose."

Another form of fraud or misrepresentation possibly affecting spiritual or complementary counselors was originally directed against fortune-tellers. While this book certainly does not equate counselors with fortune-tellers, it is conceivable that this statute may reach some branches of spiritual or complementary counselors. This may occur to the extent that counselors use clairvoyant, telepathic, precognitive, or prophetic techniques. The term "and other crafts" (used below) gives the statute broader reach than the specific, proscribed terms.

Many states still have such statutes. North Carolina provides one example:

> It shall be unlawful for any person to practice the arts of phrenology, palmistry, clairvoyance, fortune-telling and other crafts of a similar kind in the counties named herein. Any person violating any provision of this section shall be guilty of a Class 2 misdemeanor. This section shall not prohibit the amateur practice of phrenology, palmistry, fortune-telling or clairvoyance in connection with school or church socials, provided such socials are held in school or church buildings . . . (§14-401.5)

We know this is statute is criminal in nature because it is a misdemeanor penalty for conviction. There are two other important facets of this statute pertinent to practitioners of spiritual or complementary counseling. First, while counselors may not practice palmistry or phrenology as part of their practice, clairvoyance is another matter. To the extent that counselors predict or use techniques that lead the client into predictive or prophetic exercises or discussions, they may fall within the prevue of this statute.

For example, a defendant describing himself as a "parapsychologist" and a "counselor" was convicted of fortune-telling under New York State law. That state law provided for convictions for those who claim "occult powers" for pay to answer questions, to give advice on personal matters, or to exorcise or influence evil spirits (*People v. Sanchez*, 1994). While the conviction was reversed on technical grounds (fatal defects in the **indictment**), this case is strong reinforcement that those who practice in the prophetic, occult, or paranormal arts are still subject to criminal penalties. It bears repeating that many spiritual and complementary counselors may approach the bitter edge of such statutes.

The second facet of this statute lies in its exceptions: amateur practice in schools and churches. This is an indicative exception. It would seem that the statute wants to exclude "fortune-telling" activities related either to educational or to worship activities. The statute specifies that exempted activity must take place in a school or a church (or, no doubt, other religious sites, if pressed). This exemption is probably of little value to private counselors and of very limited use even to counselors working for religious or educational institutions. The plain language of the statute requires the exempted behavior to take place in a church or school. The legislative intent may be to allow fortune-telling or prophesy for religious or educational purposes or not to sanction fund raising activities based upon that behavior. This is another example where schools and students sometimes possess privileges and exemptions of which counselors must be aware.

☐ **Criminal Sexual Conduct During Counseling**

Sexual assault or criminal sexual misconduct are possibly the most publicized, if not the most prevalent, crime alleged against counselors. Practitioners of spiritual or complementary counseling are amenable to such charges for two reasons. First, their clients may misinterpret counselor actions. This is true for any kind of counseling, whether alternative or spiritual or more conventional. However, for some counselors who take a "wholistic" approach to counseling, it is not uncommon to hold hands, hug, or touch head, shoulders, or back.

So suits for sexual misconduct have been filed against counselors who may have had no physical contact with their clients at all. Some school counselors even make it a practice to keep their office doors open while counseling in order to avoid being suspect.

Second, sometimes alternative and spiritual interventions lend themselves to less rigid boundaries and more tendency for clients to hug or to touch a counselor than more cognitive forms of therapy. Some spiritual or complementary techniques use something close to the "laying on of hands." Bullis (1996) reported that a relatively limited number of clinical social workers touch their clients for healing purposes ($M = 1.2$; $SD = 5.0$). (See also Appendix C.)

A case likely to increase a counselor's fear of being sued involves the criminal appeal that had to determine when a hug is just a hug, or a criminal act. In *State v. Ohrtman* (1991), the defendant was charged, but not convicted, of fourth-degree criminal sexual conduct for sexual contact during counseling. The state appealed his acquittal.

The complaint alleged that on the third counseling session the male defendant gave the female client a hug "during which he compressed her breasts against his chest. It is alleged that his penis was erect during the hug" (*State v. Ohrtman*, p. 2). However, no unlawful touching of the penis was charged. After a detailed examination of the statutory history of the law under which the defendant was charged, the court of appeals affirmed the trial court's ruling. They ruled that the entire case turned on the legislative intent of criminal "touching," The court found that "touching" had also to involve an additional sexual act. They also found that "touching" merely to express "fondness and affection ought not to be threatened with sanction" (p. 4).

So why would a case ultimately decided in favor of the counselor tend to make counselors extra cautious? The answer is simple. Who wants to put themselves in a legal, economic, social, and professional position of *twice* defending themselves in a criminal action? Most counselors would rather be safe than sorry. This case (and others like it) has what lawyers call, a "chilling effect" upon physical contact between counselor and client. Of course, it must be stated again, that the public policy, and subsequent law, favors protecting the client from harm. To the extent that clients need to be protected from the negligent or even predatory intentions and actions from counselors, such laws will need strict enforcement.

This case and discussion may serve as a cautionary tale specifically to some spiritually or complementary counselors. Laying on of hands, holding or moving hands above the client's body, or just holding hands in prayer may be part of the counselor's therapeutic repertoire. Even under the most benign circumstances, such interventions may be misinterpreted or misconstrued; thus, the counselor must make such decisions with full awareness of possible ethical or legal consequences.

So what are the choices of the prudent counselor in deciding to affectionately hug, hold hands, or otherwise nonsexually touch a client? They may be summarized as follows, from the least legal risk to the counselor to the most risky:

1. Don't touch clients at all, under any circumstances.
2. Conduct such contact only under rare and unusual circumstances. These might include if the client approaches and hugs the counselor when the counselor is taken by surprise. Apparently, many counselors have selected this approach. According to Bullis' survey of Virginia clinical social workers (1996), only 13.5% are professionally comfortable touching a client for "healing" purposes. The percentages drop even further when asked if they were personally comfortable (10.9%).
3. Conduct such conduct only under specified and circumscribed circumstances. These include when the counselor has fully and thoroughly agreed to such nonsexual, noncriminal contact. "Nonsexual" is discussed in some detail here and in the next chapter. By "noncriminal" contact, the author means contact that does not involve assault or battery, among other things. Essentially, this involves informed consent, the topic of the following section. Informed consent, a doctrine valued sometimes more in its breech than its adherence, discloses: (a) what is to be done (i.e., what kind of touching), (b) why it is done (it must be therapeutic), (c) under what circumstances it will be done, and (d) any ill effects it may have. Often, a signed document accompanies the consent.

If this preparation seems to take the spontaneity out of it, keep in mind that this is a book on legal and ethical practice and that court cases do not arise when the client is fully satisfied. The problem is, a counselor can never really be sure when and if the client may precipitously or subsequently withdraw his or her "consent."

☐ Informed Consent

Of critical importance in adjudicating sexual harassment, and other legal issues, is *informed consent*. Informed consent is an assent that is based upon adequate information, such as any harmful informed consent is a serious matter and may need additional serious attention among profession health care workers. In a recent study of physicians in routine office visits, nine out of ten doctors failed to discuss issues thoroughly enough to make informed decisions.

In a study of 1,057 primary-care physicians, reported in the December 22 issue of *Journal of the American Medical Association* (Braddock, Edwards, Hasenberg, Laidley, & Levinson, 1999), some important pieces in the decision-making process were missing. The study indicated that there was little discussion of the pros and cons of a medical decision or mention of side effects of an alternative medication. "New strategies, including more effective and efficient use of educational materials and decision aids in office practice will need to be developed and tested as part of the solution" (Associated Press, 1999h). This book offers two specific suggestions at the end of Chapter 5, as educational and testing tools, to address the issue of informed consent. One cannot help but wonder how well the counseling professions would fare under similar circumstances.

The legal application and significance of informed consent is illustrated in the case in which Ms. Matthies (***Matthies v. Mastromonaco***, 1998) broke her hip and her doctor ordered bed rest. Surgery, which the doctor argued was contraindicated because of her age and physical condition. The doctor did not explain possible adverse complications of bed rest to her. During the bed rest, the chosen procedure, Ms. Matthies' right femur displaced, the result being that the right leg became shortened. She had to have two hip replacement surgeries. She has to live in a nursing home and is confined to a bed or chair. Ms. Matthies sued under the theory that the doctor negligently failed to get her informed consent to the bed rest by not specifically informing her that surgery was an alternative.

The doctor argued that is not necessary in noninvasive treatment cases (such as bed rest). The trial court agreed and returned a verdict of no cause of action. The appeals court reversed and **remanded** the case for a new trial saying that informed consent applies to noninvasive as well as to invasive treatments.

The doctor appealed the case to the Supreme Court of New Jersey. That court, too, held for Ms. Matthies, writing that the medical provider should explain both invasive and noninvasive procedures, including risks and likely outcomes of those procedures, even when the chosen procedure is noninvasive (*Matthies v. Mastromonaco*, 1998).

In a premise stated earlier, "so the medical profession goes, so goes the counseling profession," we have noted that legal issues affecting the medical profession often presage legal decisions in the counseling profession. The *Matthies* case indicates that it may well be necessary to fully inform a client of the benefits and risks of treatment alternatives, particularly those facts that the counselor knew or should have known (see *scienter* in Glossary), at the time of the decision. A fuller discussion of scienter is undertaken in the next chapter.

☐ Practicing Medicine Without a License

Given the rather somber, even scary, nature of our legal discussion thus far, it might be fun to begin this section with outlandish and egregious examples of people who were able to practice medicine without a license—and get away with it! In one case, a 54-year-old man was arrested in Florida after practicing medicine for 17 years without ever having gone to medical school and after delivering literally hundreds of babies. He was sentenced to three years and three months in federal prison and had to pay $5 million in restitution (Fake Doctor, 2000).

In another case, a man convicted of involuntary manslaughter and for practicing medicine four previous times, was again arrested for the unlicensed practice of medicine. U.S. marshalls arrested the man in a Hollywood clinic after he was given bus fare to transfer himself from one California prison to another (Hollywood Clinic, 2000). It might seen that in our computerized society, where there is so much information accessible on our professional and personal lives, that records on who and who is not authorized to practice their professions would be readily available and that the consumer would be safe from imposters. Apparently not.

There are as many varieties of practicing without a license as there are licenses under which to practice. Criminal statutes against the unlicensed practice of medicine can come under many guises, many of which apply to counselors. Counselors who offer advice or therapeutic techniques that cross the line into medicine can face and have faced criminal charges. This criminal charge may come from unexpected quarters which can apply to spiritual and alternative counselors in any number of contexts.

For example, the proprietor of a food store, Joseph Pinkus, was convicted of a violation of the medical act when he offered advice on the diagnosis and treatment of various illnesses, including stomach upset and pressure around the heart. Pinkus advised the "client" to eat various foods and vegetables—some of which he sold. He was convicted in New Jersey for practicing medicine without a license and the Supreme Court of that state upheld his conviction (*Pinkus v. MacMahon*, 1943).

A similar case involved a dentist who wrote a book titled "One Answer to Cancer" which contained information about the diagnosis, treatment, and offered treatments to cancer and other diseases. Additionally and significantly, the dentist did not differentiate his "dental" credentials from those of a "doctor." The book left open the impression the dentist was, in fact, a medical doctor. The state board of medical examiners brought an action against the dentist. The trial court issued a permanent injunction against further "practice of medicine" and the Texas court of appeals upheld the injunction stating that even the First Amendment does not allow a nonmedical doctor to offer such diagnoses and treatments (*Kelley v. Texas State Braddock of Medical Examiners*, 1971).

These two cases are particularly interesting and informative in our day when so many are writing books and offering nutritional advice on illnesses. These cases are a cautionary tale (as so many of these cases are) for counselors practicing spiritual or complementary counseling. By its very nature, it is consistent for such counselors to address issues of health and physical ailments through diet, nutrition, or others means. Additionally, it is conceivable that counselors may commit such opinions and ideas to writing or the spoken word, such as in the Kelley case. While simply trying to help clients explore other options, counselors may inadvertently be "practicing medicine."

Here, let's maintain our realistic perspective. This author grants that it is quite possible for counselors to offer advice to clients on physical ills, through suggestions, pamphlets, radio advice, articles, or books, without any legal ramifications. It is well to remember that law is made mostly when people complain—that is, sue. Counselors may do the very same things that the practitioners in the above two cases did, without any legal problems. It is well to remember that the lack of indictment does not mean that the conduct is legal. A lack of investigation or indictment only means that the conduct is not yet challenged.

To review the lessons of the preceding cases: (a) it is imperative that the counselor understand the difference between practicing medicine and practicing psychotherapy. Put another way, counselors should only practice within the bounds of their license; (b) a license to practice psychotherapy is not a license to diagnose physical illnesses— even though the bio-psycho-social-spiritual model (Bullis, 1996) may be a predicate for authentic spiritual or complementary interventions; and (c) counselors need to strictly construe the *media* and *method* of their therapeutic advice. It is reasonable that the more public the advice, the more attraction it will generate. That attraction can be well and good, but it can also bring unwanted scrutiny. A review of both the *content* and *media* is necessary to protect against being "blind sided" by an investigation.

☐ Reckless Endangerment

In *People v. Tychankski* (1991) the highest court in New York State (the Court of Appeals) upheld the conviction of Lena Tychankski, a hospital volunteer. The defendant was convicted of reckless endangerment, a misdemeanor, after she disconnected the life support system of an AIDS patient. She believed that the patient had been healed by prayer.

While counselors—even in their capacities as institutional counselors, hospital volunteers, social workers, clinical psychologists, or other clinicians in hospital or other care health institutions—would never conduct themselves in this manner, they may know some who might. Counselors who favor alternative and spiritual interventions may acquaint themselves with those who might be tempted to think about actions like the defendant in the above-cited case. Such counselors should be aware, at the very minimum, of the laws that can be broken even by attempts of the actions above described.

☐ Peyote, Marijuana, and Other Hallucinogens

Some religious and spiritual traditions use drugs to effect healing (F. Huxley, 1974). Marijuana and peyote, both legally prohibited drugs, are most commonly used in this sacred context (Bullis, 1996). Such traditions assert that these drugs are both central and sacramental to their worship and should be protected by the First Amendment (Bullis, 1990b). Courts have agreed, with considerable limitations.

A recent case illustrating such exceptions is *U.S. v. Brown* (1995). Brown helped to establish Our Church, producing medicinal herbs and plants (including marijuana and peyote) which "possessed . . . properties of spiritual enlightenment," which the church distributed to the sick. He was convicted and sentenced to 121 months in prison.

The 8th Circuit Court of Appeals affirmed Brown's conviction, even though he appealed on 1st Amendment grounds. He submitted that both the First Amendment and the Religious Freedom Restoration Act (discussed in Chapter 1) protected his use of these controlled substances. Brown was mistaken.

The federal Court of Appeals held that controlling illegal drug use was, indeed, a compelling and consistent state interest. The Court also concluded that, under the facts of this case, the defendant's use of peyote, even under admittedly "sacramental" use, was not constitutionally protected.

A criminal defendant found the same result by the 10th **federal Circuit Court** of Appeals (*U.S. v. Meyers*, 1996). Meyers was found guilty of possession with intent to distribute marijuana, and aiding and abetting possession with intent to distribute marijuana. The district court denied Meyers a defense based upon his religious freedom defense. Meyers, at that time, filed an affidavit stating that he is the founder and Reverend of the Church of Marijuana and that it is his sincere belief that his religion "commands him to use, possess, grow, and distribute marijuana for the good of mankind and the planet earth" (*U.S. v. Meyers*, p. 3). He appealed his conviction based upon, inter alia, that the trial court erred in prohibiting his religious freedom defense and that the Religious Freedom Restoration Act (RFRA).

Meyers' religious freedom appeal centers upon his assertion that the criminal prohibition of his religious conduct unduly burdens his freedom of religion. The court of appeals denied Meyers' religious appeal under both the constitution and the RFRA. The court held that, the RFRA notwithstanding, the 1st amendment religious protections do not relieve an individual from complying with valid and neutral laws. The court found that the criminal laws under which Meyers was convicted did not single out any religious group for discrimination and that the laws applied equally to everyone.

Additionally, the court of appeals concluded that the Church of Marijuana and, in particular Meyers' social and philosophical beliefs, do not rise to the level of "religious" beliefs. The court of appeals, as we have seen in the Preface, distinguished between a "philosophy" or a "way of life" but held that those ideas do not rise to the legal definition of "religion." Thus, on the two previous counts, the court ruled that Meyers' religious defense would fail on their own merits, and affirmed the lower court's ruling.

This line of cases suggests several concerns for spiritual or complementary counselors. First is the obvious notion that counselors who take part in ceremonies using illegal drugs run the risk of criminal prosecution. Even with legitimate appeals to the RFRA, many drug convictions are upheld. Even seemingly religious or spiritual motivations for taking illegal drugs can bring felony possession indictments. The United States' "war on drugs" has raised both the vigor of prosecutions and terms of imprisonments, particularly in federal drug cases. Counselors should be scrupulous in avoiding any such entanglements, even if for religious purposes.

Second, clients may want the counselor to advise or procure illegal drugs for their "spiritual edification." After all, clients will seek out spiritual or complementary counselors in order to explore alternative interventions. Some clients may want the counselor to take such explorations one step further and want the counselor to help them to explore spirituality through the use of hallucinogenic or psychedelic drugs.

There is a long history of the connection between drugs and spiritual experience. Many popular and distinguished writers have detailed their experiences with hallucinogenics in spiritual terms. A classic book by Aldous Huxley titled *The Doors of Perception* (1954) describes his experimenting with mescaline, an active ingredient of peyote. Some 20 years later Baba Ram Dass (formerly Harvard professor Richard Alpert) wrote *Be Here Now* (1971) where he described his association with Timothy Leary and their experiments with LSD, and on into his discipleship with an Indian holy man. The year *Be Here Now* was published, Carlos Castaneda traveled to Mexico and began an apprentiship with a Yachi sorcerer called don Juan Matus. The tales of this discipleship in a series of books (e.g., *The Teachings of Don Juan, A Separate Reality, Journey to Ixtlan, Tales of Power*) became bestsellers and sparked enormous interest in drugs known to the sorcerer including jimpson weed (*Datura inoxia*), a form of peyote (*Lophorphora williamsii*), and a mushroom of the genus *Psilocybe* (Castenada, 1972).

In a more "academic" context, Masters and Houston (1966) published *The Varieties of Psychedelic Experience* (in a takeoff on William James' psychological classic *The Varieties of Religious Experience*) where they detailed the effects of LSD on perception and human development. While these authors in no way advocated drug use, taken as a whole these works and others like them introduced readers to the psychological and spiritual effects of psychedelics. Thus, some clients may want counselors who are amenable to spiritual exploration and human transformation, to "guide" them in a psychedelic spiritual search.

Third, clients suffering from addictions may try to use or to suggest that counselors aid and abet their use of alternative medications. These alternative medications may include hallucinogenic drugs. For example, the psychotropic drug Ibogaine (from the bark of *Tabernantha iboga*) a plant from Gabon, West Africa, has been used to treat heroine addiction. Treatments with Ibogaine have been given to addicts in places ranging from the Netherlands, Panama, St. Kitts, and Slovenia—but not in the United States. Here, Ibogaine is as illegal as crack cocaine (Koerner, 1999).

Another species of hallucinogen is making its way from the Amazon jungles into South American cities and into North American spiritual consciousness. This is a tea called either *yage* (pronounced "ya-hay") or *ayahuasca* (pronounced "eye-ah-wah-ska"). The beverage is brewed from the *Canisteriopsis Caapi* vine and is being brought by into greater use by Columbia Amazon Indian medicine men and shamans. One shaman explains that yage is, "a great analyst" that can be used in "helping people cure emotional problems at the root of their illnesses." Yage is also not unknown among artists and intellectual and spiritual seekers. *The Yage Letters*, a book on the experience under its influence, was written by beat writers William Burroughs and Alan Ginsberg after their experiences with the tea in the 1950s and 1960s (Kotter, 1999).

Neither has yage excaped notice by the counseling professions. Dr. Charles Grob, a UCLA psychiatry professor, thinks the yage is worth investigating for its therapeutic benefits saying, "We might learn more about how to treat depression and other mood disorders" (Kotler, 1999).

In addition to drugs used for serious, but dangerous, purposes or as "spiritual inspiration or insight," another class of drugs begs the spiritual counselor's attention. Some clients may use what are called "club drugs" for purportedly spiritual purposes. Clinicians who aid and abet clients in the use of illegal drugs, even for "therapeutic purposes" (unless authorized to do so) run the considerable risks of criminal prosecution.

This warning is true for the medicinal or medical use of marijuana. Some jurisdictions are experimenting with legalizing such usage, such as San Francisco and Maine. In Maine, voters approved a measure to allow the medicinal use of marijuana (Wren, 2000). Pot is unlikely to be in everyone's medicine cabinet anytime soon, however. A Gallup poll shows that 69% of U.S. citizens oppose making pot legal for everyone, even though some voters are tolerant for pot use among the seriously ill (Wren, 2000). Additionally, the U.S. Supreme Court has continued to ban the distribution of marijuana for medical purposes. It did so in the summer of 2000 under an expedited ruling requsted by the Clinton administration after a lower court ruled to allow the distribution.

Such political decisions notwithstanding, the "jury" is still out both on the science and the law of medical marijuana use (Hostetler, 1999). It is likely that the pendulum will swing back and forth for some time. What can be said now, however, is that counselors are not in a legal position to aid or abet such usage, even on behalf of clients, without suffering adverse legal consequences.

☐ Child Abuse

All counselors, whatever their school of practice, are likely to come into contact with the law of child abuse. I address this issue here because counseling by spiritual or complementary means can also bring the counselor into the law exempting such prosecutions because the parents or guardians tried healing by spiritual means. It goes without saying that child abuse or neglect constitutes major legislation. All states and the federal government have various criminal sanctions against child abuse. Many commentators have discussed these statutes and we need not comment further here. Child abuse is addressed again, both in Chapters 6 and 7, as it pertains to religious affiliation ("cults") and to crosscultural spiritual practices.

Elder abuse legislation is also important, of course, but does not engender the religious or spiritual exemptions because of parental control, as we shall see in the next sections. Some parents choose to address medical concerns of their children through prayer or other spiritual means. Case law is replete with examples of churches or parents using spiritual treatments in the service of curing childhood illness—and being prosecuted for it.

Religious Exemptions to Child Abuse

The constitution provides for exemptions for religious practices of healing. Governments would be prohibited from prosecuting certain persons from exercising their religious freedoms, including those connected with the use of spiritual techniques of healing.

At least forty-seven of the fifty states allow for a defense against criminal charges where certain persons use spiritual healing techniques (Bullis, 1991a; denoted in that article). These statutes embody exemptions and are coming into increasing conflict with child abuse laws. For example, the New York state statute reads:

> In any prosecution for endangering the welfare of a child . . . based upon the alleged failure or refusal to provide proper medical care for treatment to an ill child, it is an affirmative defense that the defendant (a) is a parent, guardian, or other person legally charged with the care or custody of such child; and (b) is a member or adherent of an organized church or religious group the tenets of which prescribe prayer as the principal treatment for illness; and (c) treated or caused to be treated in accordance with such tenets.

This statute points out two aspects of this "spiritual healing" defense. One is that the defense applies to "an organized church or religious group." It may well not apply to simply a "spiritual" practitioner. Second is that the treatment must be "in accordance with" those religious tenets. These conditions serve to limit this affirmative defense. Not only does the statute require that the defendant adhere to religious norms, but the interventions must be related to those religious tenets. Spiritual motivations or interventions of the practitioner's own choosing will probably not qualify.

At face value alone, statutes may seem to offer blanket protections to those indicted for child abuse. As we have seen previously, the law does not apply so easily. In some cases its seems to afford such protection, while in other cases it does not.

Perhaps this sounds like "weasel" words. However, it is hard to state broad legal principles when the law is yet unsettled. Counselors can expect this issue to remain unsettled for some time. There are simply no hard and fast rules on this issue. This is clearly an issue where different courts from different jurisdictions rule differently.

Yet, sometimes significant and relevant information is embedded in a law case. While not explicitly part of the decision, such data can be illuminating. In *State v. Norman* (1992), the defendent, the father of a 10-year-old, was convicted of first degree manslaughter because he refused to provide medical care for his ill son. The son later died of untreated juvenile diabetes weighing only 46 pounds at the time of his death.

Mr. Norman was a member of a religious group that relied primarily upon God to head its members. Medical care was to be used as a last resort. The Washington Court of Appeals held that the father's conviction violated the U.S. constitution or the Washington State constitution. Additionally, the jury instruction that parents have a duty to provide their children medical care when a reasonably prudent person would deem it necessary accurately stated Washington law.

The case illustrates how authentically held religious or spiritual beliefs are all qualified. Just because someone holds strong, clear, and authentic beliefs, that does not provide a defense for all criminal behavior. Child welfare and safety in particular is often of greater legal value than parents' religious beliefs.

As we have seen in the cases criminalizing "psychotherapeutic deception," courts seem more and more willing to hold either parents, guardians, or counselors to a high standard to protect those in their care—especially children, even when religious motivations are claimed. In Chapter 7, we address the "cultural defense" issue in child abuse cases as well.

Having introduced this legally unsettled topic, perhaps the most useful suggestion is to form some thoughts on how counselors can address clients when they are now, or are considering, healing child illness purely by spiritiual means.

1. Do not give legal advice, but show them the relevant statutes on child abuse and its exemptions; this might alert them to the legal ramifications of their choices. Suggest they contact a lawyer.

2. As a counselor, then, you can do what you do best—explore the emotional and social meaning behind their choices and their options.
3. Consider whether the child abuse reporting statute applies for you personally.
4. With appropriate respect, you might also explore the moral and spiritual meaning of their choices in using only spiritual means. You might ask about how strong their ties are to their religious group, the intensity of their faith, and the meaning of this faith for them. Obviously this questioning is not intended as an inquisition or critique, but rather to explore the dimensions of this important faith stance in their lives.

☐ Schools: Suspensions for Wearing Insignia, and Organization Membership

One overlooked but important issue, especially for school counselors, are school suspensions and other penalties connected with wearing spiritual insignia or participation in spiritual organizations. While school suspensions are not precisely criminal convictions, they can act as such in terms of the impact on a young person's "record." Whether or not school counselors or social workers practice spiritiual or complementary counseling, they will be in positions to advise or to counsel students and administrators regarding school and student positions. These paragraphs are designed to set the ethical and legal context for school counselors to competently respond to school officials, parental questions, and student concerns in these areas.

Some courts have strictly limited nontraditional religious symbols in public schools. For example, in a 1999 ruling, a federal district court judge ruled that a school district violated the religious rights of Roman Catholic families when Bedford, New York school district teachers had third-grade students cut out images of the elephant-headed Hindu god Ganesha, constructed toothpick "worry dolls," and built an altar for an Earth Day liturgy. In issuing the ruling that there was "subtle coercive pressure to engage in the Hindu religion," the judge declared, "While reading the Ganesha stories can be part of a neutral secular curriculum, this court fails to find any educational justification for telling young, impressionable students to construct images of a known religious god" (Associated Press, 1999b). While the general trend for the past decades had been to legally protect nontraditional spiritual and religious practices, constitutional tolerance may be limited in the face of "impressionable minds" of school children.

Without question there is a national trend toward openness to historically nontraditional religious and spiritiual practices among young people. For example, *Teen-Witch: Wicca for a New Generation* (Ravenwolf, 2000), a 250-page manual, is popular reading for 10- to 17-year-olds that claims to tell everything a teen needs to be "a pentacle-wearing, spell-casting, completely authentic witch!" Including such teen-driven spells as the Bad Bus-Driver spell, the Unground Me spell, and the Just Say-No spell, it reportedly is flying off the shelves of major book retailers (Mulrine, 1999).

Speaking of pentacles, the constitutional tolerance for nontraditional traditions, at least in colleges and universities, seems to be expanding. For example, a 17-year-old Lincoln Park (Illinois) High School student successfully sued her school over her religious right to wear a pentagram (a five-pointed star) as a form of practicing her Wicca religion. The American Civil Liberties Union filed the suit on her behalf and a spokesperson said, "Christian students can wear crosses and Jewish students can wear stars of David, but Wiccans can't wear the pentagram" (Associated Press, 1999a).

The school superintendent said that the high school did not realize that Wicca was a religion and not a gang designation (Associated Press, 1999c). From the school's point of view, safety was the main concern. The ban on the pentagram was part of school-wide crackdown on gangs, drugs, and violence, according to a school memo. Black nail-polish, dog-collars, and "death-style makeup" are also banned (Associated Press, 1999c).

Obviously, much of the school concerns of gangs is due, in part, to the 1999 Columbine School shootings in Colorado. Many school officials have banned certain clothing and proscribed certain behaviors. Schools have become test cases for the new boundaries of religious and spiritiual inclusion and counseling. School counselors need to stay up-to-date on the increased tendency of courts to constitutionally protect religious apparel. While schools are increasingly under pressure to protect students, they are also increasingly under pressure to accommodate the increased religious diversity of their constituencies. This balance is rightly confusing. Two initial points may help define the confusion.

First, the boundaries between protecting the health and welfare of students and religious expression have become moving targets as society, the law, and ethics grapple with these issues. So if counselors, and school counselors in particular, are confused about the legal lines drawn between students' rights and school officials' rights in protecting students, that confusion is justified.

Second, these decisions must be made on a case-by-case basis. There is no "silver bullet" solution applicable to all situations. Blanket policies prohibiting the wearing of certain insignia, colors, or symbols, where they have religious significance, are likely to be legally challenged. While an entire chapter of this book is devoted to the legal/ethical issues raised by so-called "cults" (a term used with some reticence by the author), some suggestions follow.

1. School counselors are likely to have to address religious and spiritual issues even in public schools. As noted already in the Preface, the alleged "wall" between church and state is, at best, porous. While church/state issues are constantly fought in public schools, religious and spiritual activity regularly take place there—from after-school prayer meetings, to impromptu discussions. School counselors not only need to hear "where students are" spiritually, but need to educate themselves as to the levels of legal tolerance for such behavior.
2. School counselors must not substitute their own religious comfort for constitutional protection offered to nontraditional religions. Of course, it is easier to understand, and sympathize with, a spiritual or religious tradition with which one has been accustomed or chooses for oneself. However, the counselor's role is to understand and to appreciate "where the client is"—this must include the client's spiritual orientation as well as socially and emotionally.

   There are many ways to accomplish this—none having to compromise the counselor's own religious beliefs or practices. Perhaps the best way is to just listen to students. Students are often eager to share their impressions of the belief system in which they have been raised or to share new-found beliefs. Prudent counselors will also listen to the communities in which they practice. Counselors need to know the limits of spiritual toleration for students' beliefs, if for nothing more than to advise students on the probability on clashes with parents or community members.
3. Counselors can educate themselves about religious and spiritual practices by reading and watching videos. There is a plethora of educational material on the market. (Appendix C is designed to offer illustrative, not exhaustive, sources for such research.)

4. Counselors can read what students read. If a student finds a religious or spiritual book particularly influential, the counselor can read it. The counselor may find merit in the information it contains. Additionally, discussing *why* a work is important to students has therapeutic value of its own. Such discussions can unlock avenues of communication about the values and ethos of the client. It can also reveal emotional directions down which the student is traveling. Additionally, it can promote therapeutic rapport. Student clients appreciate that others take the time and effort to understand them or their world better. Just learning and listening is therapeutic.

5. Counselors need to evaluate the differences between gangs, cults, sects, and bona fide religion. This evaluation would not be a *legal* evaluation, of course, but could be an aid in one's own clinical evaluations as well as a help in advising school officials as to the relative differences between those groups. For example, not many would quibble with the dress of an Amish or a Hasidic student. School officials will have to make decisions on acceptable dress and jewelry, maybe even tatoos or body piercing, predicated upon First Amendment principles of free exercise of religion and not upon idiocyncratic tastes. This book devotes an entire chapter on cults, sects, and spiritual behavior.

The following considerations can help guide the school counselor:

1. Is the insignia religious or spiritual in nature? Or it more fashion that faith? This is the crux of this series of questions. This issue has two parts. The first part determines whether the symbol has sacred connotations to the wearer. This "point of view" is a crucial consideration. It doesn't matter whether the symbol is sacred to the school administrators, teachers or counselors; it matters whether the symbol is sacred to the wearer. The second part is political as much as legal and may be an issue as much for the courts as for school officials. That is how important is the symbol as a religious or spiritual article for the wearer. This is important for school officials to determine because it may determine the extent the purposed banning may become a legal issue. If the school officials correctly determine that the symbol is more fad or fashion that faith, then the insignia is unlikely to be the cause of a successful lawsuit. Simply put, students or their parents are less likely to go the trouble and expense to prosecute a lawsuit over fashion than if it is a matter of deeply held conviction.

   The following series of questions may be helpful for school officials to consider in addressing this question: (a) how deeply connected is the symbol to the personal and private life of the student? (b) does the student use the symbol as part of formal or even informal worship or religious services or acts of devotion? (c) how adamant does the student seem to be in challenging the proposed ban? (d) how adamant do the parents seem to be in supporting the student's challenge? (e) is the symbol a part of a larger belief system? (f) to what extent is the symbol employed in religious or spiritual services outside that of the student's use? and (g) Is the symbol idiosyncratic to the individual student?

2. Would the institution's regulations otherwise ban the symbol? This question asks whether or not the school or institution has a separate reason for banning the symbol. Does the symbol have an exclusive and unique gang connotation?

3. Do the shape, design, or elements making up the symbol itself present a danger in its own right? In other words, an automatic pistol made with a crucifix on the handle grip would not be allowed even with the obvious religious symbolism. Conversely, a Wicca pendant may be allowed, even if other gang-like groups also adopt the symbol as their own.

4. Is each case being handled on an individual basis? Courts are likely to frown upon a wholesale ban on any one sign or symbol if one group identifies it as its religious symbol. If a gang member uses the symbol as a gang identification, it is quite different than if the same symbol were to be adopted by a religious group. As we have stated earlier, students can be expected to wear isignia for different purposes. Some reasons may be religious, others quite secular. It is important to ask students what the purpose is for wearing the symbol and to discern its meaning for them.

5. How informed are school officials about the symbols and beliefs of nontraditional or nonmajority religious or spiritual symbols? Spiritual symbols will proliferate in an increasingly pluralistic world. The constitution has an obligation to protect *everyone's* religious symbols—especially of those religious groups who need constitutional protection because they are few in number or without political power. While those who originally wrote the First Amendment would be stunned to see the Wicca symbol in schools and on campuses, it is precisely those who might be oppressed who are in most need of constitutional protection.

☐ Defenses Against Criminal Actions

No discussion of criminal culpability and other sanctions would be complete without a discussion of defenses against such charges. Charges are only one-half the story of criminal accusation and conviction. Defenses are the other half. Defenses are legal excuses against accusations. Just like every kind of "bad" conduct does not constitute a crime, not every excuse is a legal excuse. Defenses, like accusations, must conform to statute or case law.

To repeat the purpose of this book, I do not recite criminal defenses here to exhaust the possibilities for such defenses. The incomplete menu below is provided to place counselor criminal conduct into its legal context; this information will help counselors, particularly those practicing spiritual and alternative interventions, to protect themselves and their clients.

Although it seems like "I didn't do it" might constitute the principal defense, the law is not so simple. If you are sued, you will have to *prove* your innocence, or more precisely, you will need to reasonably show that there is a reasonable doubt as to your guilt. This section describes how counselors might show their innocence if they defend themselves by the primary reason that they were not present at the scene, or the session did not go that way, or that they never did or said something. The goal is establishing proof or reasonable doubt. The following is a catalogue of suggestions as to maintaining records to do just that.

1. Maintain a complete set of process notes for every client. Recording every word and act is not necessary, but a record of *what* interventions were used, *how* they were used, and *the result* probably is.

2. Trust your gut. If a client is particularly challenging or noncompliant, you may want to maintain more detailed records.

3. Keep an accurate, detailed appointment book. Note the client, time, and location of meeting. Sometimes counselors engaged in spiritual or complementary interventions conduct such sessions outside the office, in hospitals, other institutions, outside, or in a client's home. Note the reason that such sessions are not in the office. The reason that a session took place in the hospital, for example, might be that your client had a

broken leg. If the case should ever come to court, the rationale for a non-office visit or a non-business-hour session should be explained.

4. The date book is your alibi in another sense as well. If a client alleges improprieties at a time and location where you can prove you were somewhere else, you go a long way toward **summary judgment** in your favor. For the same reason, it is a good idea to save receipts. They not only are important for taxes, but also provide proof of your whereabouts (with time dated receipts).

5. Never meet a client, even for nonorthodox interventions, at a clearly inappropriate place. As one of my seminary professors succinctly put it, "There's just no reason for a session at 10 o'clock at night in the lobby of a hotel."

6. We address the integrity defense below. This defense is designed to save the counselor from false allegations in the first place.

7. These same suggestions apply to civil defenses (discussed, in the next chapter).

Pleading "not guilty" does not necessary mean that the defendant did not commit the act for which he or she is charged. Pleading "not guilty" may also mean that the defendant claims a legal excuse for committing the act. Thus, in *people v. Cardenas,* the case study at the beginning of this chapter, the defendant appealed his conviction on the grounds that the women consented to his alleged criminal conduct. Thus, the appeal did not center around whether or not he committed the acts in question, but whether he had consent.

Another example is the hug case (*State v. Ohrtman,* 1991) described earlier. The defendant did not raise the defense that he did not commit the hug in the first place. His defense was that the hug did not meet the statutory definition of "touching" to achieve a criminal conviction. Thus, the issue before the courts was not whether or not the defendant actually committed the act, but the legal meaning behind the act. The court was aided in its determination by such technical help as a statutory and **legislative history** of the criminal "touching" laws. These legal materials give the rationale, origin, and development of the statutes through their developmental history. The court also employed such common sense aids as a dictionary. These legal and nonlegal tools offered the court guidance in its determination.

Similarly, expert witnesses are designed to guide the "triers of fact" (either a trial judge or a jury) in their determinations. Even a casual observer of dramatized courtroom scenarios or live court proceedings could demonstrate the role and value of expert witnesses.

☐ Expert Witnesses and Criminal Accusations

In medical malpractice cases, for example, medical doctors will be called upon to testify as to the "standard of practice" for a specific surgical (or other) procedure carried out upon a certain patient under certain circumstances. The defense will call their set of expert witnesses and the plaintiffs (or prosecution) will call their set of expert witnesses. This is sometimes ironically referred to as the "parade of the experts." I say ironically, because the experts often disagree with each other even over the interpretation of the same set of facts. In the end, the triers of fact must make sense out of the enormous amount of data and explanations offered by the experts and come to a determination.

Expert witnesses, of course, are called upon to offer opinions in criminal cases against counselors. In *State v. Eichman* (1990), a counselor was accused of violating the Wisconsin Sexual Exploitation by a Therapist statute. He was convicted and his appeal centered around the propriety of admitting an expert witness to define and describe "psychotherapy" as it related to the criminal statute. Remember that the professional must have been conducting psychotherapy at the time of the alleged criminal act in order to be convicted. The Supreme Court ruled that expert witnesses in this case were admissible.

The court found that an expert witness could help determine whether or not the kind of interventions employed by the defendant were consistent with the statutory definition of psychotherapy. Additionally, the court declared that expert witnesses might well be helpful in cases where the "evidence is couched in professional terminology beyond the understanding of the ordinary person. Because proof of that fact is an element of the offense, expert testimony should be admitted if given the circumstances of the case it would assist the **trier of fact**" (*State v. Eichman*, p. 150).

What, then, do expert witnesses have to do with a counselor who uses complementary or spiritual interventions? Plenty. First, expert testimony can play key roles in most, if not all, of the criminal statutes mentioned in this chapter. The prosecution of such counselors may rise and fall upon the admissibility, availability, and credibility of their side's expert witness.

Second, thus, counselors have a self interest in keeping a mental note of experts in the fields in which they practice, or of the intervention techniques which they employ. For example, if a counselor were to employ meditation or prayer in their practice, it would be wise to know who are the experts in those areas. It is also wise to know where those experts are located and to amass records of the experts' books, articles, and recordings of their seminars. Such experts may be called upon to testify—as might an eminent cardiologist in a medical malpractice case—in a suit challenging the counselor's proper use, gathering of informed consent, or precautions in the use of the intervention. These precautions form a larger context in which the counselor plays an active role in his or her own defense. After all, the counselor, not the attorney, will know who the experts are in the counselor's chosen area of intervention. While the attorney will rightly lead and execute the defense, the counselor will play an important auxiliary role.

Third, this supportive role can include spiritual and complementary therapists "defending" themselves even if they never see a complaint lodged against them. Counselors using expert witnesses have a self-interest in encouraging, participating in, aiding, interpreting, and publishing research about their chosen interventions. Research into contemporary and spiritual therapies can only help. Additionally, the greater professional and public acceptance, understanding and awareness of such interventions, the less chance there is of a judge or jury misinterpreting the counselor's use of that intervention.

A close analogy is that of expert testimony relating to profiling serial killers. There was a time when the patterns, motivations, and behaviors of such people were simply thought of as sinful, evil, or aberrant. The notion that serial killers had a well thought-out plan, got better with practice (if we can use that term), and that their behaviors were both meaningful (to them) and predictable was laughable well into the last half of the previous century. Now expert testimony is taken routinely on the patterns and *signature* as opposed to the ***modus operandi*** of well known serial killers. Judges and juries now have a greater comfort level, trust level, and ability to more adequately discern technical concepts of the social sciences.

While almost anyone can claim to be an expert, a judge does not have to allow just anyone to testify as an expert witness. As you might guess, there is a case that helps judges determine whether or not an individual has the competence and experience to qualify as an expert witness. The court serves as a "gatekeeper" in this respect. The traditional standard for the admissibility of expert testimony is *Frye v. U.S.* (1923). This U.S.

Supreme Court decision required that the scientific technique was generally accepted as reliable in the relevant scientific community. The precedent, enunciated in *Frye v. U.S.*, has been modified, sometimes substantially modified, in later cases. Rule 702 of the Federal Rules of Evidence also requires courts to use the standard of "reliability." It reads:

> If scientific, technical, or other specialized knowledge will assist the trier of fact to understand the evidence or to determine a fact in issue, a witness qualified as an expert by knowledge, skill, experience, training, or education, may testify thereto in the form of an opinion or otherwise.

As the date of *Frye v. U.S.* suggests, this case, while venerable, has had some tinkering done to it over the intervening years. In *Daubert v. Merrell Dow Pharmacauticals Inc.* (1993), the U.S. Supreme Court refined *Frye v. U.S.* to these factors in the admissibility of expert witnesses: (a) whether the theory is tested, (b) whether the theory has been subjected to peer review and to publication, (c) what the known or possible rate of error is, and (d) whether the theory is generally accepted within the relevant scientific community. Briefly put, the Supreme Court required expert testimony to be both relevant and *reliable*.

In the "hard" sciences, reliability can be more carefully measured and "tested" than in the social sciences. Not that it can't be done, but human interaction is not always as testable as chemical interaction. As everyone knows, psychologists, social workers, and other counselors have been testifying in courts for years. Many, many aspects of social science theory have been tested.

But when we speak of spiritual or complementary counseling, does the standard still apply? For example, can the reliability of Christian, Buddhist, or shamanic theory be tested? While the *Daubert* case showed the way for the "harder" sciences, might the standards be the same for spiritual or complementary counseling interventions?

Let us be clear, once again, why this discussion is important. For criminal, civil, and licensing actions against counselors, expert witnesses can offer crucial insights and verification of a counselor's methodology and interventions. Expert witnesses often are a crucial factor in tilting the scale of justice either toward guilt or innocence.

In 1999, the U.S. Supreme Court decided a case that offers more clues about how future courts may view expert witnesses in spiritual or complementary counseling. In *Kumho Tire Co. Ltd. v. Carmichael* (1999), the Supreme Court had to decide the admissibility of a "tire failure analyst." Plaintiffs in this case wanted the tire expert to testify that a defect in the tire caused a blowout causing injury and death. The defendants here (at trial it was the tire company) challenged the admissibility of the tire expert by asserting his testimony was not scientifically reliable enough. The trial court agreed and wouldn't allow the expert to testify. The federal circuit court (11th circuit) **reversed** and the U.S. Supreme Court granted certiorari.

That Court held that *Daubert* applied not only to "scientific" testimony, but to all "expert" testimony. This affirms the wide net that both *Daubert* and Federal Rule 702 casts over those who testify as experts on any issue helpful to the court. Additionally, the court affirmed that the *Daubert* standard is both flexible and non-exhaustive. This means that the judge has a fair amount of discretion about who it allows to testify as an expert. In terms of reliability, the Court held that the following factors might be used in assessing reliability:

1. Nature of the issue
2. The expert's particular expertise
3. The subject of the testimony

The *Kumho* decision offers some lessons about how spiritual and complementary counselors might strengthen their positions to offer such testimony in court proceedings.

Alongside of *Kumho*, we offer the Kelly test, specifically addressing the admissibility of "new" scientific techniques (*People v. Kelly*, 1976). This case, decided by the California Court of Appeals and prior to *Kumho*, offers insights, analogies, as well as precedence in cases involving spiritual and complementary counseling. The case held that new scientific techniques must be "sufficiently established to have gained general acceptance in the particular field to which it belongs" (p. 30, italics removed). *Kelly* is applied in the Ramona case described in the next section—a case both interesting and significant to those who use "new" interventions.

At the risk of being redundant, such expert testimony can offer the court necessary insights into the proper and improper uses of spiritual and complementary interventions and their likely impacts upon clients. These four criteria are offered in the reverse order as they may occur in a counselor's professional life.

1. *Publish.* Publications, preferably in juried journals, offer both the public and clinicians information as to aspects of spiritual and complementary counseling. Such publications accomplish one further purpose. They help to establish the credibility of the author. If asked to offer expert testimony, publications are a primary source of establishing that the author's work has been reviewed by professional peers.
2. *Conduct seminars.* Conducting seminars is a similar way to establish credibility. It offers one more advantage; this is, it offers the counselor a way to get personal feedback on their ideas and approaches.
3. *Practice.* A history of personally practicing the interventions about which an expert testifies is indispensable for establishing credibility. This factor offers the counselor some insights into how practitioners "on the ground" address particular client issues. This is the "real life" component of credibility.
4. *Get educated in the theory and practice of complementary and spiritual interventions.* Obviously, this should be a prerequisite for practice. But it is also important in establishing that the counselor is grounded in the theory and history of the interventions he or she employs.

These factors can provide the courts with an accurate and useful way of determining the proper use of spiritual and complementary interventions. In this sense, expert witnesses actually help make the law. We now turn to the specific issue of *non-expert* testimony in a hotly-debated spiritual or complementary counseling issue.

☐ The Admissibility of Non-Expert Testimony of Post-Hypnotically Recovered Memory

While the section above addresses expert admissibility, this section addresses the admissibility of "regular" witnesses, such as those who are victims of an alleged crime.

The value and veracity of post-hypnotically recovered memories has been one of the most hotly debated clinical issues of the past decade (See Lein, 1999). This book will not rehearse the clinical value of that intervention. Instead, we offer a legal analysis of how courts have held on the issue of allowing victims of crimes who have had their recollections refreshed by hypnosis or other aids. To be very clear, we address here only the admissibility of such memories, not their clinical utility.

We address this issue here for two reasons: 1) who is allowed to testify can help determine the outcome of the court action, and 2) this issue is analogous to other spiritual or complementary interventions.

In a relevant and interesting (but unfortunate) case, Holly Ramona accused her father, Gary Ramona, of molesting her as a child. Holly's recollections came after she was both hypnotized and given sodium amytal—a kind of "truth serum"). Her presenting issue was an eating disorder, and Holly was told by her California marriage, family, and child counselor that a majority of the counselor's clients experiencing eating disorders were also abuse victims. Holly attended group therapy sessions where sexual abuse victims participated. Subsequent to these events, Holly had "flashbacks" or "visual images" of herself as a five- or eight-year-old. When these "flashbacks" began, Holly was unsure whether or not these memories were real.

After the "flashbacks" she underwent a sodium amytal interview, but when told what she said during the interview was the truth or not (Holly had "memories" of her grandmother being raped by her brothers). The psychiatrist and her counselor assured her that she did not lie. Two years after the sodium amytal interview, she had additional "flashbacks" about Gary having forcible, vaginal sex with her and commenced the suit. Meanwhile, he and Mrs. Ramona divorced and he lost his job.

Gary, moving for summary judgment, asserted that *People v. Kelly* precluded any testimony regarding the repressed memories and that no substantial evidence corroborated the allegations. He claimed that the counselor implanted false memories through suggestive questioning during the sodium amytal interview while assuring Holly that she could not lie under the drug.

In deciding Gary's motion for dismissal, the trial court held that *Kelly* was inapplicable to psychological testimony, believing that conflicting expert testimony (the "battle of the experts") was sufficient to create a triable issue of fact that should go to a jury.

The Court of Appeals took an opposite view, holding that Holly's testimony of her alleged abuse was inadmissible. The Court found that it is well established that witnesses whose memories are "refreshed" by sodium amytal (or sodium pentathol for that matter) are inadmissible. Such testimony, said the court, is tainted and precluded cross-examination. The Kelly requirements were reliability and acceptance, as noted earlier. While the drug might have some acceptance in the relevant scientific community, the scientific community still cannot prove the reliability sufficient for court testimony (like the polygraph, for example).

Holly asserted that she should, regardless of the drug-induced memory, be able to testify to recollections *before* the drug interview. The Court dealt the same blow to that argument, holding that unless she had "personal knowledge" and "showed specific facts showing a triable issue" she could not testify. The court ruled that she did not satisfy her burden.

The above ruling could be compared to the case-by-case approach reached by the U.S. Circuit Court of Appeals (2d Cir.). In that case the plaintiff sued two individuals she accused of sexually molesting her as a child. At issue was whether she could testify as to memories enhanced through hypnosis. After initial treatment by her clinical psychologist and a medical doctor, her physician referred her to a hypnotherapist. The plaintiff underwent fourteen session and had no recall before or immediately after the sessions. The district court (trial court) ruled that she could not testify, and dismissed the case.

She fared no better on appeal. After conducting an analysis, partly using the precedent in *Daubert*, the appeals court affirmed the prior ruling, but did establish an approach to admissibility that makes room for latitude in allowing such testimony. These non-exclusive factors are:

1. Evaluate the purpose of the hypnosis: to refresh memory or to conduct therapy. The court warned that if the purpose of the hypnosis is to refresh a potential witnesses' memory, he or she may feel pressured to aid prosecutors, to convict the alleged perpetrator and, generally, to remember details.
2. Determine whether the witness received any hints or suggestions from the hypnotist.
3. Determine whether or not a permanent record of the hypnotic sessions were kept so that the court can discern, for itself, whether any suggestions were used. The court highly suggested video or audiotapes.
4. Determine whether or not the hypnotist was appropriately qualified.
5. Determine whether or not there is corroborating evidence to support allegations revealed in the refreshed recollections.
6. Determine if the subject is a highly hypnotizable subject. The court opined that some-one highly hypnotizable may be more apt to confabulate.
7. Consider expert testimony on the hypnotizing procedures used.
8. The court highly recommended a pretrial hearing so that parties can present their experts and to test credibility during cross-examination.

Finally, the court noted that it is party who seeks to introduce the hypontically re-freshed testimony that must carry the burden to persuading admissibility (*Borawick v. Shay*, 1995).

One of the principal determinations the court provided was its analysis of whether or not the hypnotist the plaintiff used was "qualified." The court determined he was not. Its analysis, including the above factors, is helpful in providing a framework for future hypontists. These factors are relevant for spiritual or complementary counselors.

The court echoed the district court's determination that the hypnotist was unqualified "beyond question" (p. 13). The appeals court found that, while a panoply of academic qualifications" are unnecessary to achieve admissibility, the hypnotist's formal educa-tion concluded with a high school diploma. Additionally, the hypnotist had no formal training in psychotherapy, did not read the professional literature, and used an exper-imental, electronic cranial stimulator in his practice (p. 13). The *Borawick* and *Kelly* cases offer an opulence of information for those who use hypnosis (or perhaps other related interventions) in a forensic setting. As we have noted, they also offer insights into how those who use spiritual and complementary interventions will promulgate their practices in professional circles. We address the related issue of "a false memory claim" in the section titled "Third Party Liability" in Chapter 3.

☐ Statutes of Limitation

The statute of limitations defense bars a finding of guilt or liability because the ac-tion is time barred. Most criminal and civil actions place a time limitation upon when an alleged act is perpetuated and when the act is brought to the attention of author-ities and filed. If the time limitation expires, no criminal charges or civil suit can be brought.

The purpose of placing a time limitation on legal actions is basically one of practicality. After a time, witnesses (and their memories), physical evidence, and other evidence die, decay, get lost, are forgotten, or deteriorate. Statutes of limitation usually—require, that a criminal charge or liability claim be brought in a timely manner. It is not unusual, for example, for many malpractice actions to have a two year statute of limitation.

The main issue of *Karasek v. Lajaie* (1998), is whether or not the statute of limitations, applied to medical malpractice cases, also applies to social workers. The court ruled that it did not. This ruling was no victory for the defendant counselors. The ruling allowed the plaintiff to maintain their cause of action beyond the normal time limitation afforded to medical practitioners.

The court's reasoning is instructive and relevant. The court reasoned, on the one hand, that while counselors *as professionals* are covered by the statute of limitations, their *professional activities* are not. The diagnostic and treatment modalities of counselors, ruled the court, are diverse as their professions including "psychiatrists, social workers, clerics, guidance counselors, substance abuse counselors, lay therapists, and faith healers" (3 of 5). The court specifically noted that while New York State law outlines the scope of practice for social workers and physicians, the law for psychologists does not specify a scope of the licensee's practice. It might be additionally noted that some of the named healers are not licensed at all.

The court noted that only psychiatrists' diagnostic and treatment services may rightly be termed "medical," thus falling within the statue of limitations limiting "medical" negligence to two years. It said that the other counselors' training is so diverse that, while counseling similarities might exist, they're not all "medical".

The practical effect of the court's ruling is that the court will not dismiss the suit due to the statute of limitations. They must stand trial even though one of the defendants was not served until nearly three years after the alleged harm.

The conceptual effect of this case is the notion that courts will engage the very definitional distinctions noted in the introduction. This, New York's highest court, split the nature of a counselor (social worker, substance abuse counselor, psychiatrist, cleric, faith healer, etc.) with those of their duties (diagnosis and treatment) while arriving at a result that would hold them legally responsible for professional negligence.

☐ The "Integrity" Defense

The integrity defense is the author's term for behaviors that tend to immunize a counselor from ever being charged in the first place. While the integrity defense is not strictly a legal defense, it is a defense that is a prime example, along with consent forms, of a *prevention* against ever being charged with a criminal or civil action.

The defense works like this. Anyone can sue a counselor. As we have noted, many suits are specious or unsupportable at face value, and judges can summarily dismiss them as a matter of law. This action is called a "summary judgment" and such cases do not even go to trial. However, the defendant still must hire a lawyer, suffer the embarrassment, and spend the time, money, and tears to await the trial and attend depositions. Even if the case is thrown out on summary judgment, the defendant has already suffered. The best solution is to act in such a manner that no one would even waste their time making a false accusation against you. This is the essence of the integrity defense.

Students often ask me, usually in the context of sexual misconduct claims, how they can avoid being falsely accused. These are the steps I suggest and they first call for a bit of imagination.

1. Imagine the 10 or 20 people you work with every day. A counselor should imagine his or her peers in the counseling professions. Now imagine which of these you would *think it possible* that they might be guilty of a criminal or civil infraction—such as sexual misconduct.

2. Now imagine those of your colleagues for whom you *would not believe* such an infraction is possible. What is the difference in behavior and attitude between these two groups? You have to ask yourself, "In what group do I fit?"
3. Conform your behaviors and attitudes in line with those persons whom others cannot and would not believe would commit such offenses. Some students say that they do not want to act 'n ways that are dull, boring, and no fun.
4. The significance of this exercise lies in the fact that those who falsely accuse others of misconduct (sexual and otherwise) may often, not always, choose easy targets. An "easy mark" in this sense is one whom others would believe it possible, maybe even likely. False accusers are more likely to prey upon those who are vulnerable to suspicion, who talk in indiscrete ways, who are overly flirtatious, who cannot and do not account for their time, who keep sloppy or inaccurate records, and who are too flippant in their remarks.
5. The integrity defense also eliminates or reduces clients who misinterpret the act of a counselor. In the *Ohrtman* case, for example, a misinterpretation of a hug cost the counselor one criminal trial and one criminal appeal.

There is no "silver bullet" that this, or any author, can offer to shield a counselor from criminal accusation. The best counselors can do is to know the sanctions that can be placed against them and to think of every person who seeks their help can be a possible client—and a possible plaintiff against you.

☐ Conclusion

Counselors hold positions of trust and confidence with their clients. Clients almost always attend counseling sessions under times of anxiety, pain, uncertainty, and vulnerability. In important ways, clients become dependent upon their counselors to treat them with dignity. All professional codes of ethics require counselors to treat clients with dignity, respect, and with competence. This chapter outlined and explained roles of the criminal law in ensuring such qualities.

This chapter has illustrated several specific criminal laws and cases that apply to counselors who practice complementary interventions or to clients. These cases and statutes are designed to describe how the criminal law seeks to apply public will (through statutes) to such counselors. Sometimes these laws will apply to clients who work with clients who may be charged with some criminal offense, such as child abuse or peyote or marijuana use. These behaviors, among others, have constitutional implications. The use of hallucinogens has long been a part of religious and spiritual ceremonies, and prosecutions have been challenged recently on constitutional grounds.

Counselors not only need to know how the criminal law might apply to their own interventions and therapies, but also how the criminal law might apply to clients. Counselors who understand the legal positions and constitutional protections of their clients are in better positions to address the therapeutic issues of their clients. The same is true for possible defenses against criminal actions. Not only may a counselor be asked to testify as to the client's condition, motivations, and prognosis; without knowledge of possible defenses with which clients avail themselves, a counselor cannot fully apprehend the client's situation.

Finally, expert witnesses play an increasingly important role in all criminal and civil actions. Counselors, especially those who use complementary therapies, need to know not only how the law uses expert witnesses, but also how counselors can more properly and effectively use expert witnesses on their own behalf.

☐ Legal Audits and Exercises

1. This chapter has spent much time on issues surrounding coercion or manipulation in the practice of counseling. If you had to defend any of your interventions or the processes by which you administer them, would there be any inference of such coercion?

    Place yourself in a client's shoes, or even better yet, place yourself in a criminal investigator's shoes. Has there been or is there now any form of coercion or intimidation that might be chargeable against you? Can you defend such actions on your part?

    If there is, how have you changed the *content* or the *procedure* of your practice? How can you now guarantee a substantially different outcome than previously?

2. How about unknowing illegal acts? (By the way, it *is* true that ignorance of the law is no excuse.) For example, do you know if your state has any statute against using telepathy, clairvoyance, or any kind of prophesy? Do you use meditation, prayer, Tarot, astrology, angels, or other interventions that might be construed as an illegal act in your state?

3. Audit your vulnerability to charges of fraud or misrepresentation (I address advertising issues in the licensing section of Chapter 4). This can be done by imagining that you are a potential client, browsing your newspaper ad or phone directory, or any other promotional materials. If you had to, could you adequately defend any statements made therein? Are there any items there that you would be uncomfortable in explaining to an investigator. Do you make any claims that you cannot prove? Are there any titles, degrees, or certifications that are not precisely true and accurate? Have any certifications or licenses lapsed?

4. Do any of your clients abuse their children or older adults? Do you have the state statute for abuse, neglect, and/or abandonment (and exceptions) on file? Are these clients likely to claim any religious or spiritual exemptions? Are they likely to want to call you as a character witness or as an expert witness on their behalf?

5. Speaking about expert witnesses—what would you do if a client called you to testify as to his or her state of mind surrounding a forensic situation (e.g., child custody, abuse, or other criminal action). Are you an expert? Why? What credentials have you that would qualify you as an expert witness?

    How about a character witness or a "regular" non-expert witness for you client? How might you decide whether or not to testify if asked by a client (or even serve as a witness on behalf of the government)? Would your professional ethical standards allow or disallow this?

6. If you are a school counselor or other institutional counselor (e.g., hospital or prison) can you recognize the religious or spiritual symbols worn by inmates, residents, or students? Can you distinguish between a "gang," fad, and religious or spiritual symbols?

7. Defamation exercise: Recall this previous week. Did you say, write, e-mail, or in any way "publish" any comment, suggestion, opinion, or statement that might tend to lower the opinion of a person in the eyes of his or her community, job, career, or peers? Were these statements privileged? Is your liability insurance paid up? We address insurance for counselors in Chapter 4.

8. Are you keeping process notes, session memoranda, or other indicia of your sessions that could be used to explain or interpret a charge against you? What details are you including in your notes?

9. Would these records make sense to you, say, a year or two after you have written them? The statute of limitations for such material runs for perhaps 2 or 3 years, so your notes might be needed years after you have written them. How are you preserving your notes? Are your files safe from destruction and confusion? Can you find a set of case notes if you need them?

CHAPTER

Civil Liabilities

☐ Objectives

1. To provide illustrations of how the civil law can apply to spiritual or complementary counselors. This chapter will focus upon how the First Amendment might or might not apply to counselors who discuss spiritual or religious language, images, or practices in their therapies.
2. To outline and explain the elements of a malpractice action and related legal concepts specifically as they might apply to counselors using complementary therapies.
3. To examine and describe the legal "standard of care" for counselors and how this standard is necessarily changed and challenged by counselors using therapies that are unconventional or which are not widely known or adopted.
4. To offer examples of how specific "causes of action" might apply to counselors using spiritual or complementary therapies. These causes of action include: libel and slander (defamation), violations of privacy (including cyber-privacy), intentional infliction of emotional distress, intentional misrepresentation, violation of trademark or tradename, sexual harassment, retaliation, or constructive discharge from employment.
5. To discuss some legal concepts necessary to understanding the dynamics of civil lawsuits. These include: vicarious liability and respondent superior and third-party liability.

The second principle branch of the law is the civil law. Generally, as we have indicated in the chart noted in the Preface, the civil law is in sharp contrast to the criminal law, both in purpose and, in many cases, in procedure. Whereas the criminal law sanctions *public* wrongs against society, the civil law seeks to compensate for *private* wrongs. "Negligence" is the legal term for falling below a certain standard of care. "Standard of care" is a legal term denoting the often subjective line delineating legal competency from legal incompetency.

Causes of action for negligence, professional negligence, (malpractice) are established either by case law or statute. Both sources will be examined in this chapter. To get started, illustrate how one state can abolish a purported cause of action. What a state can give, it can also take away. This Washington State statute §18.130.180(4), noted in a website (www.healthlobby.com) states: "Incompetence, negligence or malpractice . . . .

The use of a nontraditional treatment *by itself* [author's emphasis] shall not constitute unprofessional conduct, provided that it does not result in injury to a patient or create an unreasonable risk that a patient may be harmed."

What this statute, directed toward the medical professions, does is to deny a specific cause of action for merely using alternative or complementary treatments. It does not offer a right or privilege to use them, nor does it protect patients from the incompetent use of such interventions. A patient harmed by the use of such interventions can still sue for malpractice. In this chapter we will rehearse several "causes of action" which involve counselors' use of spiritual or complementary interventions. We also examine some possible defenses.

The following case study illustrates four points. First, it illustrates one prominent example of how spiritual or complementary counselors can have conflicts with their employers. Second, the case illustrates precisely what practices can come into the purview of religious, spiritual, or complementary interventions. Third, it illustrates the way in which the First Amendment's religious protections can be played out in court. Finally, the case illustrates the roles other constitutional protections play for spiritual and complementary counselors.

This case is significant to all counselors who practice spiritual or complementary counseling, particularly those who work in public institutions, including prisons, halfway houses, psychiatric hospitals, and juvenile penal facilities.

☐ Case Study: A Contemporary Civil Action of Spiritual Counseling

This case was considered previously in the Preface; this section will more specifically consider how the civil law can impact spiritual and complementary counselors. Robert Spratt, a counselor with a masters degree in social science from Michigan State, was hired as an inmate counselor by Kent County Honor Camp. Spratt described himself as a "Pentecostal Christian" and an "evangelist" who attempts to spread the New Testament gospel. While employed as a social worker at the jail, Spratt used a counseling technique he called "treatment by spiritual means." This treatment, Spratt explained, allowed the spirit of God to minister to the client and the counselor. Spratt employed other spiritual interventions including: prayer, Bible reading, and "casting out of demons."

In describing his spiritual or complementary techniques, Spratt said he usually spent initial sessions determining whether the client suffered from any mental illness. He reported that, most often, inmates suffered from anxiety or depression. Spratt offered inmates various treatment options, one of which was spiritual interventions. He testified that he only treated by spiritual means when an inmate requested it.

Spratt's spiritual and complementary interventions were the direct cause for this case. Philip Heffron, Kent County Sheriff, testified that Spratt was advised that he was not to include religious counseling with his psychological counseling during his employment; instead, he was to refer such requests to the jail chaplains. This policy was disseminated to all the jail counselors. In a factual dispute, Spratt asserted that he was never told to forsake spiritual counseling absolutely, but only to use it as a last resort.

Spratt received complaints from women for his use of spiritual counseling. Sheriff Heffron shared these complaints with Spratt and stated that religious counseling, in this context, was inappropriate—partly because Heffron's office could be sued by those offended. Spratt's version of his meeting with Heffron—again slightly different—was that Heffron did not absolutely prohibit spiritual counseling. Spratt claimed the sheriff told him only to be discrete about it.

Later, a mother of an inmate complained that Spratt tried to cast a demon out of her son. Heffron suspended Spratt for five days, explaining that Spratt's continued spiritual counseling was contrary to Department policy and not in the best interests of the Department. Spratt grieved the suspension and it was denied. Meanwhile, Spratt tried to convince the Department to allow him to continue his spiritual and complementary interventions. Additionally, he wanted the Department to obtain liability insurance for his use of such interventions—both to no avail.

Spratt was reprimanded again when he asked inmates to sign a waiver when he used spiritual interventions with them, without asking or obtaining his supervisor's permission to use the waiver. Spratt was fired the same day for continuing to use spiritual interventions. He sued the County, the sheriff, and his immediate supervisors for wrongful discharge under the specific causes of action below enumerated.

☐ Federal Non-Discrimination Law Under Title VII

Title VII of the 1964 Civil Rights Act was sweeping legislation designed to end job discrimination based upon religion as well as race, national origin, and gender (Section 703 (a)(1)). Section 701 of the act further provides that "religion includes all aspects of religious observance and practice as well as belief, unless an employer demonstrates that he is unable to *reasonably accommodate* [author's emphasis] to an employee's or prospective employee's religious observance or practice without undue hardship on the conduct of the employer's business." As is the court's purview and responsibility, the Federal District Court for the Western District of Michigan interpreted the statute in light of the specific evidence presented before it.

There was some factual dispute as to whether Spratt's spiritual counseling interventions were a function of his practice of *religion* or a function of his practice of *counseling*. The court correctly discerned that some counselors may use prayer, meditation, scripture reading, and other complementary interventions as a function of their faith, while others may use them strictly as a function of therapeutic practice. The interventions may be the same, the results may be the same, it is only the *intentions* that are different. This legal determination was crucial to the case because religious protections do not apply to interventions based upon therapeutic principles—they depend upon religious protections.

The court gave Spratt the legal benefit of the doubt and said that his interventions would be considered religious practice. The question for the court, then, was whether Spratt's supervisors made "reasonable accommodations" for Spratt's religious practices.

Given the court's reasons set forth below, they held that Spratt's supervisors correctly made such accommodations. First, the sheriff clearly advised Spratt that policy precluded county social workers from conducting therapy with spiritual interventions. Second, Spratt had been repeatedly warned against using such practices. Third, Spratt was given chances to change his interventions. Thus, the court concluded that Spratt's supervisors gave him reasonable accommodation under the circumstances of the setting under which Spratt worked.

☐ The Constitutional Claim Under the First Amendment

The next cause of action was for the violation of his constitutional freedom to freely exercise his freedom of religion. However, the court found that no one's religious freedoms are absolute. No one may interfere with other's rights. This ruling was based upon precedent. A previous case (*Campbell v. Cauthron*, 1980) held that lay witnesses may not go into a prison to preach, sing, and witness to inmates violates the free exercise of religion of those who do not want to hear. They cannot be subjected to forced indoctrination. The *Campbell* case provided the *Spratt* court with precedent upon which to base its own, subsequent ruling.

Similarly, the court ruled that while Spratt did not overtly coerce inmates into accepting his counseling methods, he did suggest that spiritual means were the preferred treatment method. The *Spratt* court further concluded that, referring to the *Campbell* decision, the potential for coercion was even greater for an employee of the institution as opposed to simply lay visitors (as in *Campbell*). Thus, if the court allowed Spratt to continue with his spiritual counseling, the County could be sued by the inmates for violating their religious rights. The court held that Spratt's rights to freely exercise his religious rights must be limited to the degree that his conduct might interfere with the religious rights of others. While Spratt used the freedom of religion constitutional guarantee as a sword, it turned out to be a double-edged one.

The court, with a similar rationale, disposed of Spratt's claim that his First Amendment free speech rights were violated. As in religious freedoms, the freedom of speech is limited. The court must find that the employer had a compelling interest to limit an employee's free speech. The court held that County had a compelling state interest if that free speech would violate others' religious freedoms. The district refused to allow two of Spratt's major causes of action. Two more remained.

☐ The "Equal Protection" Claim

Spratt's "Equal Protection" claim arises directly from the 14th Amendment to the Constitution, adopted in 1868. The relevant part of section one reads "No state shall make or enforce any law which shall abridge the privileges or immunities of citizens of the United States; nor shall any State deprive any person life, liberty, or property, without due process of law; nor deny to any person within its jurisdiction the equal protection of the laws."

This amendment gives rise to Spratt's constitutional claim that the County treated him differently because of his religion. The court held that Spratt provided no proof that he was fired because he was a Christian or a Pentecostal Christian.

The "Conspiracy Theory" Claim

Spratt's final cause of action was a claim for conspiracy. This claim, cognizable under Section 1983 of Chapter 42 of the U.S. Code is similar to the Equal Protection claim discussed in the previous section. Spratt would have to prove that he was part of a class of persons who were invidiously discriminated against. Just as the court held Spratt failed to prove such discrimination in the Equal Protection claim, so the court so held in this claim.

This case illustrates, in itself and by analogy, several key points relevant for a discussion of legal issues commensurate with spiritual or complementary counseling. Spratt sued the County and officials for five causes of action: 1) Title VII discrimination, 2) religious freedom, 3) equal protection, 4) freedom of speech, and 5) conspiracy. Each cause of action was grounded in either the constitution or statutory law. Without such specific and recognizable causes of action, the could would throw the suit out with a "summary judgement." A summary judgment is a dismissal of the suit without a trial (See Glossary). For example, if the government has a duty, say under Title VII, not to fire anyone for practicing their religion, the breach of that duty is the term for that suit. That is why the specific facts are so important in determining a case.

The success of a suit often turns on factual nuances. For example, if the facts of *Spratt* revealed that the Sheriff specifically targeted Spratt for suspension or reprimand because he was a Christian or a Pentecostal Christian (or member of any religious group), Spratt would have a viable Equal Protection claim. Additionally, if the setting of Spratt's interventions was a religious or sectarian organization, like Methodist, Jewish, Lutheran, Roman Catholic Social Services, the outcome might have been quite different.

Besides federal civil rights claims or constitutional claims illustrated by the *Spratt* decision, the law has numerous other causes of action applicable to counselors who use spiritual or complementary interventions. Another entire class of causes of action may come into play with negligence actions.

☐ Principles of Negligence Actions: Duty, Foreseeability, and Scienter

As noted earlier, there are four elements of a "tort" or a negligence action. Negligence actions are wrongful, twisted actions. In fact, the term "tort" is a Latin word for "twisted." "Tort" is where we get the word "torture." These elements, noted previously, bear repeating:

1. Duty
2. Breach of Duty
3. Proximate Cause
4. Damages

At this point we dig deeper into the legal principles that have come to characterize negligence actions: duty, foreseeability, and *scienter*. Legal duty is a legal obligation. As noted in the Preface, a purported moral or ethical duty may not rise to the level of a *legal* duty. Yet, a legal duty almost always embodies an ethical or moral duty. Legal duties must be recognized as such by courts. We examine, at length, ethical duties in Chapter 5.

Foreseeability is the degree to which an event or consequence can be predicted. The legal calculus is this: the greater the foreseeability, the greater chance for liability. A hypothetical case illustrates nicely. A counselor uses meditation to address suicidal ideation in a vividly imaginative client. The counselor uses the "tunnel of light" image to help the client relax. In the meditation, the client is assured that his death is a good thing and that he will be welcomed into the nether regions. The client shoots himself.

In the suicide note, the former client thanks the counselor for "freeing him up" with the assuring imagery of the meditation enough to actually go through with the suicide. The family of the former client sues the counselor for malpractice in a wrongful death suit.

This hypothetical case may turn on how foreseeable this meditation intervention was in the suicide act. Is the current practice of psychotherapy able to predict that such a meditative exercise likely to contribute to the suicide act? Certainly, this hypothetical case will bring out expert witnesses on both sides to opine on whether the meditation exercise was appropriate under the circumstances. (The technical term for the "appropriateness" is the "standard of care" which we discuss later in the next section). Closely associated with foreseeability is *scienter*.

Scienter describes the extent to which a defendant "knew, or should have known" that some harm might result. *Scienter* requires that counselors not turn a blind eye to foreseeable harm. In the hypothetical above, scienter would extend the foreseeability beyond the realm of what the counselor was sure might cause harm into what the counselor should have known could cause harm. For example, even if the counselor did not think that the images used in the meditation would contribute to the suicide, some inquiry into how those images might affect this particular client. Some questions addressing foreseeability and *scienter* arising from this hypothetical are: (a) to what degree did or should have the counselor been aware of the client's suicidal ideation, (b) to what degree did the counselor know or should have known that the client was vulnerable to the persuasive imagery of the meditation, and (c) to what degree did the counselor warn the client or take steps to protect the client from possible ill effects of this intervention.

These questions go to the heart of a negligence action in the use of spiritual and complementary interventions. This jurisprudential inquiry goes well beyond the well-meaning use and methodology of such interventions. This inquiry requires the counselor to ask him or herself some pointed questions about the interventions, such as:

1) Why am I using the intervention in the first place?
2) Is there a valid therapeutic reason for using this particular interventions with this particular client at this particular time?
3) Am I aware of the risks as well as the benefits of this intervention with this client?
4) Have I communicated to the client both the likely benefits and likely risks of this intervention?
5) Has the client consented to the intervention with full awareness of the available facts?

A brief but potent exercise helpful for counselors addressing these issues is to imagine explaining your rationale for the choice and methodology for using your chosen spiritual or complementary interventions to a judge or jury.

Along with this list of relevant above, there are "rule of thumb" (or, to steal a legal phrase, "bright line") reasons not to use spiritual or complementary interventions. Succinctly, they are:

1. Because they are a trend.
2. Because you think they are cool.
3. Because you think you are cool.
4. To impress or keep a client.

The inquiries and admonitions above treat such interventions as they ought to be treated, as powerful tools with potential liability attached. The remaining causes of action can be read in the light of the four traditional elements of malpractice as well as foreseeability and scienter. The following section addresses another crucial concept in the jurisprudence of a negligence action.

☐   The Traditional Standard of Care

As we have already noted in this section, the concept of "standard of care" is another significant concept in determining negligence (See glossary). The standard of care is the threshold between incompetence and competence when describing professional services. Services deemed below the standard of care spell malpractice. The standard-of-care threshold is often vague and moves relative to the specific needs and circumstances of particular clients. That is why expert witnesses testify as to their opinion on how the profession would usually treat this or that patient under their specific circumstances.

Therefore, it is imperative for counselors using spiritual and complementary interventions to clearly understand that their practice of these interventions will be judged by courts under the standard of care of other prudent and diligent practitioners. This section will conclude with some pointers on discerning the standard of care for emerging interventions such as spiritual or complementary interventions. First, however, we examine illustrative cases.

A recent case from the Canadian Supreme Court offers insight and an illustration into how courts have traditionally arrived at the standard of medical care. This case is analogous and closely related to U.S. law as well. We choose this case because it addressed an emerging intervention in the medical profession. Ms. Neuzen was artificially inseminated by Dr. Korn in 1985. Unfortunately, she also contracted HIV at a time when tests were yet unavailable for HIV and the risks were not yet so appreciated. Additionally, Dr. Korn applied those screening procedures for HIV that were generally applied by artificial insemination specialists at the time (*Neuzer v. Korn*, n.d; cited in Feasby, 1997). The *Neuzer* court had the unenviable task of determining if Korn was negligent even if he acted in strict accordance with his profession with the information at that time.

To answer this thorny issue, the court established that the Canadian standard of care for medicine is "a duty to conduct their practice in accordance with the conduct of a prudent and diligent doctor in the same circumstances." Specialists, such as those conducting artificial inseminations, must exercise the "degree of skill and knowledge of an average specialist in his [or her] field." In determining whether or not a practitioner is "prudent and diligent" or is exercising the "degree of skill," the judge or jury often hears testimony from the infamous "parade of experts." Expert testimony is a primary way that the "trier of fact" (judge or jury) uncovers the knowledge of an average specialist or exactly what is "diligent" or "prudent" practitioner.

The *Neuzer* court addressed the issue of confusing and contradictory expert testimony by holding that triers of fact cannot make a determination of liability if the medical procedure is so complex as to be beyond their ordinary experience or understanding. In law, however, there are usually exceptions, and this case is no different. If a medical practice "fails to adopt obvious and reasonable precautions readily apparent to the ordinary trier of fact" the negligent practitioner cannot claim competence in following such damaging techniques. In other words, the law will not condone business as usual" if it is reasonably known to cause harm.

This issue is an unsettling analogy to alternative and spiritual interventions. First, in unconventional interventions, how does one determine what is conventional practice? Second, in fields where schools of thought are diverse and sometimes contradictory, how does a trier of fact determine what is usual practice? Third, how does a trier of fact determine whether interventions are exercised with a reasonable degree of skill when alternative counselors use widely different styles of similar interventions? Fourth, how might a trier of fact who does not believe in the ideology of an alternative counselor evaluate its "reasonableness?"

☐ The Evolving Standard of Care

Courts are in a quandary over how to settle upon a standard of care for alternative medicine. The standard is fluid. But no counselor wants to be the legal anvil for the law's hammering out such a standard. The next case offers further insight into an evolving standard for emerging interventions.

In the following case, the defendant was trying to set aside (to dismiss) a verdict holding the defendant guilty of medical malpractice. The doctor (defendant) in this instance, treated the plaintiff's uterine cancer with a special diet protocol. In *Charell v. Gonzalez* (1997) the court noted, with irony, that if the standard for proving negligence is "whether the treatment deviates from accepted medical standards" (1 of 6). If that is the standard, then *any* unconventional, alternative, or spiritual interventions or treatment would per se violate the standard of care. The court said, ". . . it would seem that no practitioner of alternative medicine could prevail on such a question as the reference to the term "non-conventional" may well necessitate a finding that the doctor who practices such medicine deviates from "accepted" medical standards" (1 of 6). "General acceptance" is a crucial term and will be used in the below suggestions.

So how may a counselor get a better handle on the standard of care that judges and juries will use to determine liability? Keeping in mind the "accepted practice" noted in the above case will be asserted by a series of experts testifying both for the plaintiff and for the defendant, it is imperative for counselors to keep abreast with the current thinking and behaviors in the field as well as know the basics of negligence noted in this book. It is too late to find out the "accepted practice" when you're sitting on the defendant's table. The following are suggestions for knowing what expert testimony might say:

1. Examine the procedures outlined in books and articles from major journals in the field. It is imperative to keep current in the professional literature. The more prestigious the journal, the more likely testifying experts are to follow their lead. Start a collection of books and journal articles that are influential in your practice, they are your "proof" that you are keeping current with professional literature and that you are following their lead.
2. Attend seminars and continuing education events. If you use the techniques and methodology outlined in seminars you've attended, keep the notes, handouts and seminar agenda. Remember, you are building a record of proof that you have received training in such interventions and that you have followed the direction of "experts."
3. Publish your own articles or conduct seminars outlining the methodology of your own interventions. One way to proactively "defend" your intervention strategies is to become an "expert" yourself. As your methodology gains acceptance and credence, it becomes part of the generally accepted intervention operation. Keep in mind that general acceptance takes time and a "critical mass" of acceptance, it is no guarantee of being vindicated either in the court of law or court of public opinion. But it does offer a strong argument towards general acceptance.

☐ Causes of Action in Negligence Cases

In U.S. law, "causes of action" must be specific and recognized either by statute or case law. Just because a client feels wronged, even damaged, that does not mean they have a legal remedy. Plaintiffs must plead causes of action recognized by the courts.

Religious Malpractice

It might seem a likely cause of action against those practicing spiritual or complementary interventions might be described as "religious malpractice" or other such term. After all, if counselors misuse religious or spiritual interventions, they might be regarded having fallen below the standard of care. If a lawyer forgets to file a complaint before the statute of limitations expires, their client may sue them for a breach of their legal standard of care. Similarly, if a surgeon leaves a sponge in the patient's abdomen after an operation, the patient may well sue for a breach of their medical standard of care.

This cause of action styled religious or spiritual or ministerial malpractice has, of this writing, not been recognized by any court or statute. The main reason for this lack of judicial or legislative recognition is the First Amendment. Courts do not readily inquiry into the nature and interventions of clergy and theology. Courts do not want to set a standard of care for clerical counselors, who as we have noted already, enjoy an exemption from state licensure for their counseling activities. For example, a Roman Catholic priest might have one standard for addressing a member's concerns and a Wicca priest or priestess might have another. A leading case on court's refusal to set such a standard is the *Nally* case below noted.

Thus, the bottom line is that counselors will not now be sued under this cause of action. This means two things: 1) counselors will be using existing causes of actions, some of which are noted in this chapter, and 2) a cause of action related to spiritual, religious counselors, or "ministerial malpractice" is always a possibility. The author's best guess that if the lawyers can make the case that some standard of care is applicable for a situation where the threat of harm is extreme and the intervention is not a theological or ecclesiastical matter, such a cause of action may be instituted. Stated affirmatively, such a case may be connected to a duty to refer a member or adherent who threatens the life of another or threatens to take his or her own life (The *Nally* case held the opposite, but may not stand forever). Stated negatively, such a case may be connected to a duty not to engage in sexual misconduct with a member or a minor.

Libel and Slander: Defamation

Defamation is the snake of counseling causes of action. It can strike without warning and when least expected. It also can be deadly and too often overlooked. It is a cause of action for untrue publications that lower a person's reputation and can threaten someone's livelihood or ability to make a living. The older terms, libel and slander, mean written and spoken derrogatory comments, respectively. The traditional distinction between libel and slander is the difference between transitory and permanent communications. Because of modern information technology with computers and digital communications, there is now little real distinction between transitory and permanent communications, and the term "defamation" is most often used.

The purpose for prohibiting defamation is both to preserve an individual's reputation and to preserve public order. An untrue statement can ruin a person's career and private life. Additionally, defamatory remarks can be the cause for public brawls, fights, and in the old days, duels. As the famous duel between Aaron Burr and Alexander Hamilton demonstrated, the social cost of defamation can be high. Some states recognize both a criminal and civil claim for defamation. Defamation is placed in this "civil law" chapter because most defamation suits are civil suits. An example is the Texas libel statute that follows:

> A libel is a defamation expressed in written or other graphic form that tends to blacken the memory of the dead or that tends to injure a living person's reputation and thereby expose the person to public hatred, contempt or ridicule, or financial injury or to impeach any person's honesty, integrity, virtue, or reputation or to publish the natural defects of anyone and thereby expose the person to public hatred, ridicule or financial injury. (§73.001)

Counselors, particularly those practicing spiritual or complementary interventions, may inadvertently "publish" defamatory remarks. The term "publish" is a term of art. It means any form of communication to another (other than the subject of the defamatory remarks). For example, a counselor who criticizes a client's religious or spiritual orientation or who disparages another counselor's integrity to another is opening himself or herself up to defamation charges.

One social worker, finding himself the subject of an unflattering article in a newsletter for Oregon clinical social workers, sued members of that state's Board of Clinical Social Workers for defamation, breach of contract, breach of special duty, and violations of his civil rights. The trial court dismissed the claims, but the social worker, Michael Slover, appealed.

The Oregon Court of Appeals reversed the lower court, in some respects, and affirmed in part. One of the elements reversed was the lower court's dismissal of the defamation claim. The Appeals Court ruled that, while statements of opinion may not be actionable, such statements may be actionable if such statements could be reasonably seen by the recipients as being based upon "undisclosed defamatory facts" (*Slover v. State Board of Clinical Social Workers*, 1996, p. 1098).

Slover's claims center around a newsletter article titled "A Dubious Therapeutic Technique" that was published by his state licensing board. The article related that the board had received complaints about an intervention by a "male therapist" who encouraged adolescent male clients to "nurse" the therapist. This therapy, called "regressive therapy," whereby the clinician donned a female wig and placed two soft balls beneath his shirt as two "breasts." The article said the board investigated this therapy and "concluded this activity had a detrimental effect upon the boys, was counter therapeutic, and constituted inappropriate clinical practice" (*Slover*, p. 1100 n. 1).

That's not all the article said. On the same page, the newsletter published a second article titled "Report of Recent Disciplinary Action by the State Board of Clinical Social Workers." This second article mentioned Slover by name and outlined a stipulated agreement between he and the board "regarding professional incompetence and failure to provide informed consent to parents regarding inappropriate regressive therapy techniques." The second article went on to say that Slover agreed not to conduct clinical social work with clients under the age of 14 and to enter a two-year program of supervision. The article concluded that the stipulated agreement was not an admission of wrongdoing by Slover.

Slover sued the board for, among other things, defamation and breach of contract. He claimed the board breached an oral agreement to dismiss the disciplinary proceeding without making any finding that Slover engaged in any wrongdoing. The Oregon District Court dismissed all of Slover's complaints and he appealed. The Court of Appeals ruled that the claims could go forward.

The trial court dismissed the defamation claim because it said the statements were "merely statements of opinion." However, the appeals court ruled that even statements of opinion are actionable if the recipients (the readers of the article) could have reasonably thought that the opinion was based upon undisclosed facts. The Court of Appeals ruled that the readers could have concluded that the board's "opinion" was based upon defamatory facts about the techniques and their impact upon the clients, known the board, but undisclosed to the readers of the article. Moreover, the appeals court ruled that the statements that the interventions had a "detrimental effect," that they were "counter therapeutic," and "constituted inappropriate clinical practice" were not statements of opinion at all. They were statements of fact.

While the *Slover* case may not specifically involve spiritual or complementary practice, it clearly outlines the nature of a defamatory case against a clinician who uses interventions of which a licensing board does not approve. By this time in the book, the reader is undoubtably able to imagine how counselors using spiritual, complementary, or other "cutting edge" therapies might be subject to such disciplinary rulings or bad press. Spiritual or complementary practitioners may want to simply imagine replacing Slover's regressive therapies with their own practices and ask themselves the following questions. These questions are designed to stimulate some discussion about preventative strategies:

1. Would your licensing board take a tolerant, indifferent, eager, or intolerant view of your interventions?
2. Would you change any of your interventions if a licensing board member were observing? If so, why?
3. How would you react if your licensing board wrote a similar article about your interventions?
4. Have you heard, overheard, read, or otherwise noted one clinician disparaging another clinician's practice or interventions? What did you do? Did you repeat anything that was said?
5. Have you spoken, written, or sent e-mails to anyone in any way disparaging another's interventions or methods of practice?
6. Are there instances where saying something detrimental about a clinician is protected? What about a clinical supervisor? Can a supervisor give an uncomplimentary evaluation without fear of being sued?

The following case illustrates these questions more closely with a case involving spiritual healing in an ecclesiastical setting (*Marks v. Estate of Hartgerink*, 1995). John Marks' membership in a church in Iowa was suspended and he was later excommunicated. Reverend Muller introduced the practice of spiritual healing in the church; Marks objected and got involved in a movement to have Muller removed. Muller was, in fact, removed and Reverends Medendorp and Hartgerink became involved in the church. The ministers also became defendants when Marks sued them and others for defamation and intentional infliction of emotional distress. This latter cause of action is described below.

The defamation claim arose out of the contentions between Marks and church officials. For example, at various times, Marks was accused of saying one pastor is a "dirty sucker," "his life is a life wrecker, traitor, and a marriage "wrecker" (*Marks*, p. 2.). For their part, the church officials were accused of calling Marks a "lying bastard" and that, eventually, they would not receive phone calls from him and finally excommunicated him. The district (trial) court dismissed the charges on summary judgment. Marks fared no better on appeal, but the appellate court's discussion illuminates the issues.

First, the appeals court dismissed any counts connected with the excommunication. The court found that Marks had exhausted his appeals through the ecclesiastical courts. It noted that the general rule is that civil courts will not interfere with purely ecclesiastic matters, which, it further noted, includes church membership and church discipline. Therefore, for the court to interfere in Marks' excommunication would violate both the First and Fourteenth Amendments.

Second, Marks asserted on appeal that the allegedly defamatory remarks, although made in the context of excommunication, defamation involves his civil rights. Thus, it is appropriate for the court to rule on the defamation allegation. The court then said that Marks needed to prove three elements: 1) that the church officials "published" the allegedly defamatory statements, 2) that the statements were untrue, and 3) that these statements were not privileged. Marks failed to prove each of the three requirements.

The law requires that the allegedly defamatory remarks be "published" beyond the party allegedly defamed. The court found that church officials communicated the allegedly defamatory remarks only to Marks. It was Marks himself that showed the letters to others. Thus, the court concluded that the church did not "publish" the letters in a defamatory way.

It is a truism that truth is a complete defense to defamation. Church communications to the congregation that Marks was excommunicated conveyed true information. Other true statements were communicated by a letter to the congregation.

A "privilege" immunizes even defamatory statements. To qualify for an **immunity**, statements must be made in good faith and they must be statements with which the person has an interest, or has a duty to disclose under circumstances fairly warranted by the occasion. There are two types of privilege: complete and qualified. "Complete" refers to an absolute unqualified privilege. The elements for a qualified privilege are: (a) good faith, (b) an interest to be upheld, (c) a statement limited in its scope and purpose, (d) made at a proper occasion, and (e) publication in a proper manner and for a proper purpose.

This defamation suit included defendant Leslie Van Raden, a church elder. She wrote the disciplinary letter only to Marks or to other church officers who had direct interests in this matter. Moreover, the court found that she had no malice for writing the letters; it was merely her job to write such letters.

It must be said that this case does not exhaust the full compliment speaking of issues or requirements for defamation. However, this case does reiterate the 1st Amendment issues related to some negligence claims. It also offers another set of circumstances where counselors may be faced with someone suing them for defamation or where they might be likely to be the subject of defamatory remarks themselves. Categories of such circumstances for defamation follow:

1. Counselors cannot under any circumstances discuss clients in such a way that their identities may be known, unless a privilege to do so attaches or consent is given.
2. Such privileges are rare and usually statutory. Perhaps the broadest privilege for a counselor is related to strictly professional activities and with prior consent. In-patient consent forms may be part of the intake process. School counselors often discuss a student with an administrator, teacher, or other counselor. It is the opinion of this writer that consent forms should be authorized, even where such sharing may seem to be "implied." While both implied consent and express consent can amount to legal consent, express consent is often more clear, forthright, and demonstrable. In my book, express consent trumps implied any day.
3. Discuss the *process* not the *patient*. Counselors may want to share ideas on the proper use, methods, and cautions for some using spiritual and complementary interventions. Without patient consent, only general, non-identifiable information can be

used about the patients. In contrast, exactly how the counselor conducted the intervention, how the counselor introduced the intervention to the client, how the client reacted, how the counselor assured informed consent, and the effects over time can be discussed without disclosing improper information.

4. Counselors might be in positions to write, speak, or otherwise communicate critical or derogatory information or evaluations. It is important to have written (express) or implied consent to share such information, even when it may seem very necessary to do so.

5. Counselors may be in the roles where they might or might not be immunized by a complete or qualified privilege. If you work in an institution such as a school the question has probably already been addressed in a legally competent way. Find out and discover any exceptions.

Cyber-defamation, Cyber-jurisdiction, and the Right of Privacy.

Counselors' use of the Internet has opened the proverbial Pandora's box for legal and ethical issues. This section addresses only some of these issues, but does alert counselors who use the internet in their counseling practice that this technology implies legal issues. Among them, licensure (which we will address in the next chapter), fraud, defamation, and the rights to privacy. In the matter of cyber-defamation, many sophisticated counselors may harbor the notion that their e-mails to clients or to potential clients (or to anyone) are private, personal communications and cannot be defamatory regardless of the content.

To a large extent, the law treats e-mail and Internet use as an extension of defamation law. The idea being that if you defame someone over the Internet, the law of defamation applies the same as if you were to defame someone in traditional media.

In that sense, this brief section is simply a notice and a warning: that it is just as easy to defame someone with a mouse and a keyboard as it is to defame someone with paper and pen. Just because one writes an e-mail to a friend and one can delete the message with a touch of a button does not mean that (a) the defamatory comment is, in fact, "deleted" or that (b) it is a "personal" correspondence and not "published."

Certainly, as a practical matter, sending e-mails or documents over the computer courts the risk of someone else advertently or inadvertently receiving the message. That the counselor did not *intend* to send the message to this or that person is legally irrelevant. The fact is, the message was read.

Nor does the law care much about the form of the writing in regard to defamation. Whether you defame a person by writing with light, ink, or smoke signals is equally legally irrelevant.

Now a word on the right of privacy. As one might guess from the insistence of this book that all rights are finite, the right of privacy, too, is limited. Nothing in the law is absolute and that is true for the rights of the individual. Specifically, when one uses a computer at work, one can assume that the employer can and may well be monitoring (some call it spying) on your computer use. An employer has the technical ability and probably in most cases, the legal authority to "watch" your e-mails, your Internet searches, and other computer uses.

The basic legal argument is that an employer has a privilege, even a duty, to supervise what employees do, when they do it, and with what they do it with. Employers have, themselves, limited rights to observe employees to see that, for example, they are not using e-mail to sexually harass anyone or to conduct company business and not their own. Companies that use monitoring software are flourishing and so is the demand for such technology (New York Times News Service, 2000).

Even when a counselor uses their computer in their own office "on their own time," the right of privacy is limited. Certainly, the police would need a search warrant, but with *probable cause* such a warrant can be procured.

Many employers issue policies expressing what is or is not permitted with company computers while one is at work. That policy should be taken seriously.

So, the short course on cyber-defamation for counselors using spiritual or complementary interventions might include the following themes:

1. Treat any client records on disks or in hard drives with the same care, protections, and confidences you would any hard copy file. Do not keep electronic files lying about and do not keep your screen lit on private information when not attending to it.
2. Make no comment in e-mail on a client or anyone else that tends towards defamation, sexual harassment, or any other infraction. As we will note later in this chapter, a joke that seems hilarious to you, might mean a sexual harassment claim by another.
3. If you work for an agency, government entity, or for any other employer, your work may be monitored. In other words your e-mails can be scrutinized and your Internet searches can be tracked. Now, it may be that your searches run toward topics that might be, at first sight, hard to explain or even embarrassing. In searching for information on spiritual topics or complementary interventions, you may "click" onto any number of websites. If so, you might consider speaking to your's supervisor to let him or her know that your searches are for work but that they are wide-ranging and eclectic. Sometimes alerting a supervisor beforehand saves explaining afterwards.
4. As to websites—these too might run afoul of laws for several reasons. This is an area of unsettled law. But it is well worth wondering, if offering advice through books and in health food stores is "practicing medicine?" Might the same be true for maintaining a website that offers advice or counseling in the areas of spiritual or complementary interventions? Additionally, if a website offers counseling advice, say, on a meditation practice or assessment or diagnostic information, and someone relies upon that information, you may have a client via your website about whom you did not know. The question, then, if a duty is imposed upon your standard of care and that care is breached in some way, is the counselor's website the vehicle for a malpractice action? While the author has, to date, seen no cases on this issue, there may be some soon.

Another computer-driven legal issue on the horizon is that of offering counseling advice over the Internet. We will address licensing issues in the next chapter; however, we introduce major themes now.

States and licensing associations can be expected to limit inter-state cyber counseling. In fact, the federal government may even get involved in such legislation through the authority of the Interstate Commerce Clause of the U.S. Constitution. The California state Board of Psychology has prohibited out-of-state psychologists who are unlicensed in California, from offering cyber-counseling to California residents (NASW News, 2000). This state board is using its statutory authority to help preserve the health and safety of its citizens. After all, how can the state board regulate the counseling competence of counselors who may not have either office or residence in California and conduct counseling not face-to-face, but by cyberspace?

To be sure, there may be challenges to this ruling. For example, does the California Board of Psychology have the authority to disallow counselors from other states from sitting in their offices, in say Pennsylvania, and conducting counseling—even if the counseling is received in California? Isn't this like restricting radio-, t.v.-, or even book writer-counselors from offering advice to people outside their own states—if they are not licensed to practice in states where someone might listen to the radio program, t.v. show, or buy the book? Courts will have to address these issues sooner than later.

The rationale for the California Board to limit cyber-counseling is compelling. First, they have a duty to protect the public from counselors who might be incompetent. The California Board obviously cannot examine out-of-state cyber-counselors as to their suitability for counseling. Second, out-of-state counselors cannot be easily brought into the California justice system for sanctions. If a cyber-counselor does harm and is sued, a California client or California district attorney might not even know the counselor's address in order to be able to bring a civil or criminal action against the counselor. Third, it would be a hardship for the California client or district attorney to bring the out-state client to justice or even for clients to assess the competence of a cyber-counselor. Californians should not have to bear additional burdens of detecting counselor competence or for finding them if harm is done.

In a related case, a physician was convicted, fined, and placed on probation by the Oregon medical board for selling Viagra and other drugs over the Internet. The physician had advertised and prescribed drugs for impotence, hair loss, weight loss, and smoking cessation for patients he had not examined (Doctor fined, 2000). While two cases do not a trend make, a legal theme may be forming. States and licensing boards might well be securing their borders against professionals and others who might provide services to clients in their jurisdictions. Again, the Oregon Medical Board is responding to their statutory duty to provide health and welfare to their residents.

Additionally, and perhaps even more importantly, at least one major counselor insurance company will insure cyber-counselors only if they comply with state law (NASW News, 2000). Thus, if a cyber counselor in Pennsylvania were to counsel someone in California, they would be in violation and could not be insured by that carrier. This is an important disincentive. But, this debate is likely to gain steam at the same volume as Internet use.

Intentional Infliction of Emotional Distress

Counselors can also be sued for another species of negligence titled intentional infliction of emotional distress. This is now a common claim. It is improper to call this claim a negligence claim, because it is an intentional infliction of emotional distress, but it is a tort. States also recognize the "negligent infliction of emotional distress." The case of *Hester v. Barnett* (1987) offers a clear illustration of such an intentional tort. This Missouri appeals court defined this cause of action "so extreme as to exceed any reasonable limit of social tolerance" (p. 560). In the *Hester* case, this claim was sustained where it was shown that the defendant, knowing that the husband and wife plaintiffs suffered from nervousness and depression, pursued a course of action including breaching their confidences, defaming them, and invading their privacy.

This cause of action may arise in all kinds of counseling situations and we take as an example a "false memory case" against a clinical social worker and a licensed psychologist in *Tuman v. Genesis Associates*, 1995). We will revisit this case later in this chapter in the section titled "third party liability." The plaintiff here alleges that the counselors implanted "false" or "recovered" memories of satanic rituals, murders and incest. We address such memory recovery in the section on "expert witnesses" since such witnesses are an integral part of the legal determination.

With the examples of the above two cases, it can be said that counselors, and those practicing spiritual and complementary interventions in particular, may be especially vulnerable to this suit. After all, clients are seeking help from counselors precisely because they are in an emotionally vulnerable state in the first place. This vulnerability is noted by courts and requires, therefore, an increased sense of care and sensitivity to clients. In other words, the threshold for causing emotional upset for counselors is lower than that of the general public.

Second, as noted earlier, using spiritual or complementary interventions can connote a sense of the sacred or mystical upon the counselor. After all, who else but religious professionals talk about sacred things, holy things, the soul, spirituality, auras, dreams, the afterlife, etc. It is likely that clients will project, associate, or otherwise infer such "sacredness" onto the client. This may make the client even more vulnerable to persuasion and suggestions. This dynamic is not lost upon courts. If you're going to act as a spiritual person, courts will hold you to a standard that reflects that vulnerability in the client.

In any event, the *Tuman* court also refused to dismiss this claim. Here, recall, the counselor was accused of implanting false memories of satanic rituals and incest into the mind of her client. The counselor was sued her the client's father. So, this court determined that the jury could decide whether the counselor's actions were sufficient to find liability. So the court did not rule on the merits of the claim, but it did rule that, as a matter of law, it could not be dismissed. This was a defeat for the counselor.

Intentional Misrepresentation

Tuman also provides us with an outline of the tort of "intentional misrepresentation." This claim is based upon the claim that the counselor knowingly and willfully misled the daughter with the false memory intervention. This claim, with analogies in the criminal law for fraud, goes to whether the counselor knowingly (or should have known) that this diagnosis was wrong or misleading.

Our friend *scienter* is an important concept here. The counselor cannot simply claim that she had no way of knowing whether her diagnosis was right or wrong. She would be held accountable for her own diagnosis. Just as she cannot claim ignorance of the law, she cannot claim ignorance about her own assessments. She cannot claim ignorance about her own diagnosis. The trier of fact (judge or jury), will have to determine whether or not the counselor intentionally perpetrated a fraudulent diagnosis and treatment upon her client or perpetrated a recognized intervention fraudulently.

The father also sued for what he claimed was this fraudulent therapy of recovered memories. The federal district court for the eastern district of Pennsylvania allowed this claim to proceed as well.

Trademarks and Tradenames

Sometimes in the use of spiritual and complementary interventions, counselors and other persons promulgate their educational and instructive programs into companies, institutions, and organizations. Legal problems can occur when two or more such entities claim the same name for a program, company, or intervention.

The following facts are taken from the case *Self-Realization Fellowship Church v. Ananda Church of Self-Realization* (1995). Such occurred when disciples of the famed Hindu teacher Paramahansa Yogananda eventually formed two separate and distinct groups. Yogananda was the author of *Autobiography of a Yogi* and during his lifetime, the yogi formed a school called the Self-Realization Fellowship (hereinafter SRF) which had members in the hundreds of thousands, published a magazine, and sold audio and video tapes and other products.

There came a time when a leader of the SRF left that group to start his own organization called the Church of Self-Realization (hereinafter CSR). Both groups represented themselves as the yogi's disciples. SRF applied to the U.S. Patent Office and Trademark Office to claim the exclusive rights to use the names "Paramahansa Yogananda," "Self-Realization," "Self-Realization Fellowship Church," and other related names. It also sued for, and was granted, a preliminary injunction to enjoin CSR from using any of the names or terms in question. Later the trial court, a federal district court in California, dissolved the injunction and the SRF appealed.

The circuit court affirmed some of the district court's rulings and reversed others. For the sake of cogency, we examine only one aspect of the ruling. The circuit court affirmed the invalidation of the name "Paramahansa Yogananda." In doing so, the court found that a trademark implies that requires a direct association between the mark and the services specified in the trademark application and that the mark be used in a manner that would easily be preceived as identifying such services. The trademark and tradename of such U.S. companies as Coca Cola, Texaco, and Ford are illustrations. Most U.S. consumers, seeing these trademarks of such companies, will easily identify the associated company.

The court found these facts, supplied by expert testimony, to be significant in its decision: SRF did not use the term "Paramahansa Yogananda" with the traditional trademark badge next to it (i.e. the TM sign), and that SRF uses the term "Paramahansa Yogananda, founder," not the name alone.

While these facts might seem intuitively insignificant as to this case, they are legally significant. SRF's use of its founder's name was not closely tied to the SRF's identity and to its products.

Some brief and broad suggestions may help counselors get started in establishing a trademark or a tradename for his or her corporate entity or for his or her products.

1. Register with your state corporation commission and the U.S. Patent and Trademark Office. A search for competing names is part of the application process.
2. Jealously guard your name or patent once it has been issued. If another firm uses your name or mark, do not "sit on your rights," as lawyer's say. This means that if you want your mark to mean anything, you must be vigilant and pursue your claims in court to stop alleged infringements.
3. Make sure you always use the necessary indicia of the trademark or trade name such as the TM. The legal adage about "sleeping" on your rights definitely applies in the trademark arena: "You snooze, you lose."

☐ Sexual Harassment, Retaliation, and Constructive Dismissal

While sexual harassment has been treated in other counseling books (Bullis, 1992, 1995), this section will address sexual harassment in the specific venue of religious or spiritual counseling. We have previously noted that the First Amendment sometimes allows religious or spiritual organizations to have exemptions from civil rights obligations which other organizations must obey. For example, if a theological position precludes employing females, that can be protected behavior. Theological rights can sometimes trump civil rights.

But the case must be made that those rights would impede theological positions. If they do not, there may be no exemption. Such a case prevails in claims for sexual harassment, retaliation, and constructive discharge. As these claims are often related, and we have a case that claims all three, we will consider the issues as a whole in *Jeffries v. Kansas Dept. of Social & Rehab. Serv.* (1996). The plaintiff, another chaplain at a state hospital in a clinical pastoral education (CPE) program, sued a supervisor and the plaintiff above for sexual harassment, retaliation, and constructive discharge. The federal district court in Kansas granted summary judgment for the defendants.

This book cannot address the entire realm of sexual harassment as such claims can be varied, but we do discuss this case in the light of counselors who work in a spiritual or religious or governmental or educative settings. This case is also helpful for clinical supervisors. We abridge the lengthy statement of facts. Suffice to say that another student in the program hugged and kissed the plaintiff on one occasion. The plaintiff further accused that her supervisor retaliated against her when she complained to the hospital superintendent.

First the court had to define the nature of a sexually "hostile" work environment. For a harassment claim under Title VII, the allegedly hostile environment must be pervasive or, in a single incident, must be severe. Such cases are decided by any number of elements. The *Jeffries* court outlined a broad menu of such elements. Relying upon earlier precedent, the court noted a prima facie case for hostile-environment harassment include under Title VII: (a) The plaintiff belongs to a protected group; (b) was subject to unwelcome harassment; (c) the harassment was based upon the plaintiff's sex; (d) the alleged harassment was enough to affect his or her employment; (e) the employer either actively engaged in the harassment or was in a position where liability can be imputed (more of this in the next section).

The court noted that such cases are determined by the totality of circumstances and on a case-by-case basis. With these principles in mind, the court concluded that the three-second hugging and kissing did not rise to the level of sexual harassment. Additionally, the court denied the plaintiff's claim that the state was negligent in not stopping the alleged harassment because there was no indication of any harassment to protect anyone from prior to the single incident. Nor did the plaintiff allege further harassment after the single alleged incident.

The retaliation and constructive discharge claims met the same fate. While the court noted that an "adverse employment decision" is liberally construed, including a variety of actions beyond firing an employee (including unjustified evaluations, transfers and reassignments, and unfavorable reference letters), the legal line is drawn at disagreeing or disliking employment decisions. In other words, just because an employer makes decisions or says things that the employee does not like, it doesn't add up to harassment.

Similarly, while "constructive discharge" is broadly interpreted as making or allowing working conditions to become so intolerable that the employee is forced to quit. The standard is what a reasonable person would regard as "intolerable." Again, the court concluded that the plaintiff's unhappiness of how the supervisor treated her (for example taping their conversations and) did not amount to constructive discharge.

This case has specific relevance for counselors using spiritual and complementary modalities for two reasons. First, while the *Jeffries* case involved chaplains in a clinical setting, that setting did not affect the rules for sexual harassment. In that sense, here is a situation where spiritual counseling did not invoke any First Amendment protections. The court did not analyze its decision any differently from other totally secular situations.

Second, this case, like the *Ohrtman* case described in the previous chapter, is an example where touch or a hug, even done in an innocent and harmless intention and manner can lead to litigious results. Spiritual and complementary interventions are a kind of counseling where touch, hand holding, neck rubbing, hand shaking may well be done—but is it and can it be done without making the counselor vulnerable? We have noted issues surrounding such use in chapter two and we need not rehearse them here—except to reiterate (and case examples like Jeffries do just fine) that counselors need to review their rationale and their cost-benefit analyses for doing so. What, exactly, are the ends the counselor is seeking to achieve by touching the client? Can the counselor achieve the same ends by different means?

It might be the case that the reader now wonders how it is that this plaintiff sued the *institution* as well as the *individual*? The next section discusses that precise scenario.

☐ Vicarious Liability and *Respondeat Superior*

We have previously noted that the *Jeffries* court dismissed the plaintiff's claim against the state for failing to stop or address such harassment. That court noted avenues for imposing employer liability in general. We note some here: (a) any tort committed by an employee acting within the scope of employment, or (b) any tort committed by an employee where the employer was negligent or reckless. This does not exhaust the list, but it gives us an excellent introduction to this topic.

We can see how the plaintiff in *Jeffries* tried to draw the employer into the suit. Remember that it was another CPE chaplain who allegedly engaged in the claimed hugging and kissing. So how is it possible to sue a state agency itself for the alleged wrongdoing of an employee?

No discussion of the causes of action in a civil suit would be complete without a mention of the related concepts of vicarious liability and *respondeat superior*. These claims can name supervisors, employers, and employing organizations as defendants for the negligence of employees. Under the doctrine of *respondeat superior* ("Let the master answer"), the employer ("master") is held legally responsible for the wrongful acts of the employee ("servant"). Liability is attached even where there is, otherwise, no wrongdoing by the employer. Besides the ever-popular "deep pockets" rationale, *respondeat superior* is a liability based upon the notion that, while an employer benefits from an employee's labor, so too, they must bear the responsibility for an employee's bad acts.

The test varies from state to state, but the plaintiff must show that the employee was acting "within the scope of employment," at the time of the bad act. For example, in *Block v. Gomez* (1996), a Wisconsin appeals court held that a therapist, who initiated sexual contact with a client during the course of therapy and who knew that the clinic in which he worked forbad such contact, acted "within the scope of employment" as a matter of law.

In contrast to *respondeat superior*, vicarious liability extends liability for fault on the part of the employer when they wrongfully hire, fire, or supervise an employee. This liability is based, then, upon affirmative duties on the employer's part. In either case, however, the employer is often hit with large monetary damages. Thus, these increasingly used principles are of major and enduring concern to the supervisors and employers of counselors.

So how might these concepts apply specifically to counselors who use spiritual or complementary interventions? The answer is when counselors raise the issue of their work as "religious" or "spiritual." As ever, First Amendment issues complicate, and often change the legal calculus. For example, a Roman Catholic diocese raised that defense on appeal when the lower court granted summary judgment in favor of the diocese. The female plaintiff alleged that a hospital chaplain used his position as her counselor to instigate and to further a sexual relationship with her. She alleged, among other things, that the diocese negligently supervised the chaplain and that the diocese should be held liable under the doctrine of *respondeat superior* (*LLN v. Clauder*, 1996). The trial court ruled that both claims would excessively involve the court in church-state entanglements and dismissed those claims on First Amendment grounds.

The court of appeals ruled that the negligent supervision claim was not barred by the First Amendment, and the claims raised material issues of fact that can only be resolved at trial. The court was clear that in policies and procedures, a court cannot inquire into a strictly theologically driven practice. For example, the hiring of a priest would be under the complete discretion of the church. This, of course, is the reason that no sexual discrimination claims would be allowed for women who wanted to be hired as priests in Roman Catholic Churches. The First Amendment protects religious groups in hiring practices based upon clearly Theological grounds.

The court was not so sanguine about negligent supervision and retention once priests were hired. They allowed that a religious organization might be sued if it knew or should have known that an employee posed a public danger. Such suits, the court found, might not necessitate an impermissible inquiry into religious or spiritual doctrine or policy.

What does this have to do with counselors? In review, first, many counselors who use spiritual or complementary interventions may work for religiously- or spiritually-based organizations. Such organizations are varied, and include Catholic Charities, Lutheran or Jewish Social Services, the American Friends Service Committee, and any number of such organizations. Those organizations could be sued, either under vicarious liability theory, should their counselors act negligently. First Amendment defenses might be raised by such organizations. While such organizations might be free to hire under church guidelines, their supervision of counselors and their retention in their positions might well be scrutinized at trial.

This same rationale applies to private and governmental employers. Supervisory personnel, the corporate entity, department or board of directors can be sued under the theories of vicarious liability or *respondeat superior*. Thus, such employing organizations need to scrutinize their own supervision policies. This scrutiny includes, but is not limited to, the following two factors:

1. any information that might lead the employer to believe that the counselor poses a threat to clients. This is called "foreseeability" and would be a major focus of any litigation.
2. any factor that might lead a jury to conclude that supervision was lax, incomplete, or inaccurate.

Such an inquiry begins right at hiring time with a scrutiny of references and other job-related material. If a reference or psychological test even hints at such a threat or the possibility of threat, the employer is obligated to act in some way to avoid harm. Suspicious information necessitates some inquiry and maybe some preventative act. Turning a blind eye to suspicious information is no defense and is, in fact, likely to incense a jury. After all religious and spiritual employers are supposed to aid and support clients, not exploit them.

Rumors of, say, sexual contact on a counselor's part must, of course, be treated on a case-by-case basis. Employers must not irresponsibly publish or circulate such rumors, but they should be checked out in a private, professional manner.

Supervision should include a fully disclosed policy of procedure and statement of what is and is not permitted by the counselor. Supervision of case loads and competence, relevance and adequacy of counseling interventions, session summaries, informed consent and other documentation is essential. It is in the employer's best interest, as well as in the public interest, to maintain such supervisory vigilance.

Here we can only describe some items in a laundry list of suggestions for supervisors and employers to address supervisory vigilance in hiring and supervision. Because this work specifically addresses spiritual and complementary interventions, we confine ourselves to those issues. Here, we address ourselves to supervisors:

1. If a candidate for hire asserts that they have special training or expertise in a spiritual or complementary intervention, check out the claim. Specifically ask references. Ask the candidate to describe in detail how they use the intervention, under what circumstances, they use it, under what therapeutic conditions, and how they protect their clients from harm.

   Assessing the credentials of hiring a clinician is art as well as a science. Since some, if not most, credentials for such interventions are not certified or licensed, it can be hard to judge whether an employee is competent to conduct such interventions. Even when some credential is available, how can you judge the value of such credentials?

   All certifying programs may not be equal. One criterion can be whether or not the government, or government agency, does the certifying. Another is whether a well-established and well-recognized private agency awards the certification (i.e., APA or ACA or the NASW). This is not to say that the certification or credentials awarded by private groups or individuals is inferior. This is to say that judges and juries may give more credence to the government or nationally established licensing groups.

   In any event, the applicant need not reach the caliber of an expert witness, but being prudent is important. Don't hire someone who is "in-training" with such interventions. Hire someone who can prove, beyond even the routine counseling credentials, they have kept up the literature for such interventions, has attended seminars, and has experience using such interventions.

2. Ascertain your agency or department's policy on using spiritual or complementary interventions. If you don't have a policy, create one. This policy should include whether or not your clinicians can or cannot use such interventions. If your agency is spiritually or religiously based, or otherwise uses such interventions as a matter of course, then are some interventions forbidden or *must* a clinician use spiritual or complementary interventions?

   If the agency is public and does not use such interventions as a matter of course, *may* a clinician use them? Under what circumstances may the clinician use them? Only when a client so requests or when a clinician thinks its best, or both? Are some such interventions permitted and some not? Why not? Is there a rationale for permitting some and allowing others that you'd feel comfortable explaining as a witness?

3. Supervise spiritual and complementary interventions closely. These are emerging interventions, as we have noted, and the standards of care are, shall we say "fluid." Closer supervision of employees using such interventions is warranted. Written notes detailing how the intervention was used, the credentials of the clinician using them, and retraining sessions both in methodology of the interventions and legal issues surrounding their use should be mandatory and documented in employment files.

4. Finally, what is the criteria for firing someone who uses such interventions incompetently, unethically, or inappropriately? It is often best to at least outline the reasons for

dismissal. Stating the minimum levels of care for such use does two things: a) it puts the clinician on notice that there are agency standards for using such interventions, and b) gives the employer some defense in court if the dismissal is challenged.

Considerations for such dismissal can reflect the issues outlined in this book, including: not obtaining genuine informed consent, not warning clients of potential dangers or alternatives to such interventions, using coercive or manipulative methods or suggestions, using such methods when other methods may be more effective, and using methods that are disapproved of by the organization or agency.

5. Clearly define the place, times, and job responsibilities of the employee. This clear limitations of what the manner and the time and location parameters of employment may help the court define the scope of employment narrowly. As we shall see in the conclusion to the *Clauder* case below, the "scope of employment" test is often dispositive of a case.

These suggestions, and other criterion suggested in this book can help innoculate the supervisor and organization against vicarious liability and *respondeat superior*. While there is no "silver bullet" against such claims, close, responsive competent supervision goes a long way to prevent such suits.

Returning to the *Clauder* appeal, the court disappointed the plaintiff, however, on the *respondeat superior* claim. The appeals court held that the sexual relationship was beyond the scope of the chaplain's employment and thus, the diocese cannot be held liable under that claim. The Clauder appeals court used a "scope of employment" test. The appeals court found that this test includes whether the act was different in kind from that authorized by the employer or if it is motivated by the employee's own gain. Under these tests, the court concluded that the priest's sexual activity was not within his scope of employment, thus that claim failed on appeal.

One might well ask, "When *would* sexual contact with a client be within a scope of employment? The intuitive answer is, of course, "never!" Given this obvious response, some jurisdictions have adopted a more liberal test for *respondeat superior* such as whether or not the employment was a preexisting occasion for the misconduct. In other words, if it were not for the counseling relationship, would the misconduct have taken place? This more liberal test may well be a trend, not a fad.

In concluding this rather complicated section, it is well to remember that under both
In concluding this rather complicated section, it is well to remember that under both theories, an *underlying* negligence must be present. Employers are not held responsible without some wrongful act taken place first. For example, the priest in *Clauder* wrongfully had sexual activity with a client. Only then is the question of employer liability addressed. If the underlying negligence is not pled and proved, employer liability is irrelevant.

☐ Third-Party Liability

An analogous legal doctrine to that of vicarious liability and *respondeat superior* is the doctrine of third-party liability. Third-party liability is legal responsibility stemming from a legal duty, not so much stemming from employment or authority, but of an extension of a duty to the plaintiff—even though not directly involved in the harm done. A case will help clarify. A traditional and initiatory case of third-party liability is the distressing case of Tatiana Tarasoff, a student at Berkeley. Her ex-boyfriend was unhappy at their breakup and told his counselor at the university that he was going to kill her. And he did, with a knife.

Tatiana's parents sued, under a cause of action for "wrongful death" (the same cause of action for which the parents of Ron Goldman sued O.J. Simpson). They sued not the boyfriend, but the University, under a novel claim for that time period. After all, the university didn't stab Ms. Tarasoff. The ex-boyfriend's psychiatrist did not stab Tatiana.

The California Supreme Court held that the university could sue under the theory of the duty to "protect" or "warn" (*Tarasoff v. Regents of University of California*, 1976). This case, and others like it, is styled "third-party liability" because the usual pattern of duty would run from the university to the client (the ex-boyfriend), not to the ex-boyfriend's girlfriend. Tatiana, in this respect is the third party. The legal innovation of the *Tarasoff* case is that now counselors need to be at least cognizant, not only of what their clients do, but of any harm that their clients pose to a third party. This case had an enormous impact on the counseling profession and now affects counselors in many jurisdictions. Certainly it has raised concerns of counselors in *all* jurisdictions.

One pertinent question is whether or not counselors have to inform *other counselors* if their client is suicidal or harmful to others. What do you think? Should such a duty to inform be imposed? Would it not help the succeeding counselor to know such information? Or should law impose yet another duty upon counselors? Shouldn't counselors be able to figure it out for themselves?

We have a case on point (*Gross v. Allen*, 1994). The simplified facts are these. A psychotherapist referred a patient with a history of depression and attempted suicide to two psychiatrists—Drs. Pitts and Allen (Meyers, 1997). After a series of attempts by the doctors to treat her, she still attempted suicide and was readmitted to two different hospitals. She continued to attempt suicide while in the hospital with repeated admissions. Dr. Allen, at one point, warned the patient's mother to take away her daughter's pills for fear of an overdose.

The patient then enrolled in an eating disorder program. Dr. Pitts insisted against this, but the patient enrolled anyway. Dr. Gross, the plaintiff and the admitting psychiatrist at the eating disorder clinic, noted that his new patient seemed depressed. He called Dr. Allen and requested a psychiatric history. The response from Dr. Allen, recorded in Gross's progress notes, was only about the patient's treatment, including medication and psycho-surgery—but not about any of the suicide attempts. The following day, the patient told Dr. Gross herself that she had overdosed on medication prescribed by Drs. Pitts and Allen. The patient lapsed into a coma and ended up with severe neurological problems.

The patient sued Dr. Gross. However, Dr. Gross filed a cross-complaint against Drs. Pitts and Allen, alleging that *they* were negligent in not informing him of the patient's suicide attempts. The California jury agreed somewhat and split the liability in percentages between the three doctors: Dr. Gross at 75%, Dr. Pitts at 19%, and Dr. Allen at 6%.

This case is both tragic and telling. While perhaps not yet a trend, it is at least on the legal radar screen. Counselors should be now aware that this case held that counselors (at least under this court's jurisdiction—a California state appeals court) have a duty to inform new caregivers that their client may pose a threat, so long as they know or have reason to know (our old friend "scienter") that the client is in treatment with someone new (Meyers, 1997).

This case holds particular warnings and interest for complementary and spiritual counselors. One question arising out of this case is the definition of a future "caregiver." In the *Gross* case, the former and future caregivers were all psychiatrists. Would the same rule apply for social workers, psychologists, or licensed counselors? How about nurses,

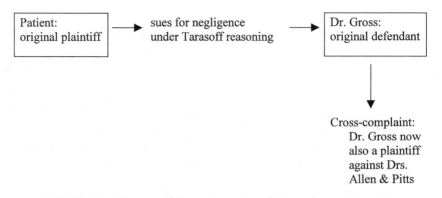

FIGURE 3.1. Diagram of Gross Case: Complaint and cross-complaint

clergy, spiritual advisors, college professors, school counselors, or A.A. sponsors? How expansive might a jury consider "caregiver" to be?

Certainly, the *Gross* case presents significant issues for counselors. This legal territory has not yet been well charted, yet the duties imposed by counselors, begun in *Tarasoff* are still unfolding.

☐ Third Party Liability and Asserted False Memory

A case closely associated with our subject here is *Trear v. Sills* (1999). A father (Mr. Trear) sued his daughter's psychotherapist (Ms. Sills), for allegedly planting false memories of child abuse in his daughter (who earlier sued her father for such alleged acts). This is a third-party action because the therapist had no "usual" line of duty to the father. We can readily understand a duty between Sills and her client (Trear's daughter). Sill's "third-party liability" was the focus of this action by Trear against Sills. So the question for the California Court of Appeal was whether Trear had a cause of action against Sills for allegedly "planting" false memories of her abuse by her father. (In an earlier action, the daughter sued her father for such allegations.)

The court left the father empty-handed. It ruled that, absent some agreement, Sills owed Treat no duty regarding allegedly "planting" such false memories, that Sills's conduct did not support a claim of intentional infliction of emotional distress, that there was no supportable claim of barratry and that there was no claim for malicious prosecution. "Barratry," according to Barron,'s Law Dictionary, is a claim for stirring up frivolous suits, and "malicious prosecution" is a claim to recover damages resulting from a suit instituted without **probable cause** and with malicious intent.

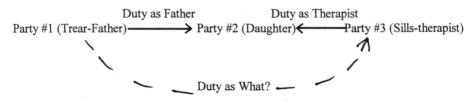

FIGURE 3.2. Diagram of Third Party Liability

In this case, the court seems to be retreating from an expansion of third-party liability. It is unclear, at this writing, if the expansion of "third party" liability will expand as it did in the 1980's to make counselors increasingly vulnerable to claims by non-clients. It seems likely, however, that any new or emerging intervention strategies, particularly those which can impact third parties (such as enhanced memories), are likely to engender suits by those third parties. For example, if a counselor emphasizes forgiveness and pardon in their practice. And if the counselor suggests or encourages the client to forgive those who have harmed them, it is not beyond reason that those third-parties might take umbrage, even extreme umbrage, against the notion that they need forgiving— especially if they feel that they did nothing for which they need forgiveness!

As no case has yet been decided on this point, it is hard to judge for sure. Therefore, it is unclear whether *Trear* is a trend or the last gasp of an old legal order.

☐ Defenses in Civil Actions

To reiterate, counselors who employ spiritual or complementary interventions may be sued under a variety of causes of action arising out of the interventions. Counselors also need to know defenses available to them. Counselors need to know these defenses because (a) they need not "roll over" in the face of false accusations, and (b) they can take proactive, preventative steps to avoid lawsuits altogether.

Just as in the criminal law, the defense of "I didn't do it" or "It just didn't happen" is always available. Just as we noted in the criminal law chapter, the use of timely and accurate process notes, date books with the time and location of appointments and setting clear boundaries with clients are good hedges against accusations. Two important concepts in malpractice cases include assumption of the risk and statute of limitation factors. These two constellations of defenses are not special to alternative or spiritual cases in particular.

☐ The Assumption of Risk

Perhaps the chief defense in alternative medicine malpractice cases is that of the assumption of risk. The legal theory of *volente non fit injuria* means that the client knew the risks involved in being treated with alternative interventions and accepted those risks (Black, 1979). Akin to the legal doctrine of "informed consent," three conditions are necessary to plead assumption of risk: 1) the client (or plaintiff) must have full knowledge of the risk, 2) the risk must be made voluntarily, and 3) the risk must be impliedly or expressly waived (Feasby, 1997).

A specific case of assumption of risk is *Charell v. Gonzalez* (1997). The plaintiff-patient appealed the jury finding that she had impliedly assumed a risk of injury when she agreed to undergo the treatment in the first place. The court did not agree. It held that, even though a jury could reasonably determine that the defendant doctor had not properly explained the risks to the plaintiff, they could also determine that she had independently educated herself about the treatment's risks. The court would not disturb the jury's findings that the patient knew risks of the diet treatment and impliedly consented to continue the treatment.

Assumption of the risk should only be relied upon in very small doses. In conducting spiritual or complementary interventions, clients may be seen to assume the risk of talking about their past religious or spiritual histories, their views of heaven or hell (or equivalents), their discomfort with their current spiritual lives, or experiments with alternative or other complementary treatments and the like. After all, deciding to engage a counselor implies a certain amount of self-disclosure and self-revelation.

It must be hastily noted, however, that counselors serve themselves best who assume least. If a client has never been to counseling previously, it is best to describe the counseling process, how it works, how a typical session might proceed, and what kind of disclosures might be expected in counseling. This education would be in addition, of course, to the usual disclosures and informed consent (See Appendix C).

When it comes to spiritual and complementary counseling a full disclosure is best. Assumption of the risk is not recommended where the processes are not commonplace and not widely known by the public. After all, the law requires that the client knew the risk, without necessarily being told, and decided to take it anyway.

Statutes of Limitation

We discussed time limitations as a defense in the previous chapter. The statute of limitations defense bars a finding of guilt or liability because the action is time barred. Most civil actions place a time limitation upon when an alleged act is perpetuated and when the act is brought to the attention of authorities and filed. If the time limitation expires, no criminal charges or civil suit can be brought.

The purpose of placing a time limitation on legal actions is basically one of practicality. After a time witnesses (and their memories), physical evidence, and other evidence die, decay, get lost, forget, or deteriorate. Statutes of limitation encourage, require actually, that a criminal charge or liability claim be brought in a timely manner. It is not unusual, for example, for many malpractice actions to have a two- or three-year statute of limitation. Determining when to "toll" or to stop a time limitation from running is worth discussing.

The main issue of *Karasek v. Lajoie* (1997), described above, is whether or not the statute of limitations, applied to medical malpractice cases, also applies to social workers. The court ruled that it did not. This ruling was no victory for the defendant counselors. The ruling allowed the plaintiff to maintain their cause of action *beyond* the normal time limitation afforded to medical practitioners.

The court's reasoning is instructive and relevant. The court reasoned that, while counselors *as professionals* are covered by the statute of limitations, their *professional activities* are not. The diagnostic and treatment modalities of counselors, ruled the court, is diverse as their professions including "psychiatrists, social workers, clerics, guidance counselors, substance abuse counselors, lay therapists, and faith healers" (3 of 5). The court specifically noted that while New York State law outlines the scope of practice for social workers and physicians, the law for psychologists does not specify a scope of the licensee's practice. It might be additionally noted also that some of the healers named in the suit are not licensed at all.

The court ruled that only psychiatrists' diagnostic and treatment services may rightly be termed "medical," thus falling within the statute of limitations for "medical" negligence. It said that the other counselors' training is so diverse that, while counseling similarities might exist "medical" under this statute refers only to psychiatrists.

The practical effect of the court's ruling is that the court did not dismiss the suit due to the statute of limitations. They must stand trial even though one of the defendants was not served until nearly three years after the alleged harm.

The conceptual effect of this case is that courts will engage the very definitional distinctions noted in the introduction. This, New York's highest court, split the nature of a counselor (social worker, substance abuse counselor, psychiatrist, cleric, faith healer, etc.) with those of their duties (diagnosis and treatment) while arriving at a result that would hold them legally responsible for professional negligence.

The Statutes of Limitation and Scienter.   Another aspect of "delayed discovery" rule results in exceptions to the standard application the statute of limitations due to the concept of scienter. As discussed earlier, scienter is the concept whereby the plaintiff "knew or should have known" that some harm may ensue. In *Scheffler v. Archdiocese* (1997) the plaintiff sued dioceses of the Roman Catholic Church and a priest for alleged sexual abuse by the priest several years earlier. Plaintiff Scheffler sued in 1994 arising out of alleged sexual abuse of a priest in 1981. The Minnesota statute covering such personal injury cases (Section 541.073(2)(a)) is explicit about when such actions must be commenced and when the statute of limitations can be tolled:

> An action for damages based upon personal injury caused by sexual abuse must be commenced within six years of the time the plaintiff knew or had reason to know that the injury was caused by the sexual abuse.

The *Scheffler* court took pains to discover whether or not he should fall within this statute's exception. The plaintiff asserted that, while he mentioned the incident to his mother a few days after it allegedly occurred, it was only after another pastor labeled the alleged incident as abusive did Scheffler act. In the intervening years, Scheffler alleged that he began a period of substance abuse, lost his self-confidence, and experienced relationship problems. He contended that he "did not know or did not have reason to know" that he was abused until 1993. The trial court refused to grant summary judgement to the priest and the church, but the appeals court reversed.

The Court of Appeals made its decision based upon earlier appellate cases, holding that a plaintiff who alleged sexual abuse by a counselor and who had told others to "watch out" for the counselor, did not have to verbalize or to formally acknowledge that he was abused in order for the statute of limitations to run (*Blackowiak v. Kemp*, 1996). Another case held that where a plaintiff provided expert testimony that a common phenomenon among abused children *not* to have recognized sexual abuse as sexual abuse. Expert testimony also persuaded the court, that a "reasonable" plaintiff, who alleged sexual abuse by a Lutheran minister would *not* have recognized that the defendant's behavior was, indeed, sexual abuse. (*Doe v. Redeemer Lutheran Church*, 1996). The *standard of proof* of the reasonable plaintiff is now widely accepted across many aspects of law. This standard is supposed to be more objective than the subjective standard of what anyone believes.

These cases suggest at least two practice implications. First, counselors should be aware that their practice behavior has legal implications far beyond the act itself. This means that counselors can be sued years after the alleged wrongdoing. This fact has important implications for counseling insurance which we explore in the next chapter. Beyond the obvious notion of care to always perform at or above the standard of care, these cases indicate the necessity of maintaining professional liability insurance. Insurance coverage must be maintained against events that may have happened many years previous.

The Minnesota cases we have been studying in this section call for a six-year statute of limitations; some other states where malpractice is involved call for a two- or three-year limitation. Whatever the specific limitation time frame, a counselor's negligent or abusive behavior in one year can haunt the counselor for years to come.

Second, the last case suggests the importance of expert witnesses. Expert witnesses provide the court and juries with testimony on technical information or insights not available to the lay person. For example, they explain psychological theory, jargon, or new concepts. Counselors need to know that courts and judges have the means and legal sophistication to discern the particular roles of counselors, particularly those representing spiritual concerns, and to hold them responsible. It is an expensive and painful irony for counselors to face their peers who testify against them.

Third, as we have noted earlier in this chapter, spiritual and complementary counselors are susceptible to similar causes of action as are clergy. With increased trust comes increased responsibilities to hold that trust carefully. With increased positions of spiritual power come increased liability for misuse of power, counselor exploitation, or transference. By whatever name, it should be clear by now that courts have less and less tolerance for counselors who use their skills, expertise, power, control, education, or prestige to unduly manipulate their clients. It bears repeating that this coercion is particularly an issue with those purporting to have a spiritual, sacred, or otherwise altruistic motive. Juries can be rather harsh on such counselors as well. The operative phrase here might be something about "a wolf in sheep's clothing."

Limitations for Unsound Mind and Fraudulent Concealment.   Yet another species of the statute of limitations is the "unsound mind" (or similar language) variety. This means that the statute of limitations is "tolled" that is, it ceases to run if the plaintiff is or has been unable to appreciate that they have been a victim of negligence. For example Rhode Island statute Section 19-1-19 states: "If any person at the time any such action shall accrue to him or her shall be ... of unsound mind ... the person may bring the cause of action, within the time limited under this chapter, after the impediment is removed."

This was the situation when several adults sued priests and a Diocese of the Roman Catholic Church years after they alleged that they were sexually abused by the priests (*Kelly v. Marcantonio*, 1999). Under this consolidated case (from a variety of plaintiffs with the same defendants), the plaintiffs allege abuse in the seventies and eighties and they brought suit in the early nineties. Under Rhode Island law all claims for personal injury must be made within three years; thus, the plaintiffs' would be time barred under normal circumstances. The federal district court so ruled on summary judgment and the alleged victims appealed.

The court of appeals considered the precedent from a previously held decision (*Kelly v. Marcantonio*, 1996) ruling that the trial court could make the determination as to whether a repressed recollection of past sexual abuse could qualify as an "unsound mind" to toll the statute of limitations. The court of appeals went on to address the state provision that allows the statute of limitations to be tolled where defendants "fraudulently concealed" a cause of action. In this case the plaintiffs alleged that the defendants not only knew the priests had committed sexual abuse previously, but also covered up their misdeeds by moving them from parish to parish. The court found for the defendants on this issue saying that the entire facts of the negligence action need not be readily apparent for the statute of limitations to run.

☐ Conclusion

Civil law perhaps holds even greater perils than the criminal for the counselors using complementary interventions. It is worth repeating that many criminal laws have analogous civil penalties attached. (For example, the Virginia defamation law provides for *both* civil and criminal sanctions. Civil law can pose greater hazards for the counselor in that, while the criminal law is strictly construed, the civil law (including malpractice actions) is expanding. For example, the law surrounding sexual misconduct, *Tarasoff* type warnings has expanded the types of behavior prone to liability. What exactly could cause liability remains uncertain; thus, how a counselor can prevent civil lawsuits or to prevent being held liable is not always clear.

Stated another way, the "standard of care" is evolving in new and complementary therapies. Without knowing exactly what constitutes "competent" or "incompetent" care, without a firm yardstick for care and competence, there will always be uncertainty in determining or preventing liability.

This chapter has offered some focus on that obscurity. The chapter has indicated major guideposts in how courts and juries determine liability. It has indicated how counselors might, even inadvertently, fall prey to successful civil suits against them. One criterion that tends to bring liability, however, seems to be when professionals take advantage of the vulnerable. Because the professional counselor is, by definition, a person invested with trust specifically to help those in crisis or difficulty, the law will take a hard look at the competence and care of counselors. Should the client or third-parties be harmed by any action or inaction by the counselor, the counselors actions will be subject to careful scrutiny.

School counselors, as we have seen, are particularly amenable to a changing set of "standards of care." Not only are they addressing people in crisis, but they are dealing with a youthful, underaged population as well. Additionally, it seems that society has increased the pressure on schools and school counselors to address difficult family and social issues. The Columbine High School shootings and other such events have added to the uncertainty and the difficulty of an already difficult job description. It is hard to "see through the glass darkly," but it might be said that the liability for school counselors probably will not diminish any time soon.

☐ Legal Audits and Exercises

1. Counselors must continue to keep apprised of legal developments in law as well as their own professions. This is particularly true for civil law and the law of malpractice. It seems that the civil law moves more rapidly than does the criminal law. Attend seminars and read legal material to keep current with law that directly pertains to your field of practice. First amendment law is particularly sensitive to change in public attitude.

   As we have noted, often expert witnesses can turn the tide in a court proceeding. It is particularly important to note what the expert witnesses say in court if you can get such material. One way to assess the "state of the art" (e.g., how acceptable is prayer and meditation for certain clients?) is to keep close watch on legal journals and professional seminars as well as journals in your counseling profession. The reference section of this book offers several suggestions for legal reading.

2. Any remarks tending to lower the reputation of another and published by the counselor are dangerous without a clear privilege. Even if the remarks are true, such publications have to be proven in court. For example, try proving that a client's religious beliefs are "stupid" or that some religious affiliation are a "cult."

3. The standard of care for counselors can be expected to change as the law accommodates itself to increased mental health use of spiritual and alternative interventions. Thus, counselors need to keep current on any intervention they use. Subscribe to professional journals, attend seminars, and be sure to keep records of the content of the seminars.

4. Enough cannot be said to encourage counselors to increase their *provable* competence in spiritual and alternative interventions. I say 'provable' not in the statistical sense of effectiveness, but in the forensic sense. Certifications, membership in organizations, knowledge of trends in the field, proof of seminar attendance, and documented experience tend toward competence as a witness. Imagine how you would state your qualifications as a witness? Do your qualifications seem like they would impress a jury? Would they add to or detract from your credibility?

5. Are you now or have you ever been in positions of legal vulnerability? In other words, are you someone who might have difficulty defending yourself against a false charge? Do you keep clear, adequate process notes? Do you keep a complete professional appointment book? Do you keep clear lines between your professional life and personal life?

Boundary limits are particularly important in conducting spiritual and complementary interventions. For example, there is an important difference between disclosing your religious or spiritual orientation in a session and actually attending a worship service or spiritual event with a client. There is a distinction to be made between shaking a client's hand in greeting, holding a client's hand if you pray with him or her, and massaging a client's back.

4
CHAPTER

Licensure and Insurance Issues

Objectives

1. To review the legal and ethical purposes of state licensure.
2. To compare and contrast the legal role and consequences between the civil and criminal law and regulatory offenses. An analogy of a criminal charge of midwives is used to illustrate.
3. To introduce state statutes that may exempt spiritual and complementary counselors and healers from licensure revocation from both public and private licensing agencies.
4. To note some causes of action for the state to impose licensure penalties.
5. To explain legal issues involved in malpractice insurance.

The purpose of this chapter is to establish how state licensing boards may limit or sanction spiritual or alternative counseling interventions. Additionally, this chapter addresses the law of insurance reimbursement relative to spiritual or complementary counseling. As we will see, licensing boards have constitutionally legitimized authority to suspend or revoke counseling licenses when they deem necessary.

Licensure is intimately connected with insurance reimbursement because both address oversight and evaluation of new or "experimental" interventions. Where a licensing board sanctions a counselor for "unprofessional practice" for using "questionable" interventions, insurance companies are unlikely to reimburse for such interventions. Likewise, if a licensing board is well acquainted with and supports certain interventions (such as some spiritual and complementary interventions), it is more likely that insurance companies will reimburse.

This chapter describes the purposes of licensure, the causes of action where counselors can loose their licenses, and the due process considerations that must be adhered to during licensing disputes. "Due process" are the constitutional procedures guaranteed to any person in a legal dispute.

This chapter will apply these considerations to a variety of ways in which counselors using spiritual and complementary interventions may run afoul of licensing requirements. These specific "causes of action" include improper advertising and misrepresentation. This chapter also addresses the political and social roles counselors may assume in order to effect greater recognition for spiritual and complementary.

As in the previous two chapters, we begin this chapter with a case study. While the subject of this following case study is a nurse and not a counselor, her legal case arose when she gave advice, not for her administration of medical procedures or drugs. Her case has other connections to the counseling professions. First, most counselors are licensed by state boards. Counselors should recognize their "due process" rights when challenged by licensing boards. This case addresses the issue of how broad the term "unprofessional conduct" can become before it does not give proper notice to the counselors of exactly what conduct is or is not prohibited. Second, this nurse simply agreed to discuss "alternative treatment(s) using natural products" with the family of a cancer patient, at their request.

☐ Case Study: The Too-Progressive Nurse

Jolene Tuma, R.N., appealed her suspension by the state nursing board all the way to the Supreme Court of Utah. She was suspended for the broad charge of "unprofessional conduct." The court found that Tuma discussed alternative treatments such as natural foods and herbs and that the patient could have trouble getting blood transfusions if the patient left the hospital. The patient died of her illness, though there was never any contention that Tuma in any way contributed to her death.

At Tuma's Board hearing, the officers also found that a reflexologist could be retained if the family so chose. The nursing board ruled that because of Tuma's actions, she interfered with the patient-doctor relationship and suspended her license for six months. Tuma appealed her suspension to a Utah district court, which affirmed her suspension. She then appealed to the Utah Supreme Court.

The primary issue for appeal was whether Tuma's due process rights were protected by the statute authorizing her license to be suspended for "unprofessional conduct" where the statute does not define what "unprofessional conduct" means. In legal short-hand, this challenge amounts to a "void for vagueness" defense. Briefly stated "void for vagueness" means that a statute is too indefinite or unclear to be applied. An analogy might be where one is stopped for speeding where the only sign reads "Don't Speed." Of course, all speeding signs specify an exact number above which drivers may not exceed. The motorist has no legal "notice" that he or she is committing a criminal offense. "Notice" is a legal concept meaning that citizens should be adequately warned about criminal offenses. Further, if police could stop anyone they felt was exceeding *what they interpreted* as "speeding," the criminal law could be applied arbitrarily, capriciously, and discriminatorily.

In making its decision the court first examined the statute under which Tuma was suspended. It prohibited the usual suspects: mental incompetence, gross incompetency, habitual intemperance in the use of ardent spirits, narcotics or stimulants, conviction of a crime involving moral turpitude, etc. Of course, the statute also included "immoral, unprofessional, or dishonorable conduct." The statute then specified what "unprofessional conduct" is: practices likely to deceive or defraud the public, obtaining fees by fraud, deceit, or misrepresentation, or misleading or untruthful advertising.

The Court found that there was no contention that Tuma was an unfit nurse. Her sole "infraction" was talking to a patient (or family) about alternative procedures to that the patient was receiving. The court then went on to find that nothing in the statute adequately warned Tuma that her license could be suspended for discussing such alternatives with a patient. Thus, the court ruled that the statute does not specifically prohibit the acts for which Tuma was charged (*Tuma v. Board of Nursing*, 1979).

Two additional points are brought out by the facts and the decision of this case. First, the *Tuma* court, and other courts as well, recognize that statutes regulating professional licenses are essentially criminal statutes. They are penal in nature in that the statutes have the power to restrict, revoke, or to suspend a person's license to practice their profession—their livelihood. Additionally, when a license is revoked or suspended, or otherwise restricted, a person's ability to find work thereafter may well be compromised. These sanctions amount to a severe penalty, even beyond the financial penalties of a negligence or malpractice action.

Second, it is encumbant upon licensed mental health professionals to know well their own state's statues and regulations affecting their licenses. To the extent that such regulations may restrict *or may be used* to restrict licenses for those who practice spiritual or complementary practice, specific knowledge of these statutes are an immediate necessity.

Clearly, the attitudes surrounding the use and promulgation of complementary and spiritual interventions are changing. This may mean that licensing boards would be more tolerant towards such interventions. Greater public acceptance of such interventions, however, may or may not translate into greater acceptance of such interventions by licensing boards. There is no substitute for vigilance about state licensing tolerance for spiritual and complementary interventions. Any determination might well depend upon the specific intervention under question. For example, the *Tuma* court may have ruled differently if she, for example, discussed dream symbolism as a complementary therapy or if she had not simply answered questions at the family's behest, but had unilaterally inserted such interventions.

In fact, licensing boards may take an entirely different tact and become more restrictive. The reasoning may go like this: as an increasing variety of spiritual and complementary interventions become more commonplace, licensing boards might become more selective about what interventions they deem "professional." One thing is for sure, the standard for making such determinations will change. Keeping legally, politically, and culturally astute about such interventions is as important as taking seminars on the latest such interventions. Technical competence is only half the operative definition of proficiency, the other half is forensic facility.

As we shall see later in this section, it is pretty clear that Tuma would never have been charged or disciplined if she presented the same facts clearly as of the date of this book—and probably well before. Times have changed and the attitudes of the public and professional boards' attitudes toward complementary and spiritual interventions have changed. Many states have codified this change of mind into statutes—at least for the medical professions. While we have introduced this notion in the negligence section of chapter three, we restate some of those statutes below.

☐ The Purposes of Licensure

The counselor should have a clear sense of how and perhaps even under what circumstances licensing boards might impose sanctions for the improper and unsafe use of spiritual or alternative interventions. What legal "causes of action" may licensing boards or agencies use to sanction and otherwise limit the practice of spiritual and alternative interventions?

The state may constitutionally license counselors to perform their duties. Without such licenses, they may not practice. The state offers such licenses as a *privilege*, not as a *right*, to promote the public health, morals, comfort, safety and good order of society. Additionally, in offering such a license, the state regulating body seeks to provide a minimum competency level of professionals in its jurisdiction (***Borrego v. Agency for Health Care Administration***, 1996).

What the state gives, it may take away. The jurisprudence of a professional license for, say, a clinical social worker, psychologist, substance abuse counselor, or professional counselor, is analogous to a state driver's license. For example, a Florida court of appeals held that the Agency for Health Care Administration can suspend a psychiatrist's license to practice medicine if they conclude that the defendant poses an "immediate danger to the public health, safety, or welfare" (***Cunningham v. Agency for Health Care Administration*** 1996). In this case the psychiatrist was accused of unjustifiably over prescribing controlled substances to a patient.

The relevance for alternative or spiritual counselors is whether, and under what circumstances, state licensing boards may sanction counselors for performing alternative or spiritual interventions. State licensing boards and agencies are charged with controlling the competence and quality of licensees.

A driver's license, for example, is not a civil right. A state may limit the age, eye sight, and other qualifications reasonably related to safe driving. Consequently, a state may revoke, suspend or otherwise limit a person's driving privileges. The state may not arbitrarily or capriciously do so, however, and must adhere to constitutional due process requirements.

So long as the state meets the due process requirements, counselors may be deprived of their license to counsel for a variety of reasons. The following section illustrates the case of midwives. This case demonstrates how a Virginia state court addresses the case of an emerging "alternative" intervention and what legal processes take place when such interventions are challenged.

Hopefully, to reiterate the obvious (by now), the law surrounding spiritual and complementary counseling is evolving. Trends, however, can be discerned from experience of other, similar professions. You might say this is "legal education by analogy." As noted earlier, a particularly close legal correspondence to counselors is the medical profession.

☐ The Analogy of Midwives

Midwives Cynthia Caillagh and M. Elizabeth Haw stand accused of misdemeanor manslaughter charges in the death of a woman whom they aided in childbirth in the state of Virginia. Caillagh and Haw also face misdemeanor charges of illegally practicing midwifery. In April, 1999, a Virginia circuit court judge refused to dismiss the misdemeanor charges on the licensing charge after a defense motion asserted the Virginia midwifery law was unconstitutional (Neuberger, 1999).

The defense asserted that the state had no "rational basis" for the unequal treatment between midwives who are not registered nurses; additionally, the defense claimed that the state regulatory agency arbitrarily giving the state authority to criminalize anyone who "makes the smallest affirmative act to aid delivery and gets something of value afterward" (Neuberger, 1999, 131). Caillagh and Haw face a year in jail for each misdemeanor licensing conviction.

The Virginia law defines a "midwife" as "Any person who, for compensation, assists in delivery and postnatal care by affirmative act of conduct immediately prior and subsequent to the labor attendant to childbirth in conjunction with or in lieu of a member of the medical profession shall be deemed a midwife and to be practicing midwifery."

This case illustrates several points for those counselors who are practicing spiritual or alternative interventions or who wish to do so. First, a licensing board can criminalize behavior that it deems to be inherently dangerous to the public. A midwifery case is presented here because, like some alternative or spiritual therapies, it too is an unconventional intervention. It is no stretch of the imagination that some regulatory bodies might consider some complementary therapists as posing dangerous or unauthorized practice.

Second, it is clear that regulatory agencies can be challenged for their decisions to define classes of people from practicing professional acts. The widwives challenged the state's role in excluding classes of people from conducting help in childbirth. Again, it takes no excess of imagination to consider that states may exclude counselors from performing some spiritual or complementary interventions. They might consider some acts, like exorcism, hypnoses, and other mind-altering acts as inherently dangerous. We have noted statutes defining some such interventions later in this chapter.

Third, once a counselor is charged with a regulatory infraction, the regulatory agencies can be challenged for "due process" violations. That is, the agency must afford the counselor-defendant with a fair and equitable procedure.

Fourth, licensure violations do not necessarily mean legal negligence. Professional negligence, or malpractice, was discussed in the previous chapter. Actions of regulatory agencies are totally independent of claims of malpractice. For example, a counselor may be sued for malpractice and never be examined by a regulatory agency. On the other hand, a regulatory agency may examine a counselor's interventions whether or not a malpractice claim has been instituted. A very benign, but technical violation of licensure regulation, might be failure to publicly display the counselor's license in his or her office. Many states require such display of the actual license. The rationale is for the public to know if the counselor is licensed and if that license is current. Failure to do so may violate licensure law, but is not likely to draw a malpractice suit.

Fifth, the regulatory agency's main concern is to protect the public. Should a counselor use interventions that are misunderstood by their clients, that falsely raise client expectations, or misrepresent their credentials, regulatory bodies may revoke or suspend counselor licenses to practice. This fifth consideration has profound political and economic consequences for counselors using spiritual and complementary interventions.

Counselors using such interventions must always be on the lookout for ways in which to broaden the exposure and acceptance of spiritual and complementary interventions both among the general public, but particularly among peers. This is because regulatory boards and disciplinary committees are composed of peers. Indeed, insurance company reimbursement officers are not immune from public perceptions of the value of such interventions. To the extent that such interventions gain professional and public acceptance, counselors will not only be able to use them without fear of professional sanction, but also with greater expectation of insurance reimbursement.

To reiterate, counselors using spiritual and complementary interventions should make every effort to:

1. publish qualitative and quantitative research in professional journals,
2. provide both public and professional seminars on their interventions of choice, and/or
3. support those who do numbers 1 and 2.

☐ Statutory Exemptions for Revoking Licenses of Those Using Spiritual or Alternative Interventions

Some states have enacted legislation statutorily prohibiting the revocation of a professional license for practicing spiritual, alternative, or nontraditional interventions. These statutes provide the most comprehensive protections against a charge simply arising out of the use of spiritual or alternative interventions. These statutes are promulgated for the express purpose of protecting clinicians from such licensing prosecutions. These statutes are promulgated because there is the real or perceived danger of such prosecutions. Such a statute comes from North Carolina (§90-14(a)(6)):

> The Board shall not revoke the license of or deny a license to a person solely because of that person's practice of a therapy that is experimental, nontraditional, or that departs from acceptable prevailing medical practices unless, by competent evidence, the Board can establish that the treatment has a safety risk greater than the prevailing treatment or that the treatment is not effective.

Several issues arise from this statute. First, the state seems to make an initial presumption that the "nontraditional" practice is, itself, legally neutral. The burden of proof then shifts from the practitioner to the Board. Third, the Board can overcome that presumption if it proves that the nontraditional intervention poses a risk greater than a traditional intervention for the same problem.

Of course, a principle problem is that "nontraditional" is undefined. If one had to defend their use, say, of past-life regression, at least two problems must be overcome. The first is whether or not a state statute such as North Carolina's above, applied to mental health counselors. The second is whether or not "past life regression" falls within the meaning of this, or other similar, statute.

The best of all possible worlds would be for states to license specific spiritual or complementary therapies. Most states do not. However *some* states now license *some* spiritual or complementary therapies. A couple of representative statutes are below noted.

☐ Statutes Concerning Licensure of Alternative Therapies

Sale (n.d.), in his *Overview of Legislative Development Concerning Alternative Health Care in the United States*, has done us a considerable service by collating several statutes on spiritual or complementary interventions from various jurisdictions on the Internet. His work has greatly abbreviated the search for some of the below statutes.

Aromatherapy

Sale (n.d.) notes that only Maine currently licenses this modality with a prerequisite for a counseling license (Me. Rev. Stat. Ann. §13856(10) (Supp. 1994).

Biofeedback

Sale (n.d.) indicates that most of the states refer to this intervention under the practice of psychology. Statutes can be unclear as to exactly what "biofeedback" is. For example

California and Maryland permit the use of biofeedback instruments that do not pierce or cut the skin "to measure physical and mental functioning" (Ca. Bus. & Prof. Code §2903.1 (West 1990); Md. Health Occup. Code Ann. §18-101(e)(2)(iii) (1991).

Hypnotherapy

The Florida statute defines the practice of hypnosis as "hypnosis, mesmerism, posthypnotic suggestion, or any similar act or process which produces or is intended to produce in any person any form of induced sleep or trance in which the susceptibility if the person's mind to suggestion or direction is increased or is intended to be increased, which such a condition is used or intended to be used in the treatment of any human ill, disease, injury, or any other therapeutic process" (Fla. Stat. §456.32(1)).

Spiritual Healing

This book has noted statutes under the "spiritual healing" category. As noted, and as Sale (Id.) also notes that these statutes often only offer exemptions from licensing requirements for spiritual healing consistent and (as noted earlier) some "exemptions" from prosecution of child abuse for those who use "spiritual" means. However, Sale notes some important distinctions among these statutes. For example, Michigan offers the licensing exemption exclusively for "prayer" (Mich. Stat. Ann. §14.15(16171)(d). Vermont disallows the exemption for those who try curing by means of "faith cure," "mind healing," or "laying on of hands," but it *is* permitted by those who simply adhere to the tenets of their church without pretending a knowledge of surgery or the practice of medicine (Vt. Stat. Ann. tit. 26, §1312 (1989).

Vermont's exemption and its limitations fall precisely into the public licensure policy of states enunciated earlier in this chapter. States must walk a legislative tightrope between allowing freedom of religion and ensuring public well being from those authorized to practice various counseling professions.

To reiterate, spiritual and complementary interventions pose a challenge to this balancing act. As we have stated in chapter one, states are often loathe to infringe anywhere close to the freedom of religious expression, including the healing interventions often used in religious traditions. These, by their very nature, are often the very kind of interventions that spiritual and complementary counselors use. So, a daunting task for legislators is to sharpen the fine edge occupied by professional counselors using sometimes sacred interventions in a secular surrounding.

Correspondingly, the one great task for the counselor, as we have seen and will see again, is to always be clear whether they are practicing as a religious function or in their capacity as a professional counselor. Such counselors' legal and constitutional status may depend upon it.

☐ Statutory Exemptions from Licensure by Complementary Healers

What the state requires it can also exempt. Where states require counselors to possess state licenses to practice alternative or spiritual interventions, it may also exempt them, in whole or in part from those requirements. New Mexico's exemption (§61-9A-6) illustrates in part:

A. Nothing in the Counseling and Therapy Practice Act shall be construed to prevent:
   (2) an alternative, metaphysical, or holistic practitioner from engaging in nonclinical activities consistent with the standards and codes of ethics of that practice
B. Specifically exempted from the Counseling and Therapy Practice Act are . . .
   (3) duly, ordained, commissioned, or licensed ministers of a church or pastoral-care assistants providing pastoral services on behalf of a church
   (5) practitioners of the Native American healing arts

This statute exempts alternative counselors with some exceptions. Generally, the more adjectives in a statute, the more qualifications to that exemption there are. For example, in the New Mexico statute above the practitioner must practice 1) nonclinical activities and 2) consistently with the standards and codes of ethics of that practice. While this statute "exempts" alternative, metaphysical, or holistic practitioners, it probably will not exempt licensed counselors. After all, they are doing explicitly "clinical" work. The exemption for ministers would apply only in the context of a religious or spiritual organization.

Finally, this provision specifically exempts practitioners of the "Native American healing arts." While this provision does not specify whether or not the "practitioners" need to be Native American themselves or simply practicing those interventions deemed as "Native American" in nature, such an exemption opens up many areas of spiritual or alternative interventions such as herbology, prayer, "sweat lodge" practice, and dancing.

☐ Spiritual Healing Exemptions for Caring for the Ill and Suffering

Many states also exempt "spiritual healers" from health licensure. These statutes flow from the constitutional prohibition against religious interference by the state. An example of such a state statute from Massachusetts (§333.16171 (d)) follows:

> An individual who provides nonmedical nursing or similar services in the care of the ill or suffering or an individual who in good faith ministers to the ill or suffering by spiritual means alone, through prayer, in the exercise of a religious freedom, and who does not hold himself or herself out to be a health professional.

This statute is more informative of the law than usable to professional counselors. This statute only applies to those who are not representing themselves as health professionals. This statute, however, shows the high regard for the counselors prosecuting their rights under the First Amendment. Courts are loathe to circumscribe the religious practice of counselors who offer nonprofessional "religious" counseling.

A helpful website titled "Health Freedom States" (www.healthlobby.com) has compiled a number of state statutes allowing some measure of statutory liberty in practicing alternative or complementary medicine. Some of the elements of these statutes may legally or ethically be applied to the counseling and mental health professions.

Colorado's statute is one example. Not only does it provide for that its licensing board not "take disciplinary action against a physician solely on the grounds that such a physician practices alternative medicine" (§12-36-117(3)) but that "A physician who practices alternative medicine shall inform each patient in writing during the initial patient contact of such physician's education, experience, and credentials related to the alternative medicine practiced by such physician."

As noted earlier, as goes the medical profession, so goes the mental health professions." This statute emphasizes the importance of "informed consent" and "notice" that we have addressed in the previous chapter. Informing the client of a counselor's use of complementary or spiritual interventions in writing as well as credentials, experience, and education related to such practice may become a necessity in the future of counseling. Such information in the hands of a client puts the client on notice that such interventions are parts of the counselors interests and repertoire. Such notice also gives the client the requisite information for them to make an informed choice as to the nature, extent, and degree to which the counselor will be allowed to conduct such interventions upon him or her. In the end, it must be the client's informed choice as to what interventions are used and to what extent they are used in therapy.

☐ Civil and Criminal Actions for Licensure Infractions

"Causes of action" for licensing penalties are the substantive charges leveled against people for performing acts that violate licensing acts. As we have seen in the Virginia Midwifery Act, such acts only allow specific acts to be performed. Conversely, they disallow a number of acts by unlicenced persons. This section illustrates some ways in which people run afoul of such acts including:

1. Misrepresentation
2. Departing from accepted practice standards

At the very least, counselors cannot falsely misrepresent their credentials. The following case illustrates how strictly licensing agencies construe definitions of practice and how even a verbal assurance of licensing can result in a criminal action.

Defendant David Clayton was found guilty of the unlicenced practice of psychology when he performed hypnotherapy on one of his "patients." The defendant had separated from his wife and, based upon a recommendation of his sister, began sessions with the defendant. The plaintiff-client says he was "shocked" when Clayton proposed they try hypnosis as a way of "bringing out things in [the plaintiff's] mind and in his subconscious that, if brought to the front of his mind, would help [the plaintiff] be at ease in his life" (*People v. Clayton,* 1998).

To help the plaintiff feel more confident in this intervention and to help reassure him, Clayton stated, "I'm a clinical psychologist," and that he had gone to school in California, and presented plaintiff with a card that said "Hypnotherapy." Concluding that the sessions were not helping, but were rather hindering his progress, the plaintiff terminated the sessions. He also sent a letter of complaint to the state licensing board which started an investigation, eventually concluding that Clayton was not so licensed in the state.

Clayton was convicted and appealed his conviction on the grounds that the trial court should have allowed expert testimony that his acts constituted the practice of psychology. The appeals court rejected this claim because of the fact that Clayton twice verbalized that he was, indeed, a clinical psychologist.

This case also illustrates that licensing agencies strictly construe licensing requirements. Even if it were proven that Clayton had training in hypnosis in California (or anywhere) or even that he was in any way "certified" in hypnosis (or using alternative interventions), that does not amount to a state license to practice psychology.

Another case bearing on misrepresentation is when a lone practitioner, a licensed marriage and family counselor, advertised his counseling office as a "center." It caught the attention of regulators and they deemed that such advertising ran contrary to the code of ethics of the counselor's profession. One of the ethical provisions prohibited "any statement in advertising which would or may tend to mislead the public as to the individual's competence, education, qualifications, or experience" (*Magleby v. State*, 1977, p. 1109). The Supreme Court of Utah ruled that the state could rightly adopt this ethical restriction upon code of ethics this counselor's advertising and that such ethical restrictions were not an "unreasonable restraint and regulation of a recognized profession" (p. 1109). This means that the regulatory agency could adopt reasonable restrictions upon counseling advertising and still be constitutional.

The next section addresses the licensure of alternative therapies. As we have mentioned, both statutes and cases constitute the law. It will describe both statutes and cases that outline legal regimes of licensing alternative therapies. Some of these cases arise strictly in the medical, not the counseling fields. We need to remember that sometimes "as goes the medical field, so goes the counseling field." Law is sometimes made and understood by analogy—that is, the medical cases can sometime be very closely related to the principles and to the precepts of law applies to counselors. Thus, when a physician is charged with practicing nontraditional medicine, might similar legal arguments and principles be applied to some cases where counselors might be so charged?

A leading case in the legal regulation of "complementary" medical therapies is *In re Guess* (1990). It is a "leading" case first because it was decided by the highest court in a state—in this instance, the Supreme Court of North Carolina. The second reason is that the written opinion is both extensive and "on point." It directly address the issue of the power and authority (and propensity) to limit and sanction such "unorthodox" practices.

This particular case involves a licensed physician who used homeopathic medicine to treat some of his patients. Homeopathic medicine treats like symptoms with like cures. The Court used *Steadman's Medical Dictionary* (24th ed., 1982) to define the essence of homeopathy: "that large doses of a certain drug given to a healthy person will produce certain conditions, which, when occurring spontaneously as symptoms of a disease, are relieved by the same drug in small doses. This [is] . . . a sort of "fighting fire with fire" therapy" (p. 654). By contrast, allopathy would be like fighting fire with water. Allopathy is the "conventional" way of current medicine. For example, heartburn is not cured by overdosing the system with further acid, but with chemicals that are based in nature.

Dr. Guess, as a homeopathic practitioner, treated some patients with moss, night shade, and other plant, animal, and mineral substances. Even though Guess introduced evidence that no patients were hurt from his treatments; that homeopathic medicine is a recognized system of medicine in three other states and in several foreign countries; and provided anecdotal evidence that several patients experienced relief not experienced under the orthodox allopathic regimes, the Medical Board suspended his license based upon the findings that his homeopathic practice "departs from and does not conform to the standards of accepted and prevailing medical practice in this state" (p. 835). Presumably, he could resume his practice if he did not practice homeopathic medicine.

Interestingly, both the North Carolina Superior Court and Court of Appeals reversed the Board. The appeals court held that because Guess' practice hurt no patients nor endangered any, the board could not base their revocation on "merely" being "different" from other practitioners. It must be based upon conduct that is "detrimental to the public" (p. 835). The Supreme Court, however, reversed the two lower court rulings and affirmed the Board's original ruling.

In affirming the Board's decision, the Supreme Court ruled that the Board's decision was supported by "competent, material, and substantial" evidence, the Board's decision was not arbitrary or capricious, and that other physicians could testify that Guess' treatments did not conform to either accepted or prevailing practices.

Additionally, the Supreme Court held that patient's do not have a privacy right in having homeopathic treatments, even if they so choose. Patients do not have a fundamental right to unorthodox medical treatment. If the Medical Board determines that a treatment is not allowed. This being the law, the Court went on to say that the Board does not enjoy an unconstitutional monopoly such they could deny a physician homeopathic treatment options, even if patients want it.

Another North Carolina case follows the legal reasoning of *Guess*. An acupuncturist, and her patients, brought an injunctive and declaratory suit against the Board of Medical Examiners *(Majebe v. North Carolina Board of Medical Examiners*, 1992). It was a legal "preemptive strike" against the Board which had previously requested the Attorney General to investigate her for possible prosecution. She wanted to adjudicate her rights before the state did it for her. A state investigation was, in fact, initiated.

Majebe's suit was an effort to head off possible prosecution. A lower court rejected her suit and she appealed, and (as of the date of the court opinion) continues to practice acupuncture, herbology, and naturopathy. In two respects the *Majebe* court at least loosely follows its precedent in *Guess*.

First, the court ruled that the investigation launched against Majebe did not amount to an unconstitutional "selective enforcement" of the licensing statute. She basically claimed that the Board and the state were unconstitutionally "picking" on her, amounting to discrimination. In order to make such a claim stick, she would have to prove (a) that she was singled out while others doing the same thing were not, and (b) that such a singling out or malicious prosecution was done in the service of some impermissible category such as race, sex, or religion. The court found there was no evidence of this (*Majebe*, 1992, p. 408).

Second, like Guess, Majebe claimed she had a protected, privacy right to practice acupuncture and, like Guess' claim, Majebe's was rejected. The court held that the Board did not violate Majebe's privacy right to select her method of practice—or to deny her the preferred method. Quoting another case, the *Majebe* court put it plainly, "[T]here is no right to practice medicine which is not subordinate to the police power of the state" (p. 407, quoting *Lambert v. Yellowsley*, 1926).

Another homeopathic practitioner, but from another state, presaged the *Guess* decision. Roget Sabastier was criminally convicted of practicing without a medical license. Sabastier appealed his conviction on the grounds that the requirement for physicians to graduate from allopathic medical facilities in order to obtain a medical license was invidiously discriminatory. The court said that the North Carolina legislature had clearly and unambiguously articulated a preference for "conventional" schools. The court refused to disturb that preference. The court did note, however, that if the defendant wished his homeopathic profession to *be* licensed, he should petition the state legislature as was done by practitioners of chiropractic, hypnosis, osteopathy, and acupuncture (*Sabastier v. State*, 1992). Obviously, this last **dicta** (a discussion not directly applicable to the ruling) by the court has direct and, perhaps, pressing relevance for counselors using alternative and spiritually interventions. Counselors using such interventions need to think seriously about politically organizing to secure some licensing statute.

Another case, where a massage therapist was convicted of the unlawful practice of psychology, illustrates what evidence a court will consider and what it will not. "Mrs. B." went to the defendant's place of business ("The Good Neighbor Center") for a massage in order to relieve migraine headaches. Mrs. B. testified that, at the initial visit, the defendant told her that he had a degree in psychology, that he had counseled patients in the past, and that she could see him for counseling if she needed it. She eventually did after first calling him to verify that he did have a psychology degree.

The defendant was convicted of two counts of violating Pennsylvania's licensing act and fined $2,000. The appeals court ruled that the client's verbal testimony was allowable as proof, and that a document, reputed to be an admission that the defendant was not a psychologist, but rather a massage therapist, could be excluded as evidence. Additionally, the court also ruled that fee payments do not need to be for psychological services in order to meet the requirements for a licensing act violation (*Makris v. Bureau of Professional & Occupational Affairs*, 1991).

It would be misleading to believe that licensing boards have unfettered power to revoke licenses or to sanction violators. In revoking a chiropractor's license for making misleading, deceptive, untrue, or fraudulent representations in his practice, the Florida Department of Professional Regulation must have "competent and substantial" evidence (*Turner v. Department of Professional Regulation, State of Florida*, 1992). This means that the evidence upon which the conviction was based must not be frivolous, capricious, or made in bad faith, and must have probative weight.

Additionally, the court ruled that the Department had no right, in its order revoking the chiropractor's license, to add extra provisions that the revocation was "without right of reinstatement or re licensure" (p. 1137).

☐ Licensure Issues In Private Counseling Associations

State licensing bodies are not the only organizations which can revoke, suspend, censure or otherwise limit counseling licenses. Private, professional associations and organizations also may act to affect counseling licensure. The National Association of Social Workers, the American Psychological Association, the American Counseling Association, the American Psychiatric Association, or other associations can limit a counselor's license to practice for ethics violations. While professional associations are different from state licensing boards, it is generally true that good standing in both is necessary to carry on a legitimate practice. If one loses their standing in an association for an ethics violation, insurance may be hard to get and the state licensing boards may be informed as well. Indeed, as we shall see in the following case, a state licensing board may exonerate a defendant for an ethics charge, yet the private professional may sustain the charge.

This section addresses some of the legal issues involved in a dispute with one's professional association. Law cases in this area are not frequent, but seem fairly settled.

In *Budwin v. American Psychological Association* (1994) the plaintiff sued his professional association for censuring him after a parent complained about a report Budwin had written in a custody hearing. The parent accused Budwin of filing untrue information in the report recommending a custody decision to the presiding judge. The parent filed a complaint to the state licensing board, which denied the complaint. The parent's complaint to the American Psychological Association (APA), however, resulted in the censure. The plaintiff sued to overturn the censure, claiming that the APA violated the rules of fair procedure and its own by-laws and rules of procedure.

The trial court rendered summary judgment in favor of Budwin, but the appeals court reversed that decision and remanded it back to the trial court for a decision consistent with its higher ruling.

In fairly settled law, the appeals court began to outline the legal authority of private associations like the APA. First, the court found that private associations have the power to adopt regulations and when an association disciplines one of its own members it must do so in good faith and in accordance with its own laws and in accordance with the law of the land and public policy.

Budwin argued that his report was immunized as a privileged document. Thus, the APA was barred from censuring Budwin. The appeals court, reversed the trial court, and ruled that quasi-judicial immunities do not bar the APA from censuring its members.

The next section addresses **due process** considerations when courts address licensing issues. This section describes the standard of proof and double jeopardy. These due process safeguards serve as brakes to the police power of the state.

☐ Due Process Considerations

"Due process" means the procedure by which a defendant is tried and sentenced. In a criminal setting (as any crime novel reader or watcher of police television shows knows by heart) part of the due process are *Miranda* warnings. Simply put, the Miranda warnings provide two due process protections: 1) the right against self-incrimination (anything you say can be used against you), and 2) you have a right to an attorney. These due process rights, in a sense, do not bear directly on whether the person committed the crime of which he or she is accused. However, they do bear directly upon the *admissibility of evidence* tending to prove a defendant's guilt. For example, if a criminal defendant expresses a desire for an attorney during questioning and is thwarted by police from doing so, anything he or she says during that questioning may be excluded at trial. Not only that, but any fruits of that "confession" (evidence gathered because of that confession) may be excluded as well.

One of the due process considerations is the standard of proof necessary to convict. The "standard of proof" means the degree of certainty that a defendant has done what he or she is alleged to have done. In licensing cases, the standard of proof is set by each state. It could be either "preponderance of the evidence" or "clear and convincing" evidence. The first standard is the lower of the two. While these two standards cannot be quantified with precision, it can be said that "preponderance" means at least 51% sure of liability. The "clear and convincing" standard would be higher. Often, it is the higher standard that must be proven (*Turner v. Department of Professional Regulation, State of Florida*, 1992).

Another constitutional "due process" safeguard is the protection against double jeopardy. The protection against double jeopardy means that a defendant cannot be tried twice for the same crime or offense. This protection does not mean, however, that a defendant cannot be punished both by the criminal law and a licensing agency. For example where a physician was convicted for Medicare fraud, he may also have his medical license revoked or suspended (*Borrego v. Agency for Health Care Administration*, 1996). The Florida appeals court held that while a criminal sanction is punitive in nature, a licensing decision is remedial in nature. Thus, the federal criminal law could punish him and the Agency could also fine him $5000, suspend his license, and place him on three years probation.

Yet another due process issue in disciplinary proceedings necessary to claim a formal hearing. In *Iazzo v. Department of Professional Regulation*, (1994), a psychologist was accused of having "dual relations" (a business relationship) with a client and was brought before regulators. The psychologist requested a formal hearing and disputed factual allegations but did not complete an "election of rights" and other forms and so the Department wanted to deny him a hearing on the allegations. The appeals court ruled that the psychologist's outcome might be substantially effected by the hearing and that the hearing should take place. This court admirably chose substance over form in assuring the psychologist's procedural the due process were vindicated. However, the learning from this case in no way implies a nonchalant attitude about filling out forms and completing requested notices form the licensing board. Those matters should be attended to as if your license and career depended upon it.

The section above is designed only to offer a hint at some of the procedural requirements involved in disciplinary hearings. The section is not exhaustive, but illustrative of the kinds of issues due process raises.

In earlier chapters, this book described 1st amendment (religious) exemptions to child abuse and other criminal acts. The following section describes statutory exemptions to licensing requirements. It addresses the little litigated area of religious rituals and the practice of medicine. This area is of considerable importance to counselors who may see their practice as more religious than spiritual. This section outlines the legal position of conducting a religious activity that might also be construed as the practice of medicine. We use the illustration of circumcision, performed by a rabbi, to describe the applicable law.

This chapter previously addressed the issue of statutory exemptions for revoking licenses for using spiritual or complementary interventions. We now describe a related species of statutes—those that statutorily exempt people for using such interventions. Keep in mind that many these two kinds of statutes embody constitutional (usually First Amendment) protections for religious counseling. Creating statutory provisions makes it easier for counselors to know if and under what circumstances they may practice such interventions. Such statues can be a great help in determining counselor's legal status.

☐ Statutory Exemptions to Conduct "Spiritual" or "Alternative" Therapies

New Mexico (§61-9A-6) offers such statutory language:

   A. Nothing in the Counseling and Therapy Practice Act shall be construed to prevent:
      (2) An alternative, metaphysical or holistic practitioner from engaging in nonclinical activities consistent with the standards and codes of that practice.
   B. B. Specifically exempted from the Counseling and Therapy Practice Act are . . .
      (3) duly ordained, commissioned or licensed ministers of a church or lay pastoral-care assistants providing pastoral services on behalf of a church
      (5) practitioners of the Native American healing arts.

This statute emphasizes three points. First, the exemption is for "nonclinical" activities. Second, is the emphasis upon the standards of practice and the codes of ethics. These documents, thus, are a necessity in asserting this exemption. Third, the exemption includes Native American "practitioners." While this provision does not specify whether or not the "practitioners" need to be Native American themselves or simply practicing those interventions deemed as "Native American" in nature, such an exemption opens up many areas of spiritual or alternative interventions such as herbology, prayer, "sweat lodge" practice and dancing. Case law also suggests limited exemptions for certain spiritual practices, as the next section will demonstrate.

☐ Case Law Exemptions for Religious Rituals, the Practice of Medicine, and Religious Protection

Under what circumstances may a counselor argue a claim for religious protection for interventions they conduct? For example, when is a procedure a medical procedure and when is it a religious or spiritual procedure? This difference, as we will see in the next case, is vital to the outcome. We have addressed some issues where people have argued that their behavior (including drug use) was protected under the First Amendment. We now expand our discussion to include such cases where people are sued civilly.

In one such case, the parents of a circumcised child sued the medical center where the procedure was performed. They alleged the surgery was negligently performed. The cause of action was negligence. The trial court held that standard rules of negligence applied and that the medical center's request for summary judgment was precluded (*Zakhartchenko v. Weinberger*, 1993).

This court ruled that, even though circumcision is clearly a surgical procedure, it is a religious act when performed by a rabbi. The court held that religious ritual, "anciently practiced and reasonably conducted" is not subject to government restrictions so long as it is consistent with the public health and safety" (p. 206). The court cited the New York State Constitution, which may offer more religious protection than the federal Constitution, but it may not offer less.

The *Zakhartchenko* court has direct relevance for counselors conducting spiritual or alternative interventions. Counselors might want to claim that their interventions are religious in nature and, as such, fall under the First Amendment exemptions from licensure. This case illustrates three important elements courts may consider in protecting a religious ritual, conducted in a secular setting, from secular rules of negligence.

First, the intervention was conducted by a religious official. In this case it was conducted by a rabbi. Counsels need to take this condition seriously. While it may not be dispositive, this element is significant to a court in rendering its verdict. Thus, counselors acting in a religious capacity would be in a better position to argue that their interventions would be protected by the First Amendment. Those counselors acting in a spiritual capacity might enjoy less protection.

Second, the intervention was ancient. Circumcision, noted even by the court and included in its written opinion, is a religious ritual of great antiquity and significance to the Jewish people. To the extent that counselors can research and document the antiquity and authenticity of the religious and spiritual, rituals and intentions in which they partake, they can more strongly assert their case.

Third, the intervention must be reasonably conducted. While the court did not offer specific guidance on what is meant by "reasonably conducted," we can make reasonable hypotheses. The intervention must be conducted under circumstances consistent with its religious purpose. For example, the circumcision should be performed when it is religiously appropriate, conducted in a manner consistent with the religious tradition, and for the purposes indicated by religious tradition.

In any event, the court ruled that the rabbi would still be held accountable for negligence. Thus, even if the rabbi could not be convicted of the illegal practice of medicine, he still had to perform the circumcision competently—that is, consistent with other rabbis' conduct under similar circumstances.

☐ Insurance Issues for Counselors

Insurance issues should weigh heavily upon the mind of counselors who use spiritual or complementary interventions. Two concerns should be addressed here. First, what are legal implications of insurance reimbursement for counselors and what are legal responses when insurance is denied for non-reimbursement for spiritual and alternative interventions. Issues raised in the first issue can be more directly answered than the second.

Legal Issues Arising from Insurance Claims

A major legal issue confronting all counselors is the reimbursement from insurance claims. This section cannot hope to exhaust all the issues that can arise let alone settle them for all jurisdictions. But it can raise relevant insurance issues pertinent to spiritual or complementary interventions. As ever, a case study serves as a model from which to learn and to ask pertinent questions. The following is a fairly complicated case and, for ease of reading, some additional details for the indictments have been omitted.

Case Study: Insurance Claims for Tarot Readings and Exploring Psychic Phenomena

In the spring of 1992, a Blue Cross (hereinafter "BC") investigating a West Virginia counseling center investigator for suspicious billing practices, dispatched an investigator to the counseling center posing as a potential client. After two sessions, the counseling center issued to BC an insurance claim under the name of the defendant. (On appeal, they appear as the plaintiff.) The insurance claim listed the diagnosis as "general anxiety order" and listed two CPT (Physician's Current Procedural Terminology) code numbers for "diagnostic interview" and "individual medical psychotherapy by a physician." The impostor-investigator was never treated by a physician. The signatory on the claim form was neither a physician nor psychologist, but a licensed social worker and counselor. One submitted claim was for a session that never took place.

In the summer of 1992, the impostor-investigator returned with a female investigator and they posed as a couple. They represented that they had a "conflict" over when to have children. The defendant informed them that they had no actual "psychological problems," but suggested that they explore "psychic phenomena and Tarot card readings" (*U.S. v. Hartz*, 1995). On three subsequent sessions, there was little if any discussion of emotional problems, but the social worker discussed the presence of angels, identified personal angels, identified their personal, spiritual animals, selected Tarot cards so that the counselor could make predictions, suggested the "couple" make wishes from the Bible, and stated that she preferred to conduct this kind of therapy and that the insurance company neither knew nor cared. The counselor submitted bills for these sessions under the code for "individual medical psychotherapy by a physician."

After some of the counseling center's employees were **subpoenaed** and after the named defendant was asked for additional records, she created progress notes to correspond to the dates she billed to BC. What, if any, legal consequences should or did follow from these actions or inactions.

After reading chapters two and three of this work, several legal consequences might come to mind. The first might be mail fraud. The director was convicted on several counts of mail fraud, which she appealed. In denying her appeal, the U.S. Court of Appeals for the Fourth Circuit noted that the government needed to show (a) an existence of a scheme to defraud, and (b) use of the mail to execute that scheme. The second test was not disputed, but she claimed there was insufficient evidence of a "scheme" to defraud.

The government's evidence of a "scheme" hung on three possibilities. The first was that the defendant intentionally used false CPT codes in order to defraud BC. The second was that the defendant knowingly misdiagnosed clients in order to obtain payment that would otherwise be denied. Third, that the defendant knowingly billed BC for sessions that did not occur. The court reviewed the government's first assertion found it was sufficient to sustain the conviction so did not review the two remaining. Appellate courts are efficient in that respect.

In finding the requisite evidence for "scheme," the court considered that the defendant signed the bills under question. The court also found that no physician treated the "clients." It also found that the interventions were not "medical psychotherapy" but were "essentially explorations into the realm of psychic phenomena."

It should also be noted that the court recognized that circumstantial evidence can be used by juries to infer an intent to fraud. The court allowed that the defendant's alleged practice of billing BC for Tarot card readings could be seen by a jury as a specific intent to defraud.

The defendant was also convicted of obstruction of justice related to her backdated progress notes. In affirming her conviction on this charge as well, the appellate court noted that a jury could reasonably conclude that the defendant intended to impede justice simply by creating the post-dated reports themselves. Additionally, the court found that, circumstantially, the jury could infer a *mens rea* from important omission from the reports, namely the spiritual and biblical counseling.

This case offers several considerations for the counselor using spiritual and/or complementary interventions. First, obviously, is to avoid fraud. This admonition can easily get lost in the crush of time, paperwork, and philosophy, ideology, or ignorance of the law. Time and paperwork concerns are beyond the scope of this work. Suffice to say two things: 1) accurate and timely reports are the responsibility of the one signing the billing sheets; it is a shame to find oneself under investigation by insurance companies or licensing boards or law enforcement for want of a good secretary or secretarial habits, and 2) fraud requires intent, and good-faith mistakes are not intent. However, too many "little" mistakes, over too long a period may give rise to investigations or even allow a jury to reasonably conclude bad faith. With this in mind, a good secretary can avoid the impression of bad faith.

Now, let us address philosophy, ideology, or ignorance of basic principles of law. Some counselors may feel so strongly that spiritual or complementary means of interventions are beneficial for clients that they may be tempted to "fudge" treatment notes or data on billing sheets. This is a hazardous practice if the counselor knows or should have known that the interventions should not be reimbursed. When the counselor accepts the check from the insurance provider, the counselor agrees to play by their rules. This is a contract—enforceable by both the insurance company and state and/or federal law. Because she *mailed in* the billing sheets, her crime went federal. Even if she did not use the mails, she may have been charged with simple fraud, not mail fraud.

As to the obstruction of justice charge, the defendant seemed to compound her negative legal position by post-dating progress notes—and making errors in them that could seem evidence that she was covering something up. This seeming cover up was interpreted by her jury, and sustained by the appeals court, as evidence of a *mens rea*. In 20–20 hindsight, it seems that she may have been better off by just admitting that she did not keep progress notes.

Counselors often ask the author whether it is legally advisable to keep written records or "progress notes," or whether such notes are a legal liability. Such written evidence cuts both ways. Such notes could be used to help to exonerate a counselor or to convict them. A general consideration might be: Why would a counselor want not to commit to writing something that he or she has done in a session? If a counselor had to prove that something did or did not happen in a session, contemporaneously written documents can be important evidence for the counselor.

The above case offers some insights. The grand jury wanted session notes to discover what was done during the sessions. If the counselor had even sketchy, contemporaneously written notes as to main issues of the session and interventions employed, the jury might have had a more tender attitude toward the defendant. Something is better than nothing. And even nothing is better than documents created whose timing could lead one to have suspicions of an appearance of impropriety.

Of course, a necessary and legitimate issue arising from the above case is whether, or under what circumstances, insurance companies will reimburse for spiritual and complementary interventions. There is no hard and fast rule.

☐ The Legal Environment of Spiritual and Complementary Reimbursement

There are two strains of policy that seem to be emerging in issues related to reimbursements by third-party payers relative to counselors using spiritual or complementary interventions. The first is that as spiritual and complementary interventions get more "mainstream," it seems likely they will be more reimbursable. The second is that the trend for efficiency and economy or value in health care is not likely to change any time soon. As of this writing, Congress and the courts have not decided to allow patients to sue their HMOs, but some moves are afoot to allow more latitude for health related costs. Some liberalization for coverage and reimbursement is likely to take hold. It is unlikely, however, that we will return to the days when any and all hospital and mental health expenses will be reimbursed without controls, oversight, and economies. Here again, the law surrounding these issues is fluid.

Fluid, yes, but totally obscure? No. We have relied somewhat on the analogies of the medical field to discern trends in this book. We do so again to gauge the willingness of insurers to reimburse complementary medicine and mental health care.

In 1997, Washington State passed sweeping legislation that required insurers to provide insurance coverage for every type of treatment that the state licenses. Called the Alternative Provider Statute (hereinafter Act), it mandated coverage for all licensed providers including chiropractors, acupuncturists, and naturopaths. Insurance companies claimed that the Act would raise costs and pursue inappropriate treatments as well as violating federal laws prohibiting states from regulating employer-funded health plans (Kingrey, 1999).

Insurers took the plan to court and lost. The federal district court ruled for the insurers (**Washington Physicians Serv. Ass'n. v. Gregiore**, 1997), but the 9th Circuit Court of Appeals overruled (**Washington Physicians Serv. Ass'n. v. Gregiore**, 1999). The insurers appealed to the U.S. Supreme Court, but that court declined to hear the case (Kingrey, 1999). So the legal challenge is over. Questions, of course, remain. What is the process for reimbursement for such providers? Will the voters or the state legislature amend the statute over time? Does such covers, as a practical matter, cover counselors who offer spiritual or complementary interventions? This last question, of course, is the one that most concerns us here. Washington State, over time, will have to furnish such answers.

In the meantime, what is the answer for counselors in whatever state they practice? This question is best answered by a series of questions.

1. Does the insurance company limit the kind of interventions? If there is no prohibition, then as they say, "what is not prohibited, is permitted."
2. If the reimbursor does limit such reimbursements, then closely attend to those limitations. "Closely attend" means to take them seriously. If there is a question as to what the stated limitations are, ask.
3. It may help to describe the interventions in some detail. Without guile or obfuscation, use language that is meaningful to the company so that they will know about what you are talking about.
4. If you ask the question, you must be ready for the answer. If the answer is no, abide by the decision. Maybe you can appeal it to the next supervisor. But never resort to fraud. The worst that can happen if you are not reimbursed is that you ask the client to pay out-of-pocket. Maybe the counselor will have to "eat" the costs of some sessions. That result is not as dire as an investigation by the insurance company for fraud with attendant civil and criminal charges.

☐ Insurance Law for Counselors

All counselors will have some type of insurance. This section addresses the counselor's personal, professional insurance coverage, and reminds the counselor about some of the pitfalls in insurance coverage, especially for those who use spiritual and complementary interventions. The section also provides information on the issue of exclusions in insurance policies.

Bullis (1993) outlines issues for professional counselors and insurance coverage including asking if lawyers' costs or the costs of defending yourself is covered, asking if the policy covers both negligent and intentional torts, and considering *personal* insurance even if your employer has coverage in the event that you and your employer's legal interests diverge.

Here we emphasize retroactivity, exclusions, and legal fees for licensing board hearings as these have direct applicability to counselors using spiritual or complementary interventions.

If possible, begin your insurance coverage from the instant you began to practice. This is retroactive coverage and it is extremely important. It is important that your policy cover not only current acts, but past acts as well. If you can get it, its well worth it. As we have seen, the statute of limitations for torts can run for years. So a client you saw over a year ago or more can sue you. *If you were not covered when you saw the client, you may well not be covered when he or she sues you.* Say, for example, you were using spiritual or complementary interventions in recent years ago when such use was newer and less well-known. As we noted, the standards are fluid and, as it happens, sometimes such standards are determined by courts, not by counselors. You need to be covered for past as well as future acts.

Even if you have a limited practice, insurance is essential. It might be helpful, sometimes, to see "clients" as "potential plaintiffs." "It's a sobering, but effective exercise. It only takes one client to ruin your career.

Covering is also about "exclusions" to coverage. Just because you get insurance, it does not mean that all your acts as a counselor are covered. Your policy covers what it says it covers—or, as we will see, the policy covers what the courts say it covers.

☐ Legal Environment for Denial of Coverage

In *Newyear v. Church Insurance Co.* (1998), the plaintiff, an Episcopalian priest, asked the federal courts sitting in Missouri to decide if his insurance company's (the defendant's) coverage included defense and indemnity coverage for claims against him by two women. They accused Newyear of sexual misconduct in the causes of action for intentional infliction of emotional distress and breach of fiduciary duty. The district court granted summary judgment in favor of the defendant insurance company. Newyear appealed to the 8th Circuit.

The justiciable issue was: Did the insurance have to cover claims for sexual misconduct? That court examined the specific language of the policy to make its determination. One particularly operative condition of the policy was the stipulation that coverage included "acts, errors, or omissions of ordained Episcopalian clergy acting within the scope of their duties of the Named Insured and arising out of the pastoral counseling activities of these individuals." The policy did not include a definition of "scope of employment" so the federal court looked to Missouri law for precedent.

Missouri law, said the circuit court, interprets "scope of employment" as whether or not it furthered the business interest of the employer." The court found that allegedly committing sexual misconduct did not further the Church's business interests and found for the insurance company.

Several suggestions flow from the *Newyear* case that apply to counselors using spiritual or complementary interventions. First, inquire as to the *kinds* of interventions that might be excluded under the policy. In all these matters, *scrutinize* the terms and conditions of the policy. It is insufficient to stick the policy in a drawer somewhere and assume you know its contents. It is also insufficient to simply assume that the policy will cover any and all interventions. If you still have a question, ask representatives from the insurance company and get the answer in writing. If you discover that your interventions are not covered, ask that they, in fact, be covered. Failing that, either don't practice using the specified interventions or pay to get them covered somehow.

Second, scrutinize the policy for any limitations on *place* of appointment or service. You need to know if the policy excludes counseling activities outside of the office or agency environment. Counselors using spiritual or complementary interventions may see clients in a variety of settings. These need to be covered. The same suggestions for retroactive coverage above apply.

Third, as the *Newyear* case suggests "scope of employment" as a limiting factor in coverage. What about liability arising out of conducting seminars, workshops, etc.? You may want to get, in writing, what the policy means by "scope of employment" from the insurer. It is worth the trouble for counselors to do so, as many seminars and workshops are of an "experiential" nature.

If, for example, a counselor conducts a seminar on "Finding your personal aura," that close, personal, or experiential interaction might evoke a far more powerful emotional response than, say, a lecture on "Jungian archetypes in the poetry of the beat poets. "Not that the lecture itself would be uninteresting, even fascinating. Having an experience of prayer, meditation, or introspection can lead to intense feelings or intense memories. Is then the seminar leader responsible for stopping the seminar to address the concerns of one participant? Often, experiential learning is more likely to produce lawsuits than lectures. The more hands-on the approaches, the more deeply affected the impact and, thus, harmed the client is likely to be. The point is that counselors who address spiritual issues are likely to evoke strong emotional responses in clients, compelling legal action for any number of reasons. Having coverage insurance for such eventualities is no legal luxury.

Many professional insurance providers also offer coverage for legal fees for hearings in front of licensing boards. This coverage is especially important for those who use emerging interventions or interventions not generally practiced. A complaint or investigation by a licensing board is no time to find out that you have to personally bear the cost of an attorney to help you prepare for the hearing. As we have seen in *Tuma* and other such cases, a "trial" at a disciplinary hearing may be the preferred way for a client or the state to object to your practice. There are few reasons why a lawyer should not help guide or represent you at such a hearing. There are many reasons why they should.

Even if you will plead "not guilty" because you did not do the alleged infraction, due process considerations might still be important. Only an attorney can adequately advise you in raising them.

For additional payments, most insurers should be able to provide such coverage. Some insurers may even add on the coverage *gratis* to its customers. Finally, as in all things about insurance, check the coverage amounts. As a rule, given the liability awards these days, coverage per occurrence should be figured in the millions and the coverage for lawyers to defend you at a licensing hearing should be figured in the thousands.

Conclusion

Licensure, from both government and private organizations, is designed to maintain levels of quality and integrity of professional conduct and, above all, to protect the public. Both public and private organizations can revoke, or otherwise limit, licensure. Such organizations conduct hearings to discover facts and law to arrive at such licensure decisions. These licensing decisions have their own rules and procedures. But, although not conducted in a court room, they must not offend general, constitutional standards—of equal protection and due process, for example.

Licensing agencies, of course, may establish requirements for licensure and may also allow for exemptions. This chapter notes those exemptions and exceptions where they might apply to spiritual and complementary counselors.

That insurance coverage is mandatory, obviously, goes without saying. This chapter focused upon the dire necessity for counselors to understand the legal underpinnings of an insurance contract, including major reasons for denial of coverage.

Legal and Ethical Audits and Exercises

1. Conduct an insurance audit with the use of spiritual and complementary interventions in view. This means that your insurance agent or broker should know the style of practice and your venue of practice. They need to know you use emerging interventions (spiritual or complementary) and the counselor should ascertain if

these interventions present any coverage problems. Also, if the counselor conducts workshops, seminars and the like, they should ascertain if these are covered as well.

2. Begin personally collecting evidence, empirical evidence if you can get it, of the validity and use of such interventions. While states generally are not licensing spiritual or alternative counseling practices, practitioners should be gathering political and legislative expertise in order to at least show the value and validity of such interventions.

3. Consider the use of public relations skills to familiarizing two separate parties to the use and value of spiritual and complementary interventions: 1) colleagues (those who may judge you professionally and who may testify for or against you as expert witnesses) and 2) the general public (potential plaintiffs and/or clients).

   Some suggestions follow: Read and subscribe to professional journals that address spiritual and complementary interventions, attend continuing education events, organize such events addressing spiritual and complementary, and writing "letters to the editor" of professional journals and to state newsletters for professional organizations.

4. Count on your interventions becoming public. Even though your sessions are private, since the client can say anything to anyone, be prepared to have your interventions discussed by others—who may approach your licensing board. So, practice imaging your counseling sessions as public events with licensing board members (of a plaintiff's lawyer) sitting in with you.

5. Continually monitor and improve your formal training in the interventions you conduct. What seminars and what continuing education events have you attended in the past year that specifically address the improvement of your interventions? Encourage your state professional organization to sponsor such training events. Go ahead, be a squeaky wheel!

CHAPTER

Ethical Implications and Ethical Models for the New Millennium

☐ Objectives

1. To introduce the role of ethics applied to counseling.
2. To provide models in order to unravel the ethical dynamics (e.g., the "Ethical Ecology" and the "**Duty Determination**" models).
3. To describe some legal/ethical duties that may attach particularly to counselors using spiritual or complementary therapies.
4. To propose a procedure for an ethical relaxation/visualization program.
5. To propose a procedure for using spiritual or complementary "media therapies."

This chapter outlines ethical issues connected with counseling conducted utilizing spiritual or complementary principles or interventions. First, this chapter emphasizes that spiritual and religious interventions, while being treated differently from other counseling interventions by the law, should be treated differently in the area of ethics as well. Second, this chapter emphasizes the importance of religious and spiritual cosmologies, anthropologies, and consciousness, and how such concepts can influence, and even determine, an ethical decision.

Third, this chapter discusses and describes two operational models to analyze, to understand, and to determine an ethical issue. These two models are simple to use, but not at all simplistic. The "Ethical Ecology" model and the "Duty Determination" model are practical, useable, and appropriate approaches to unravelling the many strands and components of an ethical issue. These are techniques to use in making and managing ethical decisions.

☐ Case Study: Satanism, Suicide, and Some Ethical Considerations for School Counselors

A Maryland high school student became involved with Satanism "causing her to have an 'obsessive interest in death and self-destruction'" (***Eisel v. Board of Education***, 1991,

p. 449). The female student told some friends that she wanted to kill herself. These friends told their school counselor who related the information to the student's counselor. The student and one of the friends later shot and killed themselves. The father of the suicide victim sued two counselors at the adolescent's school in a Maryland state court. That court granted summary judgment in favor of the defendants. The father appealed the case.

If you were the appellate judges, how would you have ruled? This case offers an important legal/ethics illustration of duty. It brings together a constellation of different issues which we have already addressed and which we will further address in this chapter. Some of these questions are summarized below:

1. What are the legal/ethical "duties" (responsibilities) of the school counselors?
2. What, specifically, are the duties of the school counselors to the students? To the school officials (their employers)? To the parents of the students? To the community?
3. What, then, might be some "causes of action" if someone would sue in a case arising from the facts of the *Eisel* case? How might you have handled the situation differently if you were the 1) school counselors, 2) principal, or 3) the other students who were aware of the potential suicides?
4. Against whom should or would parties sue in this case?
5. What are some duties by society or the legal system owed to the school counselors?
6. What, then, might be some of the counselors' defenses?

The *Eisel* case will be described in greater depth later in this chapter. The above questions are designed to initiate critical thinking on the ethical issues arising from real-life situations. The rest of this chapter provides ethical underpinnings and critical-thinking skills in order to help readers understand and to address such issues.

The following section asserts that using spiritual or alternative interventions requires new considerations—called a cosmology—in ethical perspectives. Then, we examine a specific method, using cosmologies, in order to address ethical issues.

This chapter does not offer answers. It offers insights. Specific answers only fit specific questions. The varied, relatively new, and professionally unfolding nature of spiritual and alternative interventions precludes hard, fast answers. The field is too new for "grand, unified ethical theories," at least not yet. It is better to establish a procedure to exploring specific solutions, not pronounce the solutions. Such pronouncements seem facile and premature, at least at this point.

☐ A Shift in Practice Interventions: Ethical Implications

Shifting to spiritual or complementary interventions requires shifting consciousness, cosmology, and ethical underpinnings. Violence is done against spirituality when one considers its principles to be just another intervention. The U.S. Constitution offers special protection to religious groups and behaviors precisely in order to honor the special place that citizens hold religious and spiritual concerns. This same constitutional protection does not apply to Freudian theory, Adlerian theory, eclectic theory, or other treatment modalities. This privilege is afforded to spiritual and religious practice because their very nature has a "sacred," "religious," or "spiritual" quality differentiating them from other therapies.

Three assumptions underline the ethical nature of spiritual and alternative interventions. These assumptions operate whether or not they are articulated in ethical concepts, policies, or procedures. They are that ethical acts and considerations: (a) accrue to the benefit of the client, not the counselor, (b) when clients undertake spiritual or complementary therapies, the counselor enters into the belief systems of the client, and (c) the outcome is more connected with the nature of the counselor than with the nature of his or her interventions. Ethics seeks, first and foremost, to protect the more vulnerable, less adept person. This is why the professional is always the one held responsible for what happens in sessions. If clients beg and plead for counselors to employ a certain intervention (against the counselor's professional judgment), to have sex with them, or to do anything jeopardizing the client's material health or well-being, it is the sole responsibility of the counselor to act above reproach. Both the law and ethics hold counselor to this standard. Moreover, that standard is unlikely to shift anytime soon.

Second, the counselor, in conducting spiritual or alternative interventions, must more actively and more seriously engage in the client's own cosmology or world view. This is a different approach than other intervention roles. For example, it is usually not necessary for a long discussion on how the client feels about Freud, Adler, or Jung for a counselor to begin interventions along these approaches. However, for a counselor to use prayer, scripture, some forms of meditation, and other alternative means, they must have a clear understanding of how the client views the ideas behind these interventions. To reiterate what must now be clear, the client's own spirituality is an active, perhaps dispositive, ingredient in this process.

Third, the nature of the relationship and spirituality of both the client and the counselor is at the heart of spiritual or alternative interventions. Such interventions are not methods imposed from outside, but arise from the inner life, experience, and insight of both parties. Thus, spiritual and alternative interventions, in and of themselves, don't heal. What heals is the inner strength, power, and energy released in and through such interventions. To put it simply, "love heals, techniques do not." This means that the motivations, intentions, ideologies, and attitudes of the counselor are relevant to the healing process. As we have mentioned, the client's attitude and ideology are not the exclusive ingredients for therapeutic progress—the counselor's own attitudes and ideologies are also significant. This insight is embodied in the Scientific versus Spiritual Model noted below.

Whether a client or counselor calls this process forgiveness, grace, agape, pneuma, compassion, or any of a thousand other different words, the experience is essentially the same. This insight is suggested by empirical evidence.

☐ Empirical Data on the Ethics of Spiritual or Complementary Interventions

Empirical research on the ethics of using spiritual or alternative interventions has been slim. Bullis (1996) offered two sets of data (now reported in Appendix C) from a random sample of Virginia clinical social workers. Among the 25 spiritual or religious interventions listed, respondents stated they were most *professionally* ethically comfortable with exploring the client's spiritual background (99.1%), recommending participation in spiritual groups (e.g., meditation groups, 12-step programs, men's and women's groups—95.4%), exploring a client's religious background (94.7%), exploring spiritual elements in dreams (93.6%), and helping a client develop ritual as a clinical intervention (e.g., house blessings, visiting graves of relatives—90.9%).

The survey instrument also measured a clinician's *personal* ethical comfort with both spiritual and religious interventions. Usually, there was a strong relationship between the respondents' professional and personal comfort with those interventions. For example, for these same interventions noted above, in examining their *professional* comfort, clinicians also scored high in *personal* comfort: exploring the client's spiritual background (99.1%), recommending participation in spiritual groups (e.g., meditation groups, 12-step programs, men's and women's groups—95.4%), exploring a client's religious background (94.7%), exploring spiritual elements in dreams (93.6%), and helping a client develop ritual as a clinical intervention (e.g., house blessings, visiting graves of relatives—90.9%).

Another relevant, ethical aspect is that spiritual interventions almost always were more ethically comfortable than were religious interventions. This difference again highlights the absolute necessity of differentiating between "spirituality" and "religion." A counselor needs to ask and to acknowledge those times when a client asks for, or consents to, a spiritual or a religious intervention. Examples of a fairly wide difference in ethical comfort is the use of bibliotherapy ("mediatherapy" is discussed at the end of this chapter).

Two interventions, both addressing mediatherapy, illustrate the difference between spiritual and religious interventions: The use or recommendation of *spiritual* books is professionally ethically comfortable to 88.6% of respondents, while only 55.0% were comfortable using or recommending *religious* books . Similarly, using *spiritual* language or metaphors was professionally ethically comfortable to 88.4%, and so comfortable to only 66.4% when *religious* language is involved.

Empirical data offers another significant insight. Of all the variables (religious or spiritual affiliation, personal ideology, etc.), the factors with the closest correlations to the use of religious and spiritual interventions are (a) how personally and professionally comfortable clinicians are with using spiritual and religious interventions, and (b) the extent to which clinicians view such interventions as a positive factor in therapy. Thus, there is a connection between the counselor's own ethical outlook and cosmology and his or her use of alternative and spiritual interventions.

Many people refer to the backbone of medical ethics, but many have never actually read the opening line of Hippocratic oath in its entirety:

> I swear by Apollo the physician, and Aesculapius, and health, and all-heal, and all the gods and goddesses, that according to my ability and judgment, I will keep this oath and this stipulation . . . " (Adams, n.d.)

This code's reliance upon divine interventions in the medical field is instructive in connection with that profession's early therapeutic model. Clearly, this therapeutic model laid heavy emphasis upon the ideology and even faith of the professional in giving care to patients.

So we end up where we began in the previous section. Spiritual and alternative interventions are not "cures" imposed from outside, but arise from the inner life, experience, and insight of both parties. While the inner life of the client is relevant, the inner life of the counselor is relevant as well. The counselor's attitudes and ideologies are an integral part of the therapeutic process.

We now turn to a discussion of cosmology and an "ethical ecology" consistent with these new models of intervention.

☐ The Ethical Importance of Cosmology: Why a New Model of Ethics Is Required

Conforming spiritual or alternative interventions to ethical principles designed for conventional interventions is anachronistic and unrealistic. Using spiritual or alternative interventions can not just connote a shift in interventions. It connotes a shift in consciousness. As noted earlier, religion and spirituality have never been considered by the law to be just another ideology or another intervention. *Religious* ideology and interventions are constitutionally protected precisely because religious thought and behavior are fundamentally different from secular ideologies—and counseling interventions. An outline describing such ideologies and behaviors has been set forth in the Preface.

We should add anthropology, consciousness, and cosmology to that list. Religious and spiritual ideologies and behaviors have very definite and distinct beliefs about how human beings were made, and about human goals and human destinies. One only has to read the first two chapters of Genesis to read such accounts. The same is true for the first line of the Buddhist scripture, the *Dhammapada* (Radhakrishna, 1950) which I retranslate: "Who we are is conditioned by how we think." This scripture dates back to about the early 5th century B.C.E. Compare that quote with the statement by the 20th century physicist Max Planck, "All matter originates and exists only by virtue of a force which brings the particles of an atom to vibration and holds this most minute solar system of the atom together . . . We must assume behind this force the existence of a conscious and intelligent mind. This mind is the matrix of all matter" (Braden, 2000).

It is a truism that scientific cosmologies, also, have underdone severe transformations since the early 1900s. Studies in quantum physics and astronomical physics and cosmology suggest a world that is much more relational, interactive, and just plain amazing than that reflecting the mechanical, empirical, and deterministic laws of Newtonian physics (Kafatos & Nadeau, 1990). The trouble is, most of us are still slaves to Newtonian thinking.

Each of these cosmologies, wrought in their own way, asserts a cosmology that is "radically relational." A radically relational paradigm is one in which, literally, everyone and everything is connected and influences each other. The result of this relationship is a cosmos permeated with purposefulness and consciousness. Religious and spiritual beliefs also acknowledge that the universe itself was made, is functioning, and will hold the ultimate ends of some conscious purpose. Bullis (1996) describes the relationship of the Norse cosmology, with its personified tree, eagle, and squirrel, to how different such a worldview can be from our Western, scientific worldview. The symbols of Norse cosmology, for example, are not fairy tales. They represent a complex and sophisticated paradigm of different levels of consciousness, interdependent and connected to one another. Norse cosmology recognizes the reality of a universe that is organic and vigorous, but that is constantly changing, reorganizing, dying, and being born again. Norse cosmology, among others, is an enviable counseling cosmology.

☐ Cosmologies in Conflict

The above discussion is useful and informative. Science and research is advanced with timely, useful data. We need not rehearse here the wonders and true marvels of modern science. What we *will* rehearse here, however, are some underlying ethical assumptions.

This section describes paradigms consistent with spiritual or alternative interventions. Paradigms will, in this book, be called "cosmologies." Cosmologies are depictions of how the universe works. Historically, these cosmologies have emphasized the spiritual nature of both the cosmos and of human consciousness. These will be many, varied, and multicultural. This chapter will describe such cosmologies as Native American, ancient Israelite, Scandinavian, and contemporary American.

At first glance, these cosmologies appear to depict physical surroundings only. They appear to show simply the relationships between human beings and heavenly beings, or angels or stars. As we have seen, many also describe the relationships between ourselves and others.

This inquiry is necessary because science itself adheres and creates its own cosmology. A cosmology is a world view. It depicts how the person or culture views how the world works and their own individual and collective part in it. A cosmology includes such concepts as the beginning and end of life, the origin of the universe, how human health and intellect flourishes, and what part of the human being (if any) survives physical death.

Cosmology may also be called a paradigm. Paradigms, or cosmologies, influence how we see ourselves, how we relate to others, how we work and achieve, how we heal or not, and how we connect to the world around us.

Both science and religion influence and are influenced by cosmologies. Without knowing the client's cosmology or paradigm, one cannot know the underpinnings of the client's goals, aspirations and their own understanding of themselves or their world.

This relationship is reflected by the fierce and unfortunate conflict between the medieval church and Galileo. Galileo hypothesized, after looking through his just-invented telescope, that the earth revolved around the sun, not the other way around. The church's position was that the sun, and other celestial bodies, revolved around the earth. Galileo postulated a heliocentric solar system and the Church believed in a geocentric solar system. But that was only the beginning of the cosmological difference.

The real contest was over both epistemology and cosmology. The real question was about how we know that we know something. For the church, the Bible taught that "God created the heavens and the earth." If God created this planet, then God would not place it only as the third stone from the sun in an insignificant solar system, in a peripheral part of the galaxy, in a corner of the universe. The sun, and the rest of the universe, revolves around the earth because that's how God wanted it.

Galileo, conversely, used science to determine what spun around what. Galileo's telescope told him the facts. He calculated and he tested. Where his observations varied from his theories, the theory was discarded. Where his observations, as a matter of fact, varied from church teachings, he got into trouble. But this was the beginning of the scientific method.

The church forbade Galileo to promulgate his findings under threat of excommunication. He recanted. In 1992, however, the Roman Catholic Church formally apologized when it condemned him for supporting Copernicus (Associated Press, 1999c). Moreover, in 1999, the Pope praised Copernicus while visiting his birthplace saying, "The discovery by Copernicus, and its importance for the history of science, remind us of the ever-present tension between reason and faith" (A4).

The forgoing debate, and others like it, center upon conflicting cosmologies and present fundamental distinctions not only upon the *content* of ideas, but upon the fundamental *processes* by which reach they reach that content. That is to say, Copernicus and the Pope not only reached different intellectual conclusions, but reached them by different means for different purposes. This "ever-present tension" spoken of by Pope John Paul II, of course, includes a different "paradigm" or cosmology. Another excellent model is presented in Cohen's 1996 article titled "Holistic Health Care: Including alternative and complementary medicine in insurance and regulatory schemes. The model (below) emphasizes both the cosmologies between spiritual and traditional scientific thinking, as well as the differences between those models in "ideology" and in "interventions."

	Distinctions between the Spiritual and Secular Ideologies	
	Scientific	**Spirituality**
Epistemology	Scientific method Empirical, Analytical	Revelation
Cosmology	"Big Bang"	Divine origin
Anthropology	Physical (Genetic), Emotional	Spirit, Soul
Teleology	Well-being, security Asymptomatic Well-adjusted	Redemption Salvation Judgment

Some general comments naturally arise from this chart. First, it should be noted that this chart dichotomizes the differences between scientific and spiritual thought. The intention is to mark the differences. Many scientists hold religious and spiritual beliefs. Certainly, there are blurs between these admittedly starkly stated elements. However, it must be said that it is doubtful that science and spirituality will merge any time soon. It is equally doubtful that they should merge. Science and spirituality have their separate rooms within the great mansion of knowledge.

Second, "epistemology" means "how do we know that we know something." Said another way, epistemology means how we know the truth. For most in the Western world, we accept something as true or as fact if there is some proof or some evidence. The scientific method requires "testability" as part of its particular standards of evidence. A scientist must test a theory, either through clinical trials or through some other regime. Not only that, but other scientists must be able to achieve the same results when using the same procedures. This tends to verify results and strengthen validity.

Religious truth or "revelation," on the other hand, has its own form of validity. What makes some great religious and spiritual "truth: The Buddhist eight-fold path, the Jewish *shema* ("The Lord is God, the Lord is One) in Deuteronomy 6:4, the Christian Gospel's teaching "Truly, truly, I say to you unless one is born anew, he cannot see the kingdom of God" (John 3:3 NRSV), or the Moslem *dhikr* or "remembrances." These truths, and others like them, are validated by other means altogether. The claim is an ultimate one. The teachings arise or are connected with an ultimate, or even divine, source. Followers attest to the veracity of the teachings. The personal experience of the believers authenticate the teachings. Tradition holds the truth inviolate over time. Conformity to ultimate reality is the standard of evidence for religious truth.

Cosmology, as noted earlier, is a conception of how the universe works. Cosmologies, by their very nature, encompass most, if not all, aspects of the universe, human beings, and life itself. Cosmologies are varied. Some people construct world views with angels and devils, heavens and hells; others employ cosmologies with electrons and protons, "big bang" theories, and black holes. This book does not evaluate these varieties, but acknowledges them.

For example, the National Association of Social Work's Code of Ethics (effective 1 January 1997) denotes a value of "dignity and worth of the person" specifying that the social worker can limit the client's self-determination "when . . . client's actions or potential actions pose a serious, foreseeable, and imminent risk to themselves or others" (NASW Code of Ethics, 1.02). How and under what circumstances a social worker may limit a client's self-determination, the code does not explain. This book will assist in those determinations.

Additionally, under the NASW Code (under Section 1.05) *Cultural Competence and Social Diversity* reads in part: Social workers should obtain education about and seek to understand the nature of social diversity and oppression with respect to . . . religion . . . (part "c"). There is a widespread consensus among mental health practitioners that cultural, and therefore religious and spiritual, issues play important roles in treatments and interventions. The current ethical issues now revolve around how to understand the *individual context* of the client with respect to spiritual and religious issues. The next sections of this chapter describes ways to uncover the individual's spiritual and religious values, principles, and beliefs.

How can social workers, or any other counselor, effect client self-determination without acknowledging their spiritual values or cosmologies. If spiritual values and concomitant cosmologies are important to the client (and they will be if they choose a spiritual or complementary counselors) they must be important to the counselor.

Put another way, a counselor is ethically obligated to accept the client where he or she is unless there is an imminent, demonstrable harm. The counselor is required to at least acknowledge the condition of the client as he or she sees it. It is not up to the client to change the world view of the client. If the client accept alterations, so be it, but it is not for the counselor to remake the client in the counselor's own image.

Anthropology, for the purposes of this book, is an integral part of cosmology. Anthropology is the study of how human beings work, live, love, die, and construct cultural norms. In terms of counseling, anthropology also studies the meaning of health and illness; that is, how they term their condition: "sick," "sin," "dysfunction," "hurt," "symptomatic," etc., and how they get "well": asymptomatic, healed, saved, redeemed, etc. How a counselor describes an illness speaks volumes as to the counselor's anthropology. A counselor could describe a counselee's situation in the psychiatric terms of the DSM-IV, in terms of an imbalance of the "humors," blocked chi, an intrusion of evil spirits, or sin. The counselee could describe their own situations in any of the terms above, or in other terms altogether. Treatment modalities can be likewise described in a variety of ways.

This is not to say that the counselor need accept a counselee's cosmology. Acknowledging, even appreciating, another's cosmology, does not imply accepting or internalizing another's cosmology.

The point is that the counselor has an ethical obligation to acknowledge and to understand the counselee's cosmology—and their own. Without such an understanding the counselee either diminishes an integral part of the counselee—even dismisses the counselee altogether. Also the counselor misses a golden opportunity to develop a rapport with a client from explicitly and professionally uncovering the client's cosmology.

Third, "teleology" means the purpose or ultimate reason for things. In the scientific view, the "end" of human life is death and the end of the cosmos will come in a way that science predicts or postulates. These conclusions are rather self-evident. The ultimate purposes of human life and the divinely created cosmos is another thing altogether. In various religious traditions, the purpose is redemptive, cyclical, regenerative, or transformative. In most instances, the end of the body does not mean the end of the person. Again, the lack of empirical evidence for a soul or spirit or reincarnation is not disputed, it is irrelevant.

In a word, different ideologies yield different interpretations. Different interpretations yield different interventions.

The fourth point addresses ethical implications of the differences between these two cosmologies. Different cosmologies give rise to different ethical regimes. The bases for ethical decisions is often rooted in cosmologies. An ethical regime based upon a scientific cosmology can be different from an ethical regime based upon a religious cosmology.

What is right or true can be vastly different for those who believe truth comes from revelation, from political reality, or from scientific inquiry. Extreme examples are world wide. Jim Jones and the People's Temple group in Guyana, South America. For many, if not all, it seems incredible that so many people would follow the religious leader—even to the extent of leaving their homes in the United States and setting up a camp in the wilderness—let alone commit mass suicide.

Such an "ethic," if you want to call it that, seems unbelievable. To his believers, however, the ethic of belief and duty obey was chillingly real and true. Such beliefs are evidence of the power of cosmology to order and shape behavior. While we address "cults" or "religious groups" and religious affiliation and their relationships to counseling in the next, a significant contribution to understanding both the leaders and follows is this rendered by understanding their cosmologies.

Distinctions between spiritual and secular or scientific ideologies yield differences between spiritual and secular or scientific interventions. The chart below suggests these:

Distinctions between the Spiritual and Secular Interventions		
	Scientific	**Spiritual**
Assessment	Spirituality, among others	Spirituality at core
Intervention Outlook	Professional "cures"	Relationship intervenes
Goals of Interventions	Relieve symptoms	Reconcile with sacred
Goal of Life	Full, rich life/ American dream	Dharma, karma, surrender to divine, find "true self"
Ethics	Prevent harm to others and self	Prevent harm to body of divine, others, and self

Some points need explaining in this section of the model. First, in assessing client(s), spirituality, even for the empiricist, can be a component of the assessment. They may inquire into religious or spiritual factors among others. Such factors will be given more or less equal weight. The spiritual or alternative-oriented will place spiritual or alternative models at the center of the inquiry and allow other factors to flow from that core. This is a subtle difference, but an important one.

The intervention outlook demonstrates this difference most fully. How a counselor views their use of spiritual or alternative interventions is a clue to how they view other dimensions of practice. Simply employing meditation, prayer, or shamanic or yogic exercises does not, in itself, indicate the counselor is employing a spiritual cosmology.

Counselors are free to employ spiritual or alternative interventions without buying into the ideologies from which they arose. Whether this behavioral dichotomy is a good idea is an ethical decision with which each counselor needs to wrestle.

Counselors who uses meditation may not see mediation as a spiritual or alternative intervention at all. They may simply be convinced by the data that meditation, or even past-life regression for that matter, has been scientifically proved to their satisfaction and apply the methodology in their repertoire. In this sense, this perspective is still a scientific model—but only using a wider set of interventions. This use is a far cry from the counselor who permeates his or her practice with a spiritual orientation.

An ethical question here is misrepresentation. A client who advertises the use of spiritual or alternative interventions may imply, even inadvertently, that he or she also takes seriously his or her client's spiritual life and employs a spiritual outlook in assessments and in ethics.

The goals of life and goals of interventions differences follow. If a counselor advertises that he or she uses spiritual or alternative interventions, a client may erroneously believe that the counselor is an adherent of such a faith, school, sect, or belief system. The counselor may distinguish these interventions from his or her beliefs about them. To confuse matters even more, a spiritually oriented counselor may select rather conventional interventions. After all, as we have seen, a spiritual technique does not a spiritual or alternative counselor make.

Finally, the scientific methodology of treatment has been that the professional objectively "cures" the patient. The doctor prescribes a pill to "cure" the patient from a given symptom. The attitude or ideology or mental attributes of the "cure-giver" is irrelevant. In fact, to promote "objectivity," the professional is supposed to stand at some distance emotionally, physically, and spiritually from the patient. In some ways this model has many benefits.

However, in the spiritual model, interventions are not a "pill" or a technique that effects the treatment—it is the relationship between the client and the counselor that is at the crux of the healing process. Objectivity is still important, but it is not as important under the spiritual model. After all "objectivity," the notion that we can really separate ourselves from the effects of those around us and, conversely, that our thoughts and beliefs have no impact upon others is now under serious scientific suspicion and is practically disregarded by most religious and spiritual traditions. Even science now accepts some notion of knowledge based upon a relationship, not just an "objective" observer. Spiritual traditions have always acknowledged that the living and the dead are in some ways present to each other (as with All Soul's Day, the communion of saints) and even that the dead can intercede on behalf of the living (veneration and praying to the saints). After all, what do the cosmological connections of astrology, feng shui, Western magic, Christian magical texts of Egypt, Jewish kabbalah, and Jungian concepts of synchronicity have in common but the interrelationship between the inner human dynamics and the outer organicity of the universe?

Spiritual and alternative therapy models almost always observe the close connection between two people in close contact. This spiritual connection is sometimes referred to as a guru, disciple, chela, master, or teacher. Sometimes it is referred to as a connection between each other's auras, or even a connection in a past life. In whatever manner it is expressed, the connection must be different than the objective, dispassionate, and "surgical" perspective of the "scientific" professional.

We address aspects of counselor self-disclosure in the next section. Now we address how to uncover the client's cosmology.

One primary way in which the counselor can uncover the client's cosmology is to compare and contrast their views of the scientific and spiritual cosmology noted above. Pertinent questions can be:

1. How much do they agree or disagree with the spiritual or scientific world views?
2. How much do they accept from each of the world views?
3. How do the opinions of the client and counselor coincide? Are there significant differences between the scientific and spiritual inventions? How flexible or strict are the client and counselor on their respective positions?
4. How much do the differences matter to each? Are there ways to negotiate around the differences. Can they "agree to disagree?" If not, is referral, renegotiation or termination a remedy?

Discussion of the world views of the counselor and the client is an absolute necessity in understanding the client's situation. This discussion has the ulterior benefit of helping to create rapport. The issue of how much the counselor should disclose of their spiritual ideas is addressed in the following section.

☐ The Counselor's Own Disclosures

An issue that arises directly from the counselor's use of counseling with spiritual and alternative interventions is the disclosure by the counselor of his or her own cosmology and consciousness. Traditionally, the counselor is trained to delve into the client's psyche and spirit. But that communication, traditionally, has gone but one way. The client *discloses* and the counselor *discourses*, one might say. The counselor, traditionally, kept a barrier between him or herself and the client.

However, when the counselor makes the decision to use spiritual and alternative interventions, the dynamic of the counselor–client relationship changes. As noted earlier, definitions of spirituality and alternative interventions arise from a spiritual or otherwise alternative cosmology and anthropology. Such interventions are the fruit of these same roots.

Similarly, the relationship between the counselor and counselee might change as well. In spirituality, two souls seek the same goal. This does not mean that the relationship is equal, it means that it requires a mutual respect for the same goal and the same interventions.

These interventions require something from those who use them. They are not simply another set of utensils—like a psychic knife and fork. The interventions can change those who use them as well as those for whom they are used. In a real sense—for the client, at least—the interventions may be holy. Thus, spiritual interventions are not the same as psychological interventions. Those things of the sacred are treated differently than those of the psychological or the social. When the holy is at stake, when two people speak of things sacred, the barriers tend to diminish. A counselor may wish to tell of his or her own struggles toward the sacred in his or her own life.

This is not to say that the counselors and counselees are equal and should treat each other as equals. Counselors should be paid and they should be respected for the work they do. This does mean, however, that any professional barriers should be tested against their values vis-a-vis the values proposed by the interventions themselves.

Would the client be helped by disclosing the counselor's anthropology and cosmology? Would the client be helped if the counselor disclosed his or her own spiritual journey? Would the client be helped by knowing the counselor's struggles or doubts or certainties about his or her own faith?

Additionally, this does not mean that counselors should disclose personal, irrelevant, improper, or potentially detrimental material, it *does* suggest that personal disclosure should be reexamined in light of a very different set of interventions and cosmologies.

Spiritual or alternative cosmologies suggest a different view of ethics and law in more areas than counselor disclosure. They tend to impact a constellation of ethical issues and the very themes of law, justice, and jurisprudence itself.

☐ Cosmology and Ethics

Cosmology has a direct connection with ethics. This relationship has two components. First, ethics do not arise full-born from the head of Zeus like Athena. Ethics is grounded in the political, spiritual, and social context of the decision makers. These cosmologies are influential, if not dispositive, in how ethical decisions are made. Two primary concepts of American jurisprudence, the right to privacy, are illustrations. The *implied* right to privacy was composed from a number of *explicit* constitutional rights. There was a time, in the early 1960's, when contraception could be banned both for single and married people. The Supreme Court voided these laws under legal and ethical cosmologies including the right to marry, the right to bear children, and the right of association (***Eisenstadt v. Baird***, 1972; ***Griswold v. Connecticut***, 1965). Even these rights come from the history before the U.S. constitution was ratified. In England, prior to U.S. independence, the home was not sacred. Marriage was, often, as much a political act as a personal act. The new American experience set out to change those conventions, by offering individual freedoms. Cosmologies are the context of ethics.

Second, the outcome of ethical decisions must not "shock the conscience." This is another way of saying the fruit of an ethical decision must be consistent with a society's cosmologies.

Thus, the impact of an ethical decision must be consistent with the decision-maker's, and their society's, cosmologies—both in fruit and root.

☐ Cosmology and Consciousness

Consciousness, itself, is a component of cosmology. Consciousness, itself, is mapped and understood by various religious and spiritual traditions. Dreams, visions, clairvoyance, supernatural healings, and other paranormal experiences are part and parcel of religious teachings and scriptures.

The very counseling processes, from which our discussions often arise, are practices directly connected to religious traditions. Meditation, prayer, and various healing practices both change consciousness and can serve religious ends. Experiencing altered states, without more, will not qualify for religious protection. That *more,* succinctly put, is a direct connection to religious values, norms, and traditions.

Drawing, or otherwise representing these norms, values, or traditions (forms of cosmologies), can be accomplished by analogizing cosmologies to ecologies. Ecologies are systems—integrated patterns of interactions between numerous components. An ecology, like that of an ocean or marsh, incorporates and integrates a variety of fish, water, seaweed, birds, sun, sand, and soil. Similarly, an "ethical ecology" depicts the interrelated components of an ethical issue.

☐ Cosmologies in Conflict and Context: Making an "Ethical Ecology"

The previous discussion of legal cosmologies, such as in *Eisenstadt* and *Griswold*, gives us a current and contentious example of how different cosmologies can yield social conflict. One of the legal scions of these legal decisions is the 1973 decision in *Roe v. Wade*—the decision that invalidated many state statutes prohibiting abortion. Many think that this decision legitimized the unrestricted right to abortion; it did not. It constitutionally protected the *limited* right to abortion. It did so by grafting several legal decisions together, particularly that of the right to personal privacy (*Eisenstadt* and *Griswold*), into the abortion context. The decision has generated heated controversy ever since. For our purposes Roe can be seen as a prime example of jurisprudential cosmologies in conflict.

Making an ethical ecology demonstrates how world views come into conflict with one another and how they relate to one another. An ethical ecology is the depiction of how various components, players, or stakeholders influence any given issue. This ecology is depicted similarly how plants, fish, ducks, water, and other elements of a biological ecology might react to the introduction of massive amounts of crude oil into their environment (for example). State legislatures, interest groups, state regulatory agencies, lawyers, the public, and prospective clients (to name a few) all have. The ethical ecology has six constituent components:

1) identifying the central issue
2) naming the various components, stakeholders, or actors
3) identifying their values or motivations
4) articulating the choices
5) making a choice or decision
6) articulating the consequences

Identifying the central issue narrows the focus of the inquiry. It is not enough to ask whether there are legal or ethical liabilities attached, for example, to conducting trance workshops for the general public. At least, such a question should not arise at this point in the book. The more pertinent questions are: *Who are possible plaintiffs under such circumstances?* And *Who has the most to gain in filing such suits?*

Second, the ethical ecology will name the possible players in such litigation. Such plaintiffs might include attendees with mental illnesses, attendees who are disgruntled with the trance, those who "saw" troubling images, or those who "saw" nothing at all.

Third, what motivates each player? This question asks *why* would that type of person sue? Unrealized expectations is one answer; so is the desire to be "made whole" with compensation for a hurt. Specifically, a severely depressed felt more depressed after the trance. Maybe someone saw a vision of their own death or the death of a loved one and was severely shaken. Maybe someone who "saw" nothing at all felt cheated by the experience. Naming the motivations identifies a causation and, thus, suggests solutions. Naming the actors identifies the solutions to particular groups of potential plaintiffs.

The fourth step is to articulate the choices. This step means that a variety of choices must be discussed. Sometimes it may seem that there is only one ethical choice. When this occurs, it is likely that other options have been precluded for one reason or another. Rarely, if ever, is there only one choice to make. Most likely this means that *only one* choice is valued or recommended by the decision makers.

It is well for many choices to be disclosed and discussed. Prematurely closing off options truncates the decision-making process and stifles creativity. Articulating choices is a form of brainstorming. Brainstorming, the free association of choices and ideas is, in itself, a form of creativity. It also stimulates creativity. Discussing all the options, at the very least, eliminates unworkable solutions in a manner consistent with the full disclosure of all the pros and cons associated with each. At best, the creative stimulus of a free flowing discussion will generate whole new approaches and ideas.

This is how one cosmology or paradigm can be transmuted and transformed into a whole new cosmology. Science, at its best, uses such creative methods to generate new paradigms—say, from Newtonian to quantum physics. The "new" physics is not entirely new, of course, but a serious reworking of models that have been introduced since the 1920s. Just as Einstein stood on the shoulders of giants in his field, his shoulders are the footholds for later, even more transformative work.

Religion and spirituality tend to change and to adopt and adapt models of previous cosmologies. "New Age" spirituality, for example, while often incorporating psychological insights and even insights from modern physics, is modeled after the old religions of shamanism, Odin, Wicca, Tantrism, and others. Spirituality often acts like the third law of thermodynamics—"No energy is either created or destroyed, just changed." Spirituality may adopt new outer forms and expressions, but the inner dynamics and principles tend to remain consistent over time.

The fifth step is to actually make the choice or decision. Often a single decision must be made. A choice has to be determined. Sometimes the decision can be tentative and time can be allowed for feedback. Then, if time and circumstances allow, the decision can be refined. The "kinks" can be worked out. Sometimes the choice is irrevocable. You're stuck with it.

Either way, during the decision phase, the consequences can, and should, be recognized and articulated. It is naive to think that even the most thought-out decision will be welcomed with open-arms by all those affected by that decision. A thorough consideration of the decision will include research and speculation (if need be) about the likely consequences of the decision made.

A prepared decision is one that recognizes how each of the players on the cosmology will likely respond. Not all may like it, but at least the decision makers can be prepared for the response. They'll be less likely to be blind-sided by unforeseen consequences.

The sixth aspect of completing the ethical ecology is to spell out the consequences of the ethical decision. Speculating upon consequences, of course, will have its hazards. Having said this, forward thinking about the possible impacts of their ethical decisions is an essential ingredient in assessing ethical decisions.

There is nothing that can hurt a counselor more than to be blindsided by their decisions. A counselor who is caught unaware about the consequences of his or her decisions cannot move proactively to counter the adverse impacts of decisions—and make no mistake about it, there are *always* adverse or uncomfortable impacts.

Take the example of a counselor who offers a seminar on sacred trance to the public. If the counselor makes the ethical decision to offer the participants a handout explaining the process and expected outcomes of the seminar, does that handout became an implied contract? Then, could a participant then claim that he or she did not receive what was implied in that contract for services?

This example does not arise frivolously from the fertile mind of a law graduate. This situation actually is quite possible. Contracts do not have to be formal-looking documents with the words "Contract" written on top to be legally binding agreements. The issue does the handout on a trance-seminar *imply* a binding contract on the part of the counselor? The following is an illustration of an ethical ecology surrounding the "meditation in counseling session" example.

Ethical Ecology on the Use of Meditation In a Counseling Session

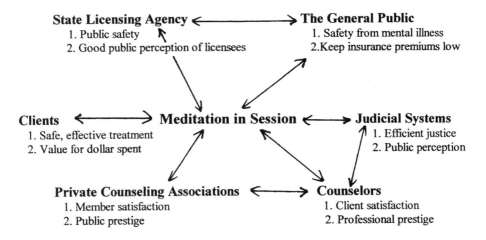

This exercise applies directly to the ethical realm. For example, identifying the varieties of motives for possible plaintiffs gives clues to expectations of the attendees. The ethical ecology helps the clinician clarify these expectations. The clinician should, thus, ask "what are the expectations of the "clients?" Some may want some clues to healing. Others may want a safe experience. Still others may want an unsafe experience. Clarifying the expectations, realistic and otherwise, can be a crucial step in formulating an ethical plan for this hypothetical trace workshop.

In the diagram above titled, "Ethical Ecology on the Use of Meditation in a Counseling Session," we chart out the interrelated dynamics of that issue. At the center, of course, is the key issue. More specifically, this issue might be read in the form of a question such as: "Should meditation be used in a counseling session?" Even more specifically the issue might be styled: "Under what circumstances might meditation be used in a counseling session?" Still further the issue might be phrased as: 'When might the state licensing board object to the use of meditation in a counseling session?" These questions pointedly frame the issue at hand.

The "players" surrounding the key issue. These include the state licensing agency, the general public, clients (or even potential clients), the private counseling associations (NASW, APA, ACA, etc.), the counselors themselves, and the judicial systems. There may be many more players, but these illustrate our purposes here. Indeed, insurance companies would also figure into this ecology. In the diagram, arrows indicate the direct relationship between the players and the central issue. Arrows also indicate the relationships between the players.

Beneath the players are examples the drives, motivations, purposes, or goals of each of the players. Again, more might be listed, but these suffice for our purposes here. For example, it seems reasonable that state licensing boards have at least the dual drives of public safety and a positive public perception of those licensed under the state regime. Each player will have his or her own drives and motivations, which may well compete or conflict with the drives and motivations of other players. These relationships and possible conflicts are the source of ethical dilemmas.

As a consequence of the scientific versus spiritual model above, it seems likely that conflicts arising out of the different players' motivations are not resolved by a decision, but through a shift in consciousness and relationships. For example, the increased value attributed to, and acceptance of, mediation in counseling was not achieved by legislative fiat but by the incremental shift in cultural, religious, and scientific values. The shift in the law, as we have seen, toward increased tolerance and constitutional of the practice of astrology and clairvoyance and the practice of non-Western religious practices, did not happen overnight.

Arrows indicate some of the relationships between and among players and their goals. Space did not allow to chart all the relationships, but some are clear. For example, there is an arrow between "counselors" and "judicial systems." Counselors have both an economic and legal interest in keeping clients satisfied. Client satisfaction is directly proportional to their willingness to return for more sessions and inversely proportional to the likelihood of bringing charges against a counselor.

☐ The Value of an "Ethical Ecology"

The ethical ecology helps clinicians craft ethical ecologies specific to clients and to specific activities. For example, if a counselor leads a seminar on meditation, he or she must consider the legal consequences. It seems clear that in conducting such a seminar for the general public, a specific set of guidelines outlining to the public what to expect and what not to expect seems mandatory. Such guidelines can adjust expectations so that the public, especially the vulnerable public, can be protected. As we have seen in the law discussions below, public protection is a high priority of jurisprudence. It is a high priority for ethics as well. The "ethical ecology" uncovers the necessity and the value of such an ethical solution.

☐ Applying the "Duty Determination" Model

The second exercise in regard to ethics involves the concept of "duty." Duty means the responsibility to act or not to act. The duty concept, as we have seen in the four elements of a negligence suit, is entrenched in law. Duty is also an ethical concept. The following process is one way to responsibly address the issue of "duty":

Identifying the Duty

Identifying the specific duty focuses the nature and the extent of the behavioral obligations of the parties. Without such specific framing, central issues may be clouded by peripheral issues. Clearly stated questions allow for clearly stated answers. Additionally, identifying precise issues offers the counselor the chance to articulate on all sides of an issue. In fact, the counselor can voice a side of an issue that they may disagree with personally; they can play the devil's advocate. Lawyers routinely argue points that they do not personally hold. Being biased in exploring ethical issues with clients offers the counselor the opportunity to experiment with many sides of issues with no harm done. Often, as my students discover, they end up with a perspective different from that with which they began. Experimentation often breeds innovation.

The earlier example of the counselor conducting the trance seminar can offer guidance here. Identifying the duty in this case would pose the question, among others, of whether the counselor has the duty to protect participants from unpleasant or unsettling experiences. The answer might be "yes . . . to some limited degree." After all, a role of counseling and seminars is to encourage new ways of thinking and experiencing the world.

So a variation on the above duty is to recharacterize it as a duty to warn the participants that they *may* experience some upsetting or unsettling thoughts. Further, the counselor may have a greater duty to protect the participants from harm arising from those thoughts. This ranking of duties is the subject of the next section.

Ranking the Duties

The second step of the process is to rank the duties disclosed in the first step. One discovers that duties are not only multiple—some duties are complementary, others are contradictory. One has to rank or order the most important of the identified duties.

Some considerations may help to rank duties. Among these are: How much damage to others may happen if a duty is or is not performed? How serious might that damage or hurt be? How many people might be harmed or put in harm's way? What is the likelihood of harm?

Who Owes the Duty?

Another important element is deciding who owes the duty. This can be a crucial element. Deciding who owes the duty can be half the battle in determining an ethical course of action. For example, who owes the duty to produce an ethically responsible trance seminar? Is it the leader of the seminar? Is it the owner of the facility in which the seminar takes place? Or is it the duty of the participants, themselves, to insist upon ethical standards?

Several people can owe ethical duties. The significance of conducting this exercise is that it narrows the list of those responsible for duties and enables the counselor to focus on only those duties for which the counselor is responsible. While no counselor can "pass the buck" to others, counselors need to accept responsibility rightly lodged with others. It is imperative, however, that counselors correctly and specifically identify their own duties.

1. For what does the counselor have authority?
2. How much control does the counselor have over the seminar?
3. How much control does the counselor have over the participants?

To Whom Is the Duty Owed?

The fourth question that must be addressed is: To whom is the duty is owed? This question is equally important as any other questions. A wrong choice here could obviate right choices elsewhere.

Clues as to whom the duty is owed are often the mirror image of who owes the duty. Where the amount of "control" is a clue to who owes the duty, the words "harm," or "influence under" are clues to whom the duty is owed. The following questions offer clues that can be applied to counselors and their clients.

1. Over whom does the counselor have authority?

2. How much control over whom does the counselor have?
3. Are there limitations on the control, if any are imposed upon the counselor?

The most clear examples come right from clinical settings. For example, where a client is seen by a counselor for spiritual conflicts but is also seen by a member of clergy for spiritual counseling. In that situation, the question is not so much *to whom* the duty is owed, but what limitations of duty may exist under these circumstances. The client's concerns are addressed by two professions. In most respects, the secular counselor need only take responsibility for what he or she does. However, there is more here than meets the eyes.

It is not enough for the secular counselor to wipe their hands of anything the spiritual counselor says or does. For example, if the secular counselor had referred the client to the spiritual counselor some duty may exist to make a "**due diligence**" inquiry into the reputation of the spiritual counselor. A "due diligence" inquiry means that the counselor must ascertain the competence of the spiritual counselor. The secular counselor may need not guarantee competence, but must inquire as to reputation of the spiritual counselor. At least the secular counselor must neither overlook nor "turn a blind eye" to any action suggesting harmful behavior.

So, where does a counselor look for terms for their ethical duties? We turn now to a brief discussion of the sources of ethical duties.

☐ The Sources of Ethical Duties

The sources of ethical duties are varied and all are important. Some sources, however, may be "more equal" than others.

Professional Codes of Ethics

The most obvious source of ethical duties are published by the profession itself. These are the codes of ethics promulgated by the various professions of counseling and mental health professional societies. For example, one may belong to the American Psychological Association or the American Counseling Association, or a clinical social worker may belong to the National Association of Social Workers. Each of these professional groups promulgates its own codes, but they often have similar themes: competence to clients, confidentiality, the safety of clients, no self-dealing, and continuing professional education among them.

The costs of violating such an ethics policy can be quite high. The professional group will hold a hearing (not a criminal or civil trial) to determine guilt or innocence. If found guilty, the guilty party can have his or her membership revoked, suspended, or otherwise limited. Additionally and significantly, the professional organization may turn over the findings to state licensing boards. If this happens, other sanctions may be imposed.

Statutory Regulations

State regulatory boards differ from professional organizations in several respects, even though the *content* of the regulations may be quite similar. First, statutory regulations have the force of law behind them. They are promulgated by a public entity, usually a state licensing board, and public funds support its offices, investigations, hearing time, and sentencing structures. As a matter of fact, if a sanction is disputed in court, the state will foot the bill for the lawyers. This is not the case in professional organizations. If they are sued, they supply their own legal counsel.

Second, statutory regulations are subject to the legislative process. Even though, in most cases, an administrative board of the executive branch is delegated to promulgate regulations governing counselors, elective officials can feel the pain of public disapproval. This is done usually through the elective process.

Third, statutory regulations have the coercive power of the state to revoke, suspend, or otherwise limit state license—not just memberships in a professional organization. We have already considered legal issues of state regulation at some length in another chapter, so we need not detour further along these lines.

Agency or Employer Policy

If not in private practice, many counselors may find themselves responsible to corporate or institutional policy and procedures as well. Counselors working in schools, for example, are subject to that institution's rules and regulations as well. These, too, however, can be challenged in court.

Public Policy

Public policy, in general, is harder to quantify. Of course, as a matter of fact, such public policy is embodied in the three sources above noted. However, the cutting edge of public sentiment and public opinion often precedes legislative and corporate efforts. The dramatic rise in alternative and complementary counseling, of course, is a case in point. Counseling programs at the graduate level, regulatory codes, and corporate policy, by and large, lag behind public perceptions and demands.

This is for good reason. The law is a conservative element in society and legislatures are deliberative bodies. They evaluate the public good. If the public demands gene therapy for genetic illness, these bodies tend to ask questions, conduct research, and consider options. Sometimes the public outcry influences the legislative process, it is intended to—but sometimes not. Sometimes public sentiment is revealed in jury verdicts, but not always.

Discerning public attitudes, for example, about what and how much the public will tolerate and even encourage alternative and spiritual counseling interventions. Such discernment is both an art and a science—but probably not rocket science. The prudent counselor will keep his or her ears to the ground of media, other colleagues, law cases, and friends with a view to changing public perceptions on counseling techniques and the shifting responsibilities of counselors.

Private Certifications

Many private companies or individuals offer certifications in specific interventions. They may also suggest ethical standards in order to either qualify for or to keep such certifications. This book will not assert criteria for the quality of private certifications, but will opine about criteria for their legal utility, particularly for use as qualifying you as an expert witness or a witness on your own behalf. Such considerations include the reputation of the certification provider in the eye of the jury or judge, its reputation in the profession, its national prestige, its contributions to the field of certification, and publications under its name.

☐ Legal/Ethical Duties that May Attach to Complementary and Spiritual Counseling

As stated earlier, the *content* of the above four sources of ethical duties may be quite similar, even though the method of promulgating them and the consequences for breaking them might be quite different.

Generally speaking, the essence of ethical duties centers around the use of the counselor's power, prestige, and control strictly for the benefit of their clients. Other words for such ethical standards is the ethic prohibiting "dual relations." The prohibition against dual relations recognizes that a counselor should not also be a client's business partner, lawyer, medical doctor, savior, or lover. By whatever term, this is an exacting standard—the details about which are below.

The sections below catalogue the primary ethical duties common to the four sources of ethical duties. This is a substantive list; not an exhaustive one.

Separation of Public Education or Counseling from Private Worship or Ideology

Counselors have a duty to discern the margins or boundaries between where their personal religious or spiritual inclinations begin and where such beliefs should end. The *Spratt* case illustrates the extent to which counselors can and cannot conduct spiritual counseling in a public setting. School counselors, and other counselors employed by the public or government, need to respect the difference between therapy and evangelism. We have already noted the "wall" between the church and state is more like a permeable membrane. Again, the First Amendment provides for no *wall*, just that the government may not abridge the free exercise of religion nor promulgate any one faith.

Counselors are not strictly prohibited from discussing any matters related to spirituality and religion with their clients. Beyond this "bright line" consideration, the duty imposed upon counselors is constitutional and ethical. This duty is also bounded by law, employer policy, professional organizations, and the therapeutic requirements of clients.

Often this distinction is unclear, but it is discernable. Counselors might ask themselves such fundamental questions as those below:

1. *Who is raising the religious/spiritual issue?*
2. *Is the religious discussion pertinent to therapeutic issues?*
3. *If I am raising a religious/spiritual issue, what is the therapeutic reason I am doing so?*
4. *Am I conducting religious, spiritual, or complementary interventions as a way to persuade the client toward a certain ideology?*

Client Self-Determination (or What Is Righteous Discomfort?)

Client self-determination means that the client set the pace, tone, and ultimate goals for their therapeutic aims. Self-determination acknowledges that clients must retain ultimate power over their lives. Self-determination recognizes that clients are not the "objects" of therapeutic interventions, but its subject. As living, breathing *subjects*, they must be treated with dignity, integrity, and honesty. Different counseling professions may use the later terms to apply to clients. The effect is the same. The return to the counselor for treating clients with this respect are trust, rapport, and compliance.

Self-determination is especially important in using spiritual and alternative interventions. First, such interventions are central to anyone's self-determination. Spirituality and alternative interventions often are intimately connected with religious belief and ideology. Religious beliefs are so connected to a person's self-determination that they are protected by the U.S. constitution. The choice between Rogerian or Gestalt interventions probably does not involve such belief systems. Second, as a practical matter, clients will be more sensitive to interventions and suggestions that conflict or interfere with their religious beliefs.

Counselors must be eager and open to sensing a client's discomfort with a particular spiritual or alternative intervention. Yet, at the same time, counselees must be told that a certain amount of discomfort is a natural part of the healing process. If healing and spiritual growth were easy and painless, there would be no need for counselors in the first place. Someone once said that a counseling session without some discomfort is nothing more than an idle chat! Indeed, the lives of religious figures and spiritual leaders tell the story of effort, discipline, and sacrifice along their spiritual journeys.

A quick method of expressing self-determination is simply to ask the client if he or she is comfortable with spiritual interventions and with any given treatment plan. This is called "notice" and "informed consent." These topics are treated elsewhere. If the client does not agree with the therapeutic goals or the means of achieving them, they can choose another counselor. Other counselors negotiate with their clients as to treatment interventions and the pace and nature of therapeutic goals. A brief contract and schedule outlining the treatment aims and specific interventions to be employed is an easy and effective way of operationalizing self-determination.

Self-determination embodies inconsistencies. The question for the counselor is when, and under what circumstances, is client discomfort righteous and when is it not? There is no "silver bullet" answer applicable in all cases. The answer comes in degrees, determined as much by art as by science.

First, the counselor needs to assess the likelihood of beneficial success of the intervention against the pain caused. Does the outcome deem it fairly certain that the pain is worth it? Or are the client's tears and disruption to his or her beliefs likely to produce only negligible benefits—and how certain can the client be that the expected results will be achieved?

Second, how long will the discomfort last? How intense will be discomfort be? How disruptive to the life of the client will the discomfort be *over the long haul*? Short lived, high intensity pain may be the wise choice for a needed result. Of course, the opposite may be true also.

Third, how *necessary* is the proposed outcome? Is the desired outcome a goal of the counselor or the client? If so, to what extent does the client "buy into" the counselor's suggestions? How much is the client surrendering their own judgment into the hands of the counselor? Or how much of the client's discomfort is based upon quite natural anxiety or habit?

Fourth, are there alternatives to the proposed interventions? Has the counselor disclosed other interventions that may achieve similar results? Is the counselor using an intervention simply because the counselor likes it (or because it is consistent with the counselor's beliefs) or because it is most helpful to the counselee?

Self-determination raises uncomfortable issues both for the client and for the counselor. But that is the necessary nature of ethics.

Loyalty—The Boundaries of Obedience

Most counselors are well aware of the operational definition of loyalty as it applies to the standard for child custody cases. That standard, now common to all states, is the "best interest of the child." Similarly, the duty of loyalty requires that the counselor act "in the best interest" of the client.

This duty has global implications for counselors. Loyalty is the ethical term that encompasses such far ranging ethical issues as sexual misconduct, moonlighting, self-dealing, and dual relations (Bullis, 1995). This is because sexual misconduct and the other issues have the duty of loyalty at the heart of the dilemma. Counselors who put their own interests, desires, or motivation before that of their client's interests are guilty of an ethics infraction. The ethical "cause of action" may vary from stem to stem, but it's the same weed.

We have seen already many unfortunate examples of counselors can place their own interests above that of clients. The *Magno* case, discussed in chapter two is a pressing example. Even without criminal charges, the ethics violations are intense and extensive. While the ethics violations of licensed, professional counselors (of whatever educational or licensure category) may be a thousand times more subtle, it may be just as damaging to the client.

Of course this is not to say that the duty of loyalty is the sole consideration for the counselor. A client's fervent desire or need for confidentiality, for example, is not the sole or ultimate consideration. The duty of loyalty is not absolute, nor are any of these duties. Each case must be decided upon their own merits and circumstances.

Fiduciary Duty

A fiduciary duty is a species of the duty of loyalty. A fiduciary duty insists that counselors act in the "best *financial* interests" of the client. While financial duties do not exhaust a fiduciary duty, they will engage us here. The concept of the fiduciary duty is like a "trust." In Roman times, the equivalents of financial managers would set up tables to take their clients' money for investment purposes. The term "fiduciary" is taken from the Latin word for "bench" or "table."

Financial duties also carry inconsistencies with them. Counselors earn their livings from their clients; however, counselors cannot take advantage of that relationship. While counselors have every right to just compensation, they cannot use their power or influence to enrich themselves to the detriment of their clients. Breach of fiduciary duties can happen when a counselor encourages the client to return for session after session for little benefit, or encourages clients to engage in joint financial ventures that would primarily benefit the counselor, or employs deceiving or misrepresentative language on insurance reimbursements to continue therapy sessions.

Counselors who engage in spiritual or alternative interventions enjoy a precise kind of authority and may be tempted to precise kinds of financial advantages. Clients who tend to relinquish spiritual authority to their counselors may also relinquish financial, sexual, or medical control to their counselors as well. Perhaps clients will ask for financial advice. Perhaps clients will ask where their charitable donations should be distributed. Perhaps clients will allow the counselor to hold onto money they have overpaid. Such counselors should flee from any overreaching authority. Counselors need to strictly limit their authority to activities within the purview of counseling practices. Pertinent questions for self-reflection might include:

1. Am I scheduling future sessions with this client for their benefit or my own financial income?

2. Am I holding any money for the client at all? Why? Who authorized this? Can you prove it? If you absolutely need to hold this money, you probably need to account for the interest accrued? Do you need a signed agreement? Does the money need to be in a blind trust?

3. Am I entering into any relationship with the client involving money or pecuniary interest whosoever? The operative definition of a "dual relation" is any relationship *beyond* that of a counselor, so any other relationship may be burdened with a presumption of unethical behavior. This is especially so for social, sexual, and financial relationships.

Duty to Protect Third Parties (or Exactly Who Are Your Clients Anyway?)

We discussed the duty to protect third parties from the harm done to third parties at the end of chapter three. Here we ask the ethical question posed by the legal doctrine of **third-party liability**. As we have noted, this doctrine is in wide use. It is the fertile ground for constructing ethical questions and for constructing an ethical ecology. This is accomplished below in part B.

Here, we speak again of the case study noted at the beginning of this chapter. The Maryland Court of Appeals ruled that "school counselors have duty to use reasonable means to attempt to prevent suicide when they are on notice of child or adolescent student's suicidal intent" (*Eisel v. Board of Education of Montgomery County*, 1991). This case has broad applicability to school counselors as well as others who address spiritual and alternative interventions in practice as well as in the public policy arena. Ethically and legally pertinent questions follow:

What are the legal/ethical "duties" (responsibilities) of the school counselors?
The *Eisel* court's decision isolated three pertinent issues related to this issue: special relationship, **foreseeability**, and scienter. It was the special relationship between the school counselors and the student that was the initial inquiry for the court. Without some kind of special relationship for care and responsibility, the court would not proceed with any further legal inquiry. Because of the school counselor's responsibilities to contact parents in the event of an expressed suicide (per school board policy), the court concluded that a relationship of responsibility and care existed. This case can be distinguished from the *Nally* case, previously mentioned due to the fact that *Nally* involved a suicidal parishioner of a *religious* counselor.

The *Eisel* case went on to find that the suicide was foreseeable because the counselors knew or should have known that she was in immanent danger of suicide. Foreseeability is the legal determination that the counselors had forewarning or foreknowledge that such an event was going to take place or was in reasonable danger of taking place.

What, specifically, are the duties of the school counselors to the students, to the school officials (their employers), to the parents of other students, and to the community?
This question goes to an ethical ecology of this case and issue it presents. This ethical ecology is an occasion to expand the relationships and consequences of the decisions made.

The short answer is that the counselors had a duty to warn others of her impending suicide to take reasonable precautions to protect her from doing so. They were obligated by school policy to warn parents. The decision indicates that parents or school officials should have been notified. This is all in an effort to place reasonable requirements to protect those in a special relationship from harming others or harming themselves.

As the next section will suggest, the counselors had a legal duty to the parents as well. They, as the student was a minor, were the ones who could sue in the event of harm coming to their children. As a matter of fact, the parents may also sued if the parents had knowledge of threats from their children.

The counselors certainly had both a legal and ethical duty to their employers. After all, their employers will be sued under *respondeat superior*.

The community itself, absent some connection to the deceased students will probably not have a cause of action. But they may have an **"ethical claim"** against the counselors. They may feel a sense of betrayal if they feel the counselors let them down and played their children at unreasonable risk.

Ethical Ecology
For
School Counselors re: Student Suicides

Inspired by Eisel v. Bd. Education for Montgomery Co., 1991

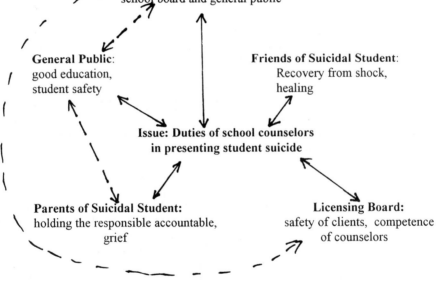

Some of these myriad relationships are depicted in the above ethical ecology. Without getting too convoluted with lines and arrows, this rendering attempts to outline the connections between the central issue under review and the players or components of the ecology.

First, the five main players are depicted: school administrators/employers, friends of the suicidal student, the state licensing board, parents of the suicidal student, and the general public. Some of their motivations or drives are also indicated.

Second, solid arrows point in both directions of influence. It is nearly always the case that struggling with an issue changes the outlook of those who must do the struggling. In this unfortunate case, grief will particularly punctuate the ethical struggle.

Third, broken lines and arrows indicate some relationships between and among the players themselves. These relationships can be as deep and profound as those between a central ethical issue and the players. Here, we note the relationships between school administrators/employers and the general public, between the licensing board and the administrators and employers, and between the parents of the suicidal student and the general public.

These relationships can be varied, but it is reasonable to assert that parents of the student will be known by segments of the general public and will be offered sympathy by the public at large. This grief and concern, it is not unlikely to assume, will turn into serious and persistent questions about the safety of all children in that school district. Because there is almost always a close relationship between school boards and the public—most communities now directly elect their school boards—it is likely that any concerns and political pressure felt by the public will also be felt by the school board. The board will, in turn, require their administrators to respond in some way. Finally, the state licensing boards may feel some political pressure to respond with additional training, education, etc., by their licensees. It is not unknown that among these pressures and political concerns is the fear of civil litigation or even criminal sanctions.

What, then, might be some "causes of action" if someone would sue in a case arising from these facts? The cause of action claimed by the student's parent was for wrongful death, basically a negligence claim. The action was brought by the parent of the student. They had standing to bring the suit because it was their daughter who died. It was "wrongful" in the sense that the claim is made that her death could reasonably have been avoided by those who had the duty to do so.

Ron Goldman's family sued O.J. Simpson also under a wrongful death claim. The legal theory in the Simpson case was that Mr. Simpson had a legal duty to cause no harm. In the *Eisel* case the legal theory was that the counselors had a duty to prevent harm from occurring.

Against whom should or would parties sue in this case? Parents sued the counselors and, under the theory of *respondeat superior*, the school board. There was no contest that the counselors were **agents** acting on behalf of the school board. Liability flows upward like sap in the springtime.

While the parents of the friends of the suicidal student did not sue, one cannot help but wonder if they might have succeeded if they chose to sue. We have discussed in previous pages, the duty of protect third parties. Would a court, for example, recognize a suit for the pain and suffering or negligent infliction of emotional distress of the friends against the school district as well? They would be third parties, as they were not the direct clients of the counselor.

What are some duties by society or the legal system owed to the school counselors? Ethical duties may run both ways. The legal duty ran only one way. The ethical duties, however, sometimes benefit both parties. If the counselors owed a duty to the students and their families, then what, if anything, does the society or the employers owe the counselors? Here, the law equivocates.

This case does not reach this question, but let's take the facts and use our imaginations. What does the school board owe the counselors? For our purposes here, they owe the counselors what the law calls "correct supervision." Put another way supervisors and companies have been sued for negligent supervision where an employee fails to train or control someone whom they supervise at or above the legal standard of care.

The question here is how well the cause of action would be styled negligent supervision. In any event, it is probably the case that the *Eisler* school system will re-educate school counselors as to their duties in suspected suicide cases.

The community may have an ethical duty to support the school counselors as well. If a community is suspicious of school counselors and withholds pertinent information from them about their students, then a counselor's effectiveness can be compromised. An ethical ecology will always include the immediate community in its cosmos.

Counselors who address spiritual issues and school counselors may find themselves in just such a position. Religiously or spiritually distressed persons may believe that they have a duty to attack satan or evil in the guise of another person or group. Or they might feel they need to do God's work in avenging some wrong or other. For example, if the person who assassinated Shimon Perez was under care of a counselor in the United States, would he be able to find "safe harbor" where people would be reluctant to disclose his whereabouts or to testify against him. Where there are sharp social or political divisions among members of a community, law enforcement officials in particular and the judicial systems in general have difficulty in conducting proper investigations, gathering evidence, and finding and securing witnesses. In many cities, criminals continue to go unpunished because people mistrust the criminal justice system or fear reprisals. This effect upon the judicial systems is another example of the ethical ecology and its many organic, interrelated constituencies.

What might be some of the counselors' defenses?   Two principle defenses come to mind. These do not necessarily reflect the defenses raised at the *Eisler* trials. They are intended to encourage the reader's legal imagination. We do not know how they would fare, because they must be adjudicated under a specific claim and a specific set of facts.

The first is confidentiality. The counselor could claim that she was legally and ethically obligated to say nothing to anyone about the suicide ideation because of student privacy. The counselor might point to professional codes of ethics or even to state mandates requiring school counselors to keep student sessions secret. This defense would probably fail in most cases. The balance between potential client harm and the rationale for confidentiality in the first place seems clearly to weigh in favor of getting the student help.

The second potential defense might be that the suicide was not immanent. The counselor could claim that, in her professional judgment, her "reading" of the situation was that the suicide attempt was not immanent nor serious. We have not considered the record of any conversations the counselor had with the student. So we raise this defense, as we raise the previous defense, as a hypothetical matter only. Certainly, the law does not require counselors to be clairvoyant and accurate prognosticators. This issue, most likely, would be a matter of fact for a trier of fact (judge or jury) to decide. In such a hypothetical trial, expert witnesses would be called by both sides to find what the prudent practitioner, under these circumstances, would have done. Did this particular counselor fall above or below that standard of care?

We now return to the menu of possible ethical duties begun some pages ago, before the *Eisler* case appropriately diverted us.

Circumscribed Confidentiality

Some counselors may still harbor the anachronistic notion that all communications between themselves and their clients are confidential. This is fundamentally erroneous.

At best, the duty of counseling confidentiality can best be described as a "circumscribed confidentiality." Circumscribed confidentiality means that the counselor's duty to keep clients' secrets has considerable limitations. Most counselors know that, under some circumstances, they must break confidentiality where suspected child or elder abuse or neglect is involved, where a threat to a third party may be immanent (as noted above), or to prevent their client from hurting themselves. These limitations should now be part of counselor's training and practice.

A further area of important limitations to a duty of confidentiality is when a counselor is served with a subpoena to testify in court. A subpoena is a summons to testify in court. A subpoena could be served either for a civil or criminal action. A subpoena has the force of law. If the counselor does not comply by testifying, the counselor may be prosecuted for "contempt of court." Contempt of court is a felony.

There are many reasons why a counselor may be served with a subpoena. Unfortunately, they are getting more and more common. If the counselee is suing someone else, for example if they were in a car accident and are claiming mental distress or anguish. If a couple wishes to sue for custody of children, they may want their counselor to testify. If the counselee is requesting workman's compensation, or if the counselee is under court-ordered counseling, a court may grant a subpoena for the counseling records and/or for the counselor to personally testify. If a counselee commits a crime, the counselor may likely receive a subpoena. These are only some of the circumstances in which a counselor may be required to disclose client secrets—and in open court.

Privileged Communications

We turn now to an area of law and ethics squarely in the domain of spiritual counseling. **"Privileged communications"** is a legal term denoting communications that are not subject to subpoena or other legal scrutiny. Public policy and the law are very stingy in handing out privileged communications. Usually only husbands and wives, lawyers and their clients, and clergy and their penitents have such privileges. The legal justification for the "priest-penitent privilege" is to recognize the need to privately disclose to a spiritual counselor his or her flawed acts with the expectation of spiritual consolation was enunciated by the U.S. Supreme Court (**U.S. v. Trammel**, 1980).

We discuss "clergy privileged communications" here because some counselors may consider that, because they discuss religious topics with clients, that the privilege applies to them. For a more thorough discussion of the religious privilege see Bullis (1990c) and for a complete, state-by-state citation for all clergy-privilege statutes see Bullis and Mazur (1993).

In a recent decision significant to all counselors, the U.S. Supreme Court extended the federal privilege to psychotherapists, specifically clinical social workers, in the course of psychotherapy (**Jaffee v. Redmond**, 1996). The court weighed the interests of a judicial system that requires witnesses against the public policy of people seeking psychotherapy. The court came down in favor of the client's limited confidentiality. In the *Jaffee* case a man, Allen, was killed by an on-duty police officer, Redmond. Redmond later received counseling from a clinical social worker, Beyer. The special administrator for Allen's estate sued Redmond and others under the theory that Allen used excessive force when she shot Allen. Beyer conducted about 50 clinical sessions with Redmond. When the plaintiffs found out about these sessions, they wanted to have Beyer testify at the trial. Beyer refused and the new law suit followed.

The court was clear, however, that the privilege is likely to be a limited one. It stated, "because this is the first case in which we have recognized a psychotherapist privilege, it is neither necessary nor feasible to delineate its full contours in a way that would 'govern all conceivable future questions in this area'" (*Jafee v. Redmond*, 1996, p. 18). And in a footnote (p. 18) the court warned it would be "premature to speculate" about how this newly adopted privilege might be limited—"for example, if a serious threat of harm to the patient or to others can be averted only by means of a disclosure by the therapist" (p. 18, n. 19).

For example, in one case, the failure of rabbis to maintain confidences raised a material issue of fact upon which the rabbis might be sued for breach of fiduciary duty and intentional infliction of emotional distress (*Lightman v. Flaum*, 1999). According to a New York State trial court, confidential clergy disclosures to a congregant's husband and to a divorce court can amount to "outrageous" and "intolerable" behavior that fulfills the requirements for the tort of intentional infliction of emotional distress.

It often comes as a surprise to counselors that their communications do not enjoy such legal privileges, but they do not. The general rule is to require professionals to testify in court, to report child or elder abuse, or other confidential matters if the state requires it.

The proof begins with statutes and concludes with case law. Any state statute will suffice to illustrate, but let's look at Washington State's, as it is relatively clear and cogent and we will be seeing it in action in a case cited in the next section (§5.60.060 (3), 1989 supp):

> A clergyman or priest shall not, without the consent of a person making the confession, be examined as to any confession made to him in his professional character, in the course of discipline enjoined by the church to which he belongs.

Even in this succinct rendering of the privilege, several considerations arise. First, this is a state law. Most privilege statutes are found on the state level. Counselors are thus strongly admonished to check the status of the confidentiality with their respective states.

Second, there is no reference to money exchanging hands. The statute is unaffected by whether or not the clergy receives any payment for his or her services. Payment is a moot point.

Third, while the privilege itself is narrowly construed by courts (in keeping with the public policy of encouraging people to testify in court) the term "clergy" is sometimes broadly construed. So, even though a counselor does not have the title of "Rev." in front of his or her name, that does not necessarily settle the matter. As we shall see in the following paragraph, it is the leadership relationship to the counselor's faith group that is dispositive.

Now we have some statutory basis upon which to consider the availability of the clergy–penitent privilege for those counselors who use spiritual and alternative interventions. First, are they clergy? Usually, this answer is no. There may be, however, some circumstances where the answer may be "yes." The answer may be affirmative if the counselor is affiliated with a religious or spiritual organization. Certainly, there are clergy members who are also counselors licensed by their respective states. The present author falls into this category. Other clergy may be working in religiously affiliated counseling centers. Some counselors may be leaders of more nontraditional faith-groups such as Wicca, Native American, Shamanic, or other groups not calling their leaders by the statutory names. Under those circumstances, the context of the conversations, the role of the counselor with respect to his or her faith group, and the intention of the one offering the "confession" are relevant factors.

Courts have established some parameters to offer some criteria for counselors to consider whether, or under what circumstances, they might avail themselves of the privilege. A Roman Catholic nun, for example, cannot invoke the privilege because her denomination does not recognize her role as "confessional" in nature, according to a lower court in New Jersey (*In re Murtha*, 1971). On the other hand, the Iowa Supreme Court held that communications made to Presbyterian Church (USA) "elders" (constitutionally elected officers of the church) *can* be privileged because church elders are "ordained" into their offices and possess many of the responsibilities of ordained clergy (*Reutkmeier v. Nolte*, 1917).

There are, and will continue to be, new and relevant "twists" to the issue of emerging spiritualities and privileged communications. In June of 1999, a Wiccan priestess applied to a Virginia state court for the right to perform marriages and was denied. The question was whether Wicca was a recognized religion. The American Civil Liberties Union defended the priestess in her appeal (Akin, 1999). About a month later, the judge reversed his decision (Associated Press, 1999d).

What if, now that the priestess can conduct weddings in Virginia, during the course of marriage counseling, someone confessed that he or she had previously embezzled money from a bank and that the police were about to arrest him or her. Might the priestess claim the clergy privilege? She might, and her argument for doing so might have merit. What if either the prospective bride or groom confesses to continuing to abuse their child. Does the priestess have a duty to report? How might the issue of privileged communications apply here? We address such dilemmas in the next section.

Courts have tried to adjudicate grey areas where they were unsure of whether the conversations were made in a "counseling" session or a "confessional" session. The South Carolina Court of Appeals simply held that all the marriage counseling conversations between a husband and wife and an ordained minister would be privileged. The court decided not to try to adjudicate between those conversations that were strictly "counseling" and those that were strictly "penitential" in nature (*Rivers v. Rivers*, 1987).

A New York Supreme Court held that the "penitential" aspects of a marriage counseling conversation would be held immune from court examination, but those "marriage counseling" conversations could be disclosed in court (*Ziske v. Luskin*, 1987). The turning point for this decision was that the husband and wife were suing their physician for malpractice and the court held that they placed their marriage relationship (and presumably their marriage counseling conversations) in the public domain by the suit.

The second consideration is whether or not the "confession" was made in the counselor's professional capacity. Even if a member of the "clergy" was an ordained priest wearing his collar and robes, if the confession was made while the priest was planting roses in his backyard and the conversation was a casual one made by an atheist neighbor who had no intention of the conversation being either religious or private, the communication may not rise to the level of a **privileged communication**. On the other hand, a serious, spiritual conversation over the back yard fence with a clergy and a nonmember neighbor who has the intention of seeking spiritual guidance and solace, may well rise to the level of a privilege.

The third consideration is whether the "confession" was consistent with the group's tenets. This might seem to be a natural and normal part of all religious groups, but it is not. Not even all avowedly Christian groups have confession as a tenet of their faith. Such was the case where a convicted pedofile had conversations with a New Life Christian Fellowship pastor. The convicted felon appealed partly on the grounds that his motion to suppress the testimony was wrongly denied—and that the pastor's testimony was privileged. The court dismissed this part of the appeal on the grounds that the conversations in question were not part of a continuing and ongoing counseling relationship and that confession, as such, was not a part of his church's tenets; that keeping evidence of crime confidential is in the pastor's discretion, and that the pastor considered the conversations in question to be "disciplinary" in nature.

This might seem like legal hair splitting, but hair splitting is the nature of the law. The law turns on words and their nuances. That is another reason for counselors to clearly understand law and their relationship to it.

I'll now add a twist to this discussion by adding another factor into the legal equation. The new factor is the role of counselors as mandatory reporters of child abuse or other kinds of abandonment or abuse.

☐ Privileged Communication and Child Abuse Reporting

Privileged communication law and child abuse reporting laws are distinct. As a practical matter, however, duties of privileged communications and reporting suspected child abuse are linked. If a counselor is a mandatory reporter, their obligation to keep confidences can be severely compromised. As a practical matter, if a counselor enjoys a privilege against testifying in court, it may impact his or her availability or admissibility to testify as to a child (or other) abuse situation. On the other hand, should a counselor avail themselves of the privileged communication statute, they may well also choose not to report such abuse. (It should be acknowledged that, while this section specifically addresses child abuse, the author recognizes that elder abuse and other classes may also be statutory.)

Every one of the 50 states, plus U.S. territories, have relatively clear statutes denoting who is a mandatory child abuse reporter. The Virginia Code (§63.1-248.3, 1999 Cum Supp.) specifically defines mandatory reporters of child abuse. Most are specifically named by professional class, including "Any mental health professional and 'any person employed as [a] social worker.'"

Each state specifies who is a mandatory reporter with relative clarity. These statutes, and a more detailed discussion of mandatory reporting, as they relate to spiritual or religious activity can be found in Bullis (1990c). To reiterate the obvious, all counselors need to know whether they fall into a class of person who is a mandatory reporter.

Such a determination is not as easy as it may seem, especially when spiritual and religious counseling are concerned. The following case illustrates.

Three non-ordained counselors, working at the Community Chapel, were convicted of failing to report child abuse. Each had received credible notice from counselees that children were being abused. They were given a deferred sentence of one year's probation. Additionally, one counselor was ordered to pay a $500 fine. Each appealed their conviction on the grounds that the mandatory reporting statute did not apply to them and that it unconstitutionally violated their rights of religious expression. Their appeal reached the Supreme Court of Washington State.

The court upheld the convictions of the two defendants who were not ordained ministers at the time of their violations. They reversed the conviction of the one counselor who was an ordained clergyman at the time he received the information on the abuse because clergy were held not to be subject to the mandatory reporting requirements. The court went on to emphasize that the other two counselors, even though they were counseling in a religious context, were still subject to the mandatory reporting requirements and were not exempt because of their religious beliefs or the tenets of their religious organizations (*State v. Motherwell*, 1990). Actually, the court ruled that they fell within Washington State's statutory definition of "social worker"—clearly mandatory reporters under that state's law.

This case, even though of relatively limited jurisdiction, is a gold mine for legal and ethical issues. The case illustrates again how the legal and ethical issues are bound to occur when counselors blur the lines between the spiritual and the secular. It is an easy mistake to make, yet it can be a costly one. There can be both civil and criminal penalties for breaching confidences and for mandatory reporters who fail to so report. Counselors may feel like they're between a rock and a hard place. In some ways, they may be. That's why they need to know the law.

The *Motherwell* court made clear that non-clergy counselors, even though they work in a clearly religious or spiritual context, cannot claim a religious exemption from doing so. Thus, if a non-clergy counselor works out of an office specifically motivated by religious or spiritual concerns, the counselor needs to review his or her status under reporting law relative to his or her *function*. What roles and purposes do they perform? Do they have the training and religious or spiritual *imprimatur* (ordination, induction, or other ecclesiological "badges" of religious or spiritual authority)? To paraphrase a saying: "If you are trained as a counselor, and get paid like a counselor, were hired as a counselor, and relate to clients like a counselor, then the state will treat you like a counselor." This reasoning seems likely to prevail in other jurisdictions as well.

The case also posits a wider ethical issue as well. Even if the counselors were exempt from *mandatory* reporting requirements, they are still *permissible* reporters. Each state allows all its citizens to report suspected child abuse and offers legal protection for those who do so, so long as it is without malice or recklessness. So, why not report suspected child abuse even though one is not so required? Certainly, it is the policy of the state to "cast a wide net" in the hopes of protecting these vulnerable citizens. That is why the state mandates a wide range of reporters and why it immunizes "good faith" reporters from civil and criminal charges that otherwise might arise, including breach of confidentiality and defamation. Even if a reporter is dead wrong about the accusation, he or she will be immunized so long as the report was not made to get back at someone or for other malevolent reasons.

Is there a therapeutic rationale for not reporting? Will a report damage the therapeutic relationship? Maybe, even likely. However, since most counselors are mandatory reporters anyway, the state has made a clear choice to protect children over that of the therapeutic relationship. After all, an adult can get a new counselor, an abused child can't easily get a second chance at childhood.

☐ Operationalizing Ethics and Meditation Practices

Ethics, of course, must be operationalized in specific areas of a counselor's spiritual or alternative practice. It is impossible to enumerate or to offer examples for each and every instance illustrating ethical programs. This chapter has already described the principles of ethical issues which counselors need to apply to their own practices.

Having said that, an illustration of such an ethical discourse and an example of an ethical disclosure can help counselors. This illustration below is intended to be just that. It is not intended to be a "boiler plate" document. It is intended, however, to be a catalyst for counselors to apply to the specific needs and circumstances of their specific practices.

The following is the text of a notice and informed consent document that the author has used both in spiritual and in secular settings before conducting meditation sessions (see Figure 5.1). It accomplishes two separate goals. First, it puts the participants on notice about what the session will be like by describing the flow of the exercise. Toward this end, I have described five "phases" or "stages" (see below) for the relaxation/visualization exercise. In actual practice, the I would explain in great detail how I intended to proceed in each stage. I would then ask for any questions, taking time to answer each.

Similarly, I also explain the informed consent part of the procedure by explaining the notice, informed consent, and voluntary participation sections. These sections outline the principles by which the session will be conducted. The notice section has been explained in the previous paragraph.

The "informed consent" section addresses the purpose, methodology, and any dangers inherent in the exercise. As we have seen, "informed consent" implies that a decision is an "informed" one. The participants should be told beforehand the purposes, procedures, and any potential harmful impacts of the interventions. This section, then, is extremely important and should be closely and carefully considered.

Nor, for example, should the counselor rely solely upon the discretion of the client or participant. If the counselor, in his or her own professional discretion, thinks that a person should not participate in the exercise, the counselor has the duty to effect that decision. The counselor has the authority to control what transpires in the session or exercise and must, therefore, have the responsibility to control who participates. The criteria for a contraindication to participate are many, including: the presence of mental illness (particularly of the hallucinatory variety), physical illness that might jeopardize free breathing or relaxing postures, or taking medication which might hinder breathing or sitting or laying down. Of course, a potential participant may choose not to participate.

The counselor should make it clear that potential participants can refuse to participate if they so desire. Such a decision should be welcomed with gratitude. It is unlikely that the counselor would ask for a reason why, unless the counselor and participant have an on-going therapeutic relationship and such a decision has therapeutic merit. Naturally, no reprisal or retribution should be devised against the non-participant. The non-participant can either be present in the room unobtrusively or move outside the session area. It may or may not be helpful for a non-participant to be present at the de-briefing session at the end of the exercise.

Three additional items need further discussion. First, the above document is distributed at the beginning of the session before the exercise is ever begun. Time is allotted for the full and complete discussion of this ethics statement—even at the expense of the time allowed for the exercise itself.

Second, objections may be cited that to fully inform the participants gives too much information about the exercise beforehand and that such "premature" information might ruin the experience of the meditation itself. This concern has not been born out in practice. In fact, the preliminary information often serves to raise participants' positive expectations of the experience.

Third, if someone chooses not to participate, would he or she deter the others from enjoying and benefitting from the experience? This concern, as well, has not been borne out in practice. The others simply move on. If the counselor does not overreact, participants are less likely to overreact.

This operationalization exercise, of course, is only one example of the many interventions that spiritual or alternative therapies use. Hopefully, counselors will adopt and adapt such ethical disclosures and notices to suit their own interventions. Two such additional exercises are included below.

☐ Operationalizing Ethics and Spiritual "Mediatherapy"

Offering and describing books, movies, and other media is not new to counselors or to clients. It is a well-established practice governed by the ethical constraints of the right material for the right client. They should be considered in the light of what is "in the best interest" of the client, not which one took an Academy Award. With the plethora of both spiritual and "self-help" books now available, the counselor's role is less crucial in uncovering good media, than in helping to glean what media are most helpful for a particular client under his or her particular circumstances.

Recommending or offering spiritual or religious media to clients, however, poses the additional constraint of respecting the religious or spiritual motivations of the client. Because of the personal and profound (let alone constitutionally protected) nature of religion, this is a different ethical constraint from, say, offering Adlerian or Freudian material to clients. Most counselors would not be subject to ethical discipline if they suggest psychological material of any school to clients.

This difference can be explained in terms of legitimate expectations. After all, a client should expect to be confronted with psychological or therapeutic theory when they attend counseling. Such psychological material is reasonably allowed in the course of therapy.

The same is not true for counselors. Because most counselors are clinicians and not theologians (in the formal sense) or clergy (usually), counselors must take extra precautions to offer notice and informed consent in suggesting mediatherapy. Counselors must take special ethical attention in choosing the appropriate and therapeutic mediatherapies. To paraphrase another saying, this time from George Orwell, "While all media are equal, some are more equal than others."

Counselors should consider a criteria by which to choose mediatherapy. Choosing media based upon content is always hazardous because it sometimes cannot be chosen objectively—that is, divorced from its religious or spiritual content. While content-based criteria has its place, particulary if it is contraindicated by the counselees themselves, it is tempting for an even conscientious counselor to be tempted to steer counselees away from ideologies about which the counselor has personal reservations.

Below are a set of criterion based not upon content, but upon the therapeutic needs of the client and the ethical demands placed upon the counselor.

1. *Accessibility*: The media should be understandable to the client. Even though it will be the counselor that exploits the necessary issues, the material should not be so difficult or alien to the client that the client cannot relate to it.
2. *Therapeutic utility*: The media should have relevance and applicability in the therapeutic process.
3. *Versatility*: The media should be useable for a client or clients. Not that one media should fit all clients, but a counselor cannot be expected to have unlimited supplies of movies and books available or to reference on every issue for every client. Once a given media has some applicability to some issues for some clients, it may be helpful in a number of different situations. The counselor can help apply the media to the situation.
4. *Longevity*: Some media has a surprisingly long shelf-life. It can stand the test of time. Some media address issues so clearly and deeply that they have applicability far beyond current styles and fashions (including spiritual and therapy fads). A list of books is included in the appendix.

There is one important difference between mediatherapy and meditation which lowers the threat to any client; and thus, lowers the responsibility for the counselor to ensure client safety. Mediatherapy does not, in itself, alter consciousness. Mediatherapy does not entail the dangers inherent in lowering a counselee's defenses or creating psychic vulnerability. Having said all that, the following is a menu of suggestions to conduct mediatherapy:

1. *Is the context or setting of the counseling religious, spiritual, or secular?* Again, this is an issue of legitimate expectations. If a counselor works in a religious setting (Jewish Social Services, Catholic Charities, etc.), counselees can and should expect some references to that faith. In fact, many counselees choose such organizations precisely *because* of their emphasis or connection with the faith group.

   This legitimate expectation allows the counselor greater ethical latitude in suggesting or offering such mediatherapy. Latitude does not mean license however, and it is only one factor in assessing the ethical ecology of the issue and in determining the counselor's duty toward the client.

2. *To satisfy notice and informed consent concerns, the counselor should describe and explain the methodology, goals, and any foreseeable dangers in mediatherapy.* The explanation and description should be specific to the client's own situation and therapeutic goals, not simply a generic description applicable to any client under any circumstances.

   The content of the media should be selected to fit into the client's psychic and spiritual circumstances. The counselor needs client ascent as to the proper goals for the media. For example, if the counselor wants to challenge or to confront a client with some issue, sometimes a movie can have a more immediate and intense impact. On the other hand, an anxious client is less frightened by a movie than reading a book of the same content.

   The content should also be carefully selected for its impact upon the person's faith stance. For example, if interfaith couple (say a Christian and Jew) wants to explore a general context of Ashkenazic Judaism, then a movie like *Fiddler on the Roof* (Jewison, 1971) might be appropriate. If the same couple wants to explore in a more intense and graphic history, then *Schindler's List* (Spielberg, 1993) might be appropriate. Additionally, an intense move like *Schindler's List* may not be appropriate for younger viewers, those prone to hallucinations, or those whose relatives or friends may have been involved in the holocaust. As always, the counselor should check out the media beforehand and discuss with the client any concerns the counselor might have about the client viewing the media. This discussion gives the client "notice."

   Fiddler on the Roof and *Schindler's List* are quite different movies and counselors should use them differently. By the same token, if a Christian client were to want an introduction for his or her Jewish spouse, a movie designed to offer an alternative view of Christianity such as *The Last Temptation of Christ* (or the book) may not be helpful.

   This same differentiation is also useful for exploring spiritual issues or beliefs in movies such as *The Exorcist* or *The Sixth Sense*. These movies can go a long way towards raising issues about the nature of divinity, the interrelationship of the spirit world with the human world, and spiritual and religious interventions and methods of entering spiritual domains.

3. *Has the client already seen the movie, read the book, or other media?* If the client has already seen the media in question, it may be easier to assess the impact upon the client. They have history with it already. The counselor's job in this respect, then, is to clarify and highlight those elements of the media that are most helpful to the client. Many times

a scene, theme, or dialogue specifically addresses therapeutic concerns between the client and counselor. Other times, some part of a movie or book places some concern or issue in a light helpful in the therapeutic process. Even if the client has read the book or seen the movie previously, these elements or issues may have been overlooked. Helping a client "see" something in a book or movie is, in fact, a good analogy for the spiritual or alternative therapeutic model itself—the counselor helps increase the client's awareness about aspects of life that often go unnoticed or ignored.

4. *One way to help ensure consent and compliance is to make the media list together.* Even if the client has not already read the book, seen the movie, or other media, he or she may have heard friends talk about some media that has been helpful to them. Maybe he or she has seen a talk-show or news program or read a review that interested him or her. This even briefest of lists can be an excellent start.

   Browsing in a bookstore is also an excellent way to find just the right book. Many of the larger chains of booksellers have coffee shops attached where the patron is free to examine a book at length in a comfortable setting. Of course, a public library is also an excellent way to browse and to obtain a number of good books. The only problem is you can't write in them!

5. *A "Contract for Mediatherapy" may seem like legal overkill, but it can be useful in committing to writing the principles of consent and notice.* A contract might be useful also in working with clients who may be forgetful, distracted, anxious or otherwise unsure of the process.

   The contract essentially, is in form, very similar to that denoted in the earlier section on meditation. It need not be more than a single page. A few sentences should be devoted to outlining the reason for conducting mediatherapy, a sentence or two should clearly state that the client and counselor reviewed the content of each media, that the client has agreed to see the movie or read the book and that, if the counselor chooses, the client may quit doing so at any time without any negative ramifications from the counselor. Finally, a list of procedures, including a schedule of readings, or a timetable for seeing the movie, and debriefings should be included. Naturally, it should be signed and dated. A witnesses' signature is really legal overkill!

6. *Debrief the next week or at the next scheduled session.* Debriefing serves several purposes: (a) to assess the impact of the media upon the well-being of the client, (b) to assess the therapeutic value of the media exercise on the client, and (c) to reinforce the seriousness with which the counselor takes the exercises. Client safety is always the first and most pressing concern. If a client has an upsetting reaction to the media, the sooner it is addressed in therapy the better. A full discussion of the media and its therapeutic value is the crux of the rationale for conducting the mediatherapy itself. This methodology is not addressed at length here because this book is about law, not about methodology. Finally, the counselor reinforces his or her seriousness about these exercises when they consistently debrief the exercise. If the counselor lets the discussion slide, it undermines the exercises' importance.

☐ Conclusion

Ethics and law are siblings, sometimes rival siblings. Ethical principles often underpin law. Law is often the consequence of ethical notions of a society. Ethics, like law, is based upon principles that are found in the foundational documents and cultural icons of a people—Western philosophical traditions of Plato, Aristotle, the Bible, and Grimm's Fairy Tales. Newer principles, people, and icons always evolve and change ethical values. Diverse persons and images such as the Dalai Lama, Mother Theresa, Zen Buddhism, Shamanism, John Wayne, Clint Eastwood, Audrie Hepburn, Bishop Desmond Tutu, and Princess Diana add to our ethical mix. This chapter offers primary ethical principles at play in the practices of counselors who use spiritual or complementary therapies.

Such counselors need to be thoroughly aware of their own discipline's ethical standards, how such standards are determined, specific instances of such standards, and how they might apply to new, innovative, spiritual and complementary therapies. Oftentimes, ethical standards lag behind innovations in the field. If a spiritual or complementary therapy seems to challenge or to violate the profession's ethical standards, the counselor should be fully appraised of the consequences and aware of his or her legal and ethical options.

Most of us can still remember when the popular and professional attitude toward acupuncture was something less than respectful and welcoming. Now there is at least a tentative acceptance of this practice and, in many states, acupuncturists are licensed. The same change in acceptance can be said for herbal remedies.

Counselors who know the sources and fundamental principles of their profession's ethical codes are in a better position to know to where the ethical standards are likely to evolve. Because spiritual and complementary therapies often present "cases of first impression" among their professions and licensing boards, such counselors must be able to articulate their positions with ethical language and principles that are clearly understood by those making such judgements. This chapter has presented forms, concepts, and principles toward that end.

☐ Legal Audits and Exercises

1. How would you describe your own spiritual life if you were asked to do so by a client? Are you comfortable speaking about your spiritual experiences with clients? Under what circumstances would you draw limits? Do you make a distinction between religion and spirituality? If you do, what is your criteria for doing so? How does your spiritual life impact or influence your professional life or the way in which you address client or policy issue, if any?
2. How did you get started in using the interventions you use? What experiences prompted you to begin using them? What are their advantages and disadvantages? How would you describe those clients who are amenable to gaining from them and how would you describe the clients who might be harmed by them?
   Are your spiritual or alternative interventions connected to or arising out of a spiritual cosmology? If they are, how does the cosmology impact your practice interventions?
3. Make your own "ethical ecology" of using spiritual or alternative interventions. Make an "ecology" using an ethical or legal issue relevant to you. Who are the components in your ecology? What values, motivations, or drives do they espouse? What are the relationships between the components? Do they form coalitions?
   What values in the "ethical ecology" do you find most compelling? Why? What are the values *you* insert into the ecology? How do your values clash or compliment the values of the other players in the ecology?
4. Do you have a document that explains the spiritual or alternative technique(s) that you use? What are its components? Do you have expected outcomes, possible harmful or negative effects, and a procedural outline?

5. Having dutifully performed #4, above, what makes it a helpful, ethically responsible, informational document and not a contract? What words are you using to portray the effectiveness of the interventions? Do you in any way promise or guarantee results? Do you even imply that certain results will flow from the interventions? Do you adequately disclose possible negative reactions to the interventions? Do you conduct the interventions in such a way as to mitigate against such negative impacts?

Informed Consent Form: Ethics and Procedures for Relaxation/Visualizations

A. **Notice:** Participants should be alerted as to what is next in the therapeutic process.
B. **Informed consent:** Participants should understand and consent to:
    a) the purpose of the technique, b) the methodology, c) any dangers, and d) precautions against ill effects.
C. **Voluntary participation and non-retaliatory withdrawal:** Participants should know they can withdraw with no negative consequences.

1. **Relaxation:** Proper meditative posture and successive muscle relaxing
2. **Visualization:** Imagining relaxing scenes, experiences, persons
3. **Affirmation:** Positive expression—hope, problem resolution, overcome some anxiety, imaginative role play, etc.
4. **Thanksgiving:** Gratitude for gifts already given and future boons—concretizes and embeds the boons, heightens expectancy.
5. **Returning:** Participants will be recentered and warned against doing any potentially dangerous activity until they are is safe to do so.

I have read the foregoing and fully understand its contents and implications.

Signed: _____   *Date:* _____

FIGURE 5.1. Informed Consent Form: Ethics and Procedure for Relaxation/Visualizations

Religious Affiliation, "Cults," Coercion, and Counseling

☐ Objectives

1. To define and to explain dynamics of sectarian spiritual groups (often called "cults"—this is a term the author eschews because it has become prejudicial).
2. To explore how and why a client might become involved with such groups, with the purpose of elaborating on the legal and ethical consequences for counselors who work with such clients.
3. To offer tools for the counselor to discern the usefulness or harm of such groups.
4. To explain legal aspects when counselors become "expert witnesses" for or against such groups.
5. To illustrate statutes that may directly impact some sectarian groups and their members' behavior—thus impacting potential counselors. These statutes include "ritual mutilation" and "ritualized child abuse."
6. To examine and to explain legal consequences for counselors, and their agencies, who become involved in counseling, deprogramming, rescuing, or otherwise involved with such groups.

The importance of legal considerations discussed in this chapter cannot be overstated. Several legal and ethical issues for spiritual and complementary counselors are directly and indirectly addressed in this chapter. First, various religious groups have been the subject of controversy centering upon their recruitment and retention of members as well as the content and implementation of their message.

The DSM-IV (American Psychological Association, 1994) diagnosis V62.89 "Religious or Spiritual Problem" (noted in the Preface) is an illustration of how religious and spiritual membership can result in clinical issues presented to counselors.

This category can be used when the focus of clinical attention is a religious or spiritual problem. Examples include distressing experiences that involve loss or questioning of faith, problems associated with conversion to a new faith, or questioning of spiritual values that may not necessarily be related to an organized church or religious institution.

Families of religious or spiritual group members may raise the issues in their own therapy. Group members may present issues of their own arising out of the teachings, discipline, or practice of such religious or spiritual groups. Counselors need to be aware of how such groups may trigger legal issues and ethical issues for clients and family members.

Second, coercion is a subject that this book has already addressed. Counselors need to have tools to differentiate between coercion, suggestion, and encouragement in their own practices and among religious and spiritual groups. Clients who are involved in such groups may raise these issues. Family members or friends of those in such groups may raise them. Either way, the counselor needs to be appraised of how legal and ethics views coercion, support and the considerable grey area between.

Third, issues surrounding religious groups offers the occasion to apply the legal concepts of *respondeat superior* and **vicarious liability**. These concepts are widely applicable to counselors, their supervisors, and their agencies or owners. Religious or spiritual groups offer a specific, relevant opportunity to explore these vital legal concepts.

This chapter will address legal and ethical issues arising from a client's interest, participation, or activities in cults. Given the nature of this book, we will address only cults with a religious or spiritual connection. Even this restriction, however, casts a wide net. We will include discussions and illustrate several "cults." The author places cults in quotes because the designation of a "cult" sometimes implies a negative bias toward a group. The author implies no such bias. The reader might read the word cult in this book as if it were in quotes. Religious affiliation will often be used instead.

This chapter will address the following four questions: 1) what, exactly, *is* a cult? 2) who might be susceptible to cult membership? 3) how can a counselor tell when a client's cult activity is self-destructive or just unusual? 4) If and when a client gets involved with a cult, how should the counselor respond? 5) what are the legal consequences if a counselor does try to extricate a client (or anyone else) from a cult?

The importance of this chapter may not be self-evident, especially for those whose practice does not directly involve clients whose membership in religious and spiritual groups may be seen by some as troublesome or who are school counselors who need to assess membership in groups. But the principles, discussed here, are widely applicable to counselors addressing such far-flung issues as coercion, client membership in any organization that might be troublesome to themselves or their families, First Amendment protections for religious or spiritual activities, child custody issues, criminal abuse, and counselors who work for child protective services or related agencies.

Additionally this chapter applies the legal principles of *respondeat superior* and vicarious liability to counselors. These concepts are especially important for counselors who manage or own their own business or for counselors who supervise other counselors either in government or private industry.

☐ Case Study: The Counselor, Coercion and Religious Protection

When Taylor, the plaintiff, was 21 years old, he entered the monastery of the Holy Protection of the Blessed Virgin Mary. His parents were not pleased. They hired a deprogramming organization—"an organization attempting a psychological shock treatment on members of non-mainstream religious sects in an effort to sever their involvement with a religious cult lifestyle"(***Taylor v. Gilmartin***, 1983, p. 1348). A psychologist "with apparently some experience in treating cult members" was the primary named defendant (p. 1349).

Taylor alleged that the defendants kept him in an Akron, Ohio, motel room under constant guard. His deprogrammers constantly yelled at him, threw cold water at him, deprived him of sleep, told him he was going to have shock treatment, told him he would be tracked down by the state police, shaved his beard, and tore off his clothing. Taylor's father applied to become his temporary guardian. Eventually the deprogrammers told him the temporary guardianship would be made permanent. He also alleged that the defendants moved him from Akron, Ohio, to Phoenix, Arizona, to commence the rehabilitation phase of the deprogramming. The father hoped that, as Taylor's guardian, he would be in a better position for the son to leave the monastery. Taylor finally escaped while he was in Phoenix and returned to the monastery.

The plaintiff sued agents of the deprogramming group and the deprogramming organization itself for intentional infliction of emotional distress, false imprisonment, and conspiracy to commit assault and battery, among other things. The federal district court issued a summary judgment for the defendants. The plaintiff appealed.

The appellate court's decision was not good news for psychologist nor for the deprogrammers. First, the order for the temporary guardianship was voided because Taylor was given no notice for a hearing and there were no signs of mental illness. We have discussed the importance of "notice" in the context of due process considerations. Because the order was void, the programmers were not shielded from the negligence claim of false imprisonment.

Second, the appeals court also held that the claim for intentional infliction of emotional distress should not have been dismissed. Instead this was ruled as a question of fact for the jury to decide. Third, the conspiracy claim that defendants deprived Taylor of his equal protection rights, including freedom of religion and freedom of association, failed. The court found that the court used in the guardianship was not part of any conspiracy.

The reader by now probably has a good sense of the importance of this case for counselors working with religious groups. Given the religious protections already addressed in Chapter 1, it is not surprising that the plaintiff could present a constitutional claim against the deprogrammers. These claims were for depriving him of both freedom of religion and freedom of association. This is a good example of how religious freedom is applied against counselors who use coercive tactics upon involuntary subjects. Not only does the law allow for the negligence actions such as false imprisonment and intentional (or negligent) infliction of emotional distress, but also allows for the religious (or spiritual) claim. It seems likely, moreover, that most "cults" have some arguable religious or spiritual basis. It is not hard for many such groups to allege a religious component to their beliefs or behaviors.

Moreover, this case illustrates how an ethical evaluation on the part of a mental health professional—after all, a psychologist was the primary named defendant in this suit—is fundamental to a counselor's legal sophistication. The following comments, as usual, are not an attempt at "Monday morning quarterbacking" the actions or inactions on the part of the psychologist (or anyone else). These comments flow from the general facts of this case without regard to any specific acts or allegations.

First, the "ethical ecology" provides a context in which to view the general nature of this case. Who are the players? Who are those holding the power? What are their motivations? What is the role of the counseling professional? What are the ethical values at play here? It is clear that the counselor needs to define his or her role in the "ethical ecology" with clarity and precision. Is the role defined by the one paying the bill or by the professionals themselves?

It is important to fully appreciate the dynamics inherent in any counseling situation. This appreciation includes knowing exactly what the client wants. But that determination is not the end of the inquiry. It is only the beginning. The full appreciation also includes the impact of the counselor's actions upon *other* constituents of the ecology. For example, the counselor needs to assess how independent his or her assessments, diagnosis, or testimony can be. Are there factors that may compromise such independence? For example, exactly who is paying your bill? Who has *de facto* control of your motivations and drives?

While it is important to discern the goals and objectives of the client, an expected role does not always translate into a duty. These considerations are not dispositive. This is why evaluating duties are so important.

Second, what is the duty of the mental health professional if he or she is called upon to examine, let alone deprogram, Taylor? To whom does he or she owe the duty? In this instance, is the duty owed to the one paying the bill or to the one who is the most vulnerable. It seems clear to this writer that the counselor's role and duty is primarily, if not exclusively, defined by his or her ethical and legal constraints imposed by his or her professional organizations and licensing boards as well as the legal milieu. All other considerations, including the potential for a paycheck, must be subservient to these jealous mistresses—law and ethics. No matter the gender, serving two masters or mistresses is a losing proposition.

Third, how would you rank the respective duties? If someone else was not paying the bill for this deprogramming intervention, would you as a counselor find that Taylor needed even a temporary guardian under these circumstances?

Before we get too deeply entrenched in law and ethics, we'd better pull back and better define the nature and function of what many call "cults." "As an issue is defined, so it is largely determined"—I like this quote and it's mine. It means that if you define something as evil or as derogatory, it is easier to dismiss it.

Defining or "recharacterizing" an issue is a persuasive technique as old as the hills. Some persons are defined as "patriots," others as "terrorists." It depends upon the point of view of the one naming the issue. Politicians and lawyers try to "define away" and negate their opponents' positions all the time. We will not engage in useless semantics here. We need to describe and understand how law and ethics view religious affiliation.

☐ What is a "Cult?"

A negative spin has become attached to the term "cult." We might do well to remember that many religions today started out with "cultic" elements. In the past decades, the media of the United States has reported on a variety of cults. These reports, however, have almost always been connected to the proverbial "parade of horribles": Jim Jones and the People's Temple mass suicide, Branch Davidians at Waco, the Heaven's Gate mass suicide in California, and the "trench coat mafia" and the shootings at Columbine High School in Colorado have all received much press attention.

Little attention, however, has been paid to what a cult is and what dynamics are involved in it. A "cult" comes from a Latin word for "cultivation." It has come to mean the "labor" or "worship." In that broad sense it encompasses much of religion and spirituality, particularly in its liturgical or worshiping aspects. In that sense a Moslem, for example, engages in his or her cultic activity during the month of Ramadan fasting, or a Christian engages in his or her cultic activity when they take the cup and bread in the act of Holy Communion. Returning to a technical definition of "cult" might help to clarify what one means when they term some group or activity as a "cultic."

Taken in its more popular, narrow sense, a "cult" is a splinter group or a sectarian group. Such groups may wear clothing different from the predominant society or they may engage in religious practices unknown or little-known to the rest of society. But that might also include such well-established and benign groups as the Amish or Hasidic Jews. So, how does a counselor differentiate membership in a group that chooses to live differently than "mainstream" U.S. society and groups that might pose a real, credible, and imminent threat to its members? This concern, of course, is heighted where there are minors are involved.

The answer, this author asserts, is not to judge a book by its cover. Judge a group by its activities, not by its ideologies. It seems likely, for example, that abolishing trenchcoats from highschool wardrobes will not put an end to school violence. More complex issues require comprehensive solutions. To judge the alleged harm religious affiliation might pose by what the groups wears, its insignia, its face paint, or its tatoos. This book asserts that the behaviors of how groups process their members, the process by which they are integrated into the group, and how the leaders process their authority can offer more penetrating insights into the potential harm of a group than examining more superficial means. This methodology is described as the *process* over *content* approach.

This book relates methodologies for assessing the "dangerousness" of religious groups. Basically, this book asserts that a process, not content, approach for assessing such groups is both constitutionally and therapeutically correct.

Obviously, what concerns parents and the general public about "cults" are those groups that threaten or invite violence or those groups who use coercive means to achieve membership or achieve their aims. But it is useful to remember that the First Amendment, as we have seen, is specifically designed to protect minority religious groups. While the government may have limited control or aid religion in only re-stricted ways, it must usually take a "hands off" policy. So, government intervention in "religious affiliation" is a balancing act between the rights of the individual and the need to protect society.

A particularly helpful set of "cult" criteria is (a) a leader who may become the subject of worship him or herself, (b) coercive persuasion, and (c) exploitation (Lifton, 1981). This set of criteria may well serve as a basis for a diagnostic examination for a "cult" over a "sect," or other religious group.

So, too, is the intervention of the counselor. The counselor must balance the rights of the client to engage in religious—even cultic activity—against the potential harm of that activity to the client or to society. With this balance in mind, we turn to a discussion of cultic, cliques, and religious affiliation dynamics.

How a counselor characterizes a set of behaviors can produce profound differences in how he or she approaches the person exhibiting those behaviors. "Cliques" can be quite different from "cults." Psychologists Tom Dolan and Peter Sheraf have outlined the potential costs and benefits of cliques. Cliques can help people: improve their self-esteem, increase their sense of belonging, share happiness and a support system, and learn how to react to new situations. The down side of cliques is that they can: encourage people to do things they would not normally do, create an acceptance of negative peer pressure, mask a sense of alienation, justify a less tolerant attitude of people outside their group, and to make people feel isolated if they are rejected by the clique (Farmer, 1999).

It is interesting to note that the term "clique" comes to us from an Old French word, from around 1711, "claque," which referred to a group in a theater hired to applaud at the appropriate times (Barnhart, 1995). Today, a clique is also a group that binds itself by its behaviors and image. A hypothesis comparing cliques to cults (or religious affiliations) might produce the following risky generalizations:

1. Cliques are less concerned with ultimate things than are cults or religious affiliations. Where a clique may center its activities on acceptance into the cheerleading squad or the football team or the marching band, a cult is more likely to center onto more ultimate concerns such as the purpose for human life, the end of the world, or the meaning behind some points of a sacred text.
2. Cliques are more likely to wear badges of a transient nature, while cults (religious affiliations) can have a more historic, even mythic, intention with their symbols. It seems like the wearing of a certain type of sneakers, blue jeans, or jacket is more associated with a clique. A religious affiliation will wear, carry, or otherwise honor symbols with a longer history. A traditional symbol associated with the Wicca affiliation is the pentagram—a design we discussed in Chapter 1. The pentagram is a symbol of ancient meaning and usage.
3. Cults or religious affiliations are much more likely to be granted the constitutional status of religions (as we have seen in chapter one) than are cliques. As noted in that earlier chapter, the badges of a religion, for constitutional purpose, are wide, but not infinite. Where cliques might wear the same hair cuts, jackets, and other paraphernalia, the same might be said for other groups known as "clubs" or "gangs."
4. To go out on a limb even further, this author might suggest that "gang" or a "club" will not achieve constitutional protection either. While such groups may have a longer history than a "clique," it still may not be a *sacred* history, such groups might have well-defined symbols, but not *sacred* symbols. Acts might be important, but may not convey the tradition and depth of meaning and venerability necessary for constitutional protection.

If nothing else, the foregoing may produce some discussion. The point is that there is no bright line distinction between cliques, clubs, gangs, cults, and religious groups. There are only degrees. We have here, and in Chapter 1, tried to point out some indicia that courts use to award or to withhold constitutional protection. We continue that process below with another hypothesis, three dynamics which may animate the group or "cultic" process:

1. *The religious group or "cult" against the prevailing norms.* First, some groups may separate themselves from contemporary social, spiritual, or religious norms. It is not unknown for a benign religious group to be clear that their group has some special or unique knowledge or skills that benefit themselves or others. These special skills can be very helpful in instilling the members with the need for acts of mercy and charity and the internal structures of mysticism and prayer with which to carry out such beneficial acts. These skills and knowledge, of course, can set the group against the rest of mainstream society. It is edifying to remember that the Roman empire banned the nascent Christian Church until Constantine lifted the ban early in the fourth century.

   It is worth noting that Methodists, Presbyterians, and other non-Church of England religious groups had to get a license to preach and teach in colonial America. It is no wonder that the Founding Fathers had cast a leery eye on any attempts by the government to control religious activity.

   What may distinguish harmful cultic behavior from beneficial behavior is the degree to which the group excludes the outside the world. If the group severely, consistently, and broadly restricts outside contact or influence, the group may impose a more coercive character. Most spiritual or religious groups fully engage the outside world, even if it means holding a critical attitude toward it. For example, the Amish or Hasidic Jews may choose not to have televisions, to have their own newspapers, their own language, and wish to remain apart in dress and clothing from aspects of the outside world, but there is not the sense that the members will be kept from any or most contact.

2. *The group or "cult" against families and government.* Second, the group may separate itself from the contemporary government. This, in itself, does not mean the cult is coercive. For example, the Amish won the legal right to omit the later grades of high school.

Perhaps the most significant difference, however, between a more and less coercive group is the extent to which it encourages or eliminates family contact or relationships with friends. While many religious groups have profoundly critical attitudes toward current culture (with some justification!), they do not seek a separation with their family. In fact, many times the opposite is true.

Many spiritual groups seek, in fact, to increase the solidarity with their families. Family solidarity may well help solidify their relations with the group itself. Fair enough. But family may also critique the religious group as well. It cannot be assumed that families will uncritically support the spiritual group as we saw in the *Taylor* case.

3. *The group or "cult" solidifies internal cohesion.* Third, the group may solidify the loyalty of members into the cult. Initiation can be through various means, but it seems to serve the same purposes. Initiation seeks to induct the members into some purportedly secret knowledge. This knowledge is usually special, even unique, to the cult. For example, the Jim Jones People's Temple *group* (the author actually prefers this term over "cult") apparently determined that they had special knowledge about the end of the world and that they would avoid the fallout by congregating in Guyana, South America. The rest of the world, they were led by Jones to believe, or a significant portion thereof, would probably be destroyed. Refuge, supposedly, would be found in the People's Temple.

The ways in which groups recruit and retain members vary. For our purposes here, counselors are concerned with clients who are recruited and retained by coercive means. This is a grey area of ethics and law amid a grey area of spirituality and religion. Coercive for one person, may mean spiritual discipline for another. After all, isn't the threat of excommunication or even the implied threat of hell or eternal damnation prevalent in many religions a form of coercion?

We have to go deeper to reveal the distinctions between accepting articles of faith on their own merits over and against those coerced in some harmful or untoward way. Again, it is often a gossamer line between "acceptable" or "normal" motivations and coercion. For example, it is a truism that many people attend or return to some religious affiliation after some hiatus when they begin to have children. Could having children, then, be considered a coercion to attend religious services?

A short course on what is called dangerous group is offered by Kleiner (2000, p. 49) in an article on the increasing conflict of colleges with religious or spiritual groups. In a sidebar titled "what to avoid" the magazine suggests (these are direct quotes):

1. *Charismatic, authoritarian leaders.* Requiring absolute devotion to one person, who dictates how members should think and act.

2. *Mind control and manipulation.* Using controlling methods, including physical and/or psychological isolation from family and friends.
3. *Misleading recruitment tactics.* "Love bombing," or showering prospective members with attention, the use of front names that mask group affiliation.

This criterion focuses upon persons getting involved in a cult. This brief criteria may be helpful for students and others contemplating such acts. It may also be helpful for counselors who are looking for guidelines and help in counseling students, some of whom may be minors.

Preliminary questions, suggestions, and issues particulary addressed to counselors who are in the educational environment may include:

1. This entire chapter, of course, should be read in the light of the discussion of the First Amendment, particularly in the introduction and chapter one.
2. Be a counselor and let the lawyers be lawyers. Counselors cannot be counselors while solving legal issues. Yes, try to anticipate legal issues as they arise. After reading this book you should have a pretty good idea of how to express a legal issue when you consult your school's attorney.
3. While it is good to anticipate legal issues before they arise, do not try to solve legal issues. First, this dissuades you from your proper work. Second, that's a lawyer's job. This book is trying to avoid counseling malpractice. Don't place yourself in jeopardy for legal malpractice by dispensing legal advice!
4. Share your concern over coercive religious affiliation, not only with your school legal counsel, but with school administrators. Such administrators have broad authority and should have policy and protocols for who can be on school property for religious purposes. We have addressed this elsewhere.
5. Do not become embroiled in verbal disputes with the representative of a religious group. This usually is counterproductive.
6. So, be a counselor to your students. Be a sounding board for their concerns. Engage in active listening for their hopes and aspirations, as well as their concerns. Reflect their inconsistencies and engage their critical thinking processes, in good faith, to help clarity their rationale and values. Your own biases and beliefs should play no part in such examinations. Remember, you are engaging them as an educational specialist, not as an evangelist.

Perhaps this debate is better understood, and the issues more clearly framed, if we examine the vulnerability of the adherent.

☐ Who Might be Susceptible to "Cult" Membership?

Counselors need to assess the susceptibility of their clients to coercive measures. Part of understanding the vulnerability, or one might say, acceptability of religious affiliation, is understanding the current context of the individual's life? Is there a crisis, or an impending crisis, in the person's life? Crises can put one "off balance" and momentarily deprive the person of making decisions in their best interest. Loss of a loved one, changing jobs, separation, and divorce are all examples of crises. Some say adolescence is a form of crisis, but we leave that characterization to other experts. These crises may be analogized to a decided lack of informed consent.

Is the person running to something or from something? This question gets at issues from another angle. Does the person seem to have a better idea of what they *do not* want than what they *do* want? Are they running away from some crisis, such as abuse home environment, school trouble, relationship trouble, trouble with the police? If they are so engaged in running avoiding something, they may not be aware of exactly into what they are delving.

How capable of discernment are they? This question goes to the mental status of the adherent. This in no way implies that the adherent has mental illness. But running from abusive or other crisis situations may impair a person's judgment. Would they make the choices they are making under any other circumstances? Testing the choices of a client may well fall within the scope of a counselor's role.

To avoid being judgmental, it may help for the counselor to employ the very same "testing" process he or she would use when evaluating any other decision the counselor may make under similar circumstances—for example, if the client were to want to get married, buy a house, or make any other important decision. The same sound tools that the counselor would apply could be used for helping a client "test" decisions of religious or spiritual affiliation. In fact, it may be an educative exercise if the counselor were to ask him or herself, "Why should I treat a religious or spiritual decision any differently than any other decision my client might make?"

How capable of exercising options are they? While the previous paragraphs centered upon issues of awareness and discernment. This question centers upon the issue of capabilities or power to *act upon* that awareness. Some counselees have more money, education, experience, support, and maturity than other clients. That is to say, not all clients have the same choices nor even the same chance at the same choices. Counselors cannot expect all counselees to exercise or access all choices equally. Counselors need to make their assessments not only in light of their client's ability to perceive choices in their lives, but to access those choices. When a person's choices are limited, by whatever means, they cannot be expected to choose the most self-affirming, rationale, self-interested choices.

☐ How can a Counselor Tell when a Client's Group or "Cult" Activity is Self-Destructive or Just Unusual?

In this sense we make try to calculate to what extent a client's involvement with a faith group is harmful, a waste of time, a fad, innocent curiosity or a serious search for something spiritual, or some combination thereof. Of course, this is a difficult determination, one fraught with the errors and human biases of those making the determinations. In hindsight, what would Columbine school counselors give to reassess the meaning of the "Trenchcoat Mafia" for at least two members of that group. That is one reason why this author will not use the somewhat grandiose term diagnosis but rather assessment. Actually, the best term might be the legal term "discovery" meaning to gather facts and to interpret those facts.

☐ Assessments or "Discovery"

This section describes a set of assumptions, taken from the *U.S. v. Meyers* (1996) case we discussed in the introduction, that can help put the assessment of religious affiliation in context. That case has renewed importance in our current discussion because it emphasizes three items. It bears repeating that we examine religious affiliation, not in terms of our own experience, but in terms of their constitutional status. These assumptions are described below:

1. *Process of discovery.* Discovery is the gathering of facts in order to arrive at conclusions. When gathering facts about a group or religious affiliation, it is important—like any good investigator—to gather facts then form conclusions, not the other way around. If an investigator gathers only that data which conforms to his or her preconceived notions, he or she might well miss important clues and not see alternative conclusions.
2. *Process not content.* Ask process questions that center around the behavior of the group and its processes for obtaining members and their integration into the group. Focusing upon the beliefs of the group may "blind" the investigator into determining which beliefs are right and wrong. As we have noted in the *Meyers* case, courts will not examine the content of beliefs, but how they have been arrived at, how long the tradition of belief is, how extensive and well-formed the liturgical and ecclesiological aspects are, and how comprehensive those beliefs are. In determining the likelihood of constitutional protection, these elements (and others like them) should be the focus, not whether one agrees with them.
3. *Constitution protects "religion," not a "way of life" or "philosophy."* As we noted earlier, the constitution defines its religious protections broadly, but not infinitely. The following numbered suggestions help the counselor determine the likelihood of harm to a client, not the protection courts would afford an activity. That determination would, of course, ultimately need to be argued by legal counsel.

The assessment or discovery should be "content-sensitive," but not "content-based." That is, the ideas and notions and beliefs should be taken seriously, but should not be the sole determining factor as to whether the group might be dangerous. For example, it is not uncommon for spiritual groups to have apocalyptic ideologies. "Apocalyptic" simply means revealing. Hence, the final book of the New Testament is called "Revelation" or the "Apocalypse of John." In current parlance, however, it often is connected to a catastrophic revealing of God's will. Eschatology is the proper name for the "end times;" so, an apocalyptic eschatology is a divine revelation connected to the end times (however that is interpreted).

Of course, the year 2000 saw an upsurge in millennial fervor, some of it apocalyptic in tone. In January of 1999, a group calling itself Concerned Christians was arrested and deported from Israel for allegedly planning violent and extreme acts in Jerusalem. They later left Israel without incident and the charges were dropped. No weapons were found among their belongings (Ackerman, 1999).

The legal term of discovery is also used here because it refers to the process by which information is legally relevant material is uncovered. Often this is done by serving subpoenas or simply by reviewing documents or interviewing potential witnesses. While not exactly a forensic fishing expedition, discovery trolls the legal waters with some deliberation and purpose. Often the complaint is modified with more charges once discovery reveals more charges. Similarly, a counselor continually discovers or assesses his or her client.

By the same token, the discovery should be highly process sensitive. Perhaps the first factor to note is whether there is a coercive element in the group process. Coercion could include actions that employ means of fraud, intimidation, or threat. Does the group request, recommend, or require compliance?

On a personal note, as a Presbyterian minister, I make pleas to my congregation all the time for donations to the church, to community charities, and to worthwhile groups all around the world. Without such donations the church roof would continue to leak, the electric bill wouldn't get paid, and the pastor couldn't pay his phone bill. At what point would such pleas become coercive? If I told the congregation they'd all go to hell if they didn't tithe? If I said God would punish their children if parents didn't donate? If I said God would bless them with nice homes and pay raises if they gave more money to the church? Of course, my congregation wouldn't believe me anyway!

Second, to what extent is there coercion? If group solidarity approaches coercion, to what degree does it demand? Does it want a title of 10% or does the group want its members to sell all their earthly good, donate them to the group's holding company and to follow the leader, lock, stock, and barrel to their secret encampment somewhere?

Another important question to ask is how much the cult requires of its members. Most religious or spiritual groups require something of its members. It can be taken as judicial notice that many Christian groups use the figure of 10% as a tithing mark for donations or contributions of money, time, and gifts. Thousands of churches each and every year "Stewardship season" is the time when—is there an element of "coercion" present here? Perhaps! It's the right thing to do; its the *godly* thing to do! Where does this tried and true guilt end and where does debilitating coercion begin?

One way to draw the line is to determine, "What if I give nothing? What is the punishment if I cannot and do not give a dime? Will I go to hell on this one criterion? Will I be excommunicated? Will I be harmed in any way? Or will I be allowed to worship there still? Discovering the penalties for noncompliance is a good way to assess the nature of the pressure involved.

How open or closed is the group about its leadership, decision-making processes, and finances? "Follow the money," was the mantra of Deep Throat, the character in *All the President's Men* (Pakula, 1976)—the Bernstein/Woodward account of the fall of Richard Nixon. Money is often an excellent gauge for the level of openness and well-functioning of a group.

In most churches and religious groups, the collection, accounting, and disbursement of its funds is a painfully open process. Often the group followers have painstakingly thorough accounting procedures followed punctiliously. Often, the leader is barred from most transactions with cross-signatures on checks. Often, the leader's salary and benefits are open for public scrutiny and even voting.

Does the leader require an ideology or idolatry? Akin to the above discussion on the openness of finances, the leader's sense of his or her own role and power can also reveal the character of a group. The operative difference between a person wedded to an ideology and to their own idolatry is the sense of objectivity. Can such leaders put themselves in another's shoes, or does everyone need to conform to their cosmologies? Does the leader seem to grasp at an ideology out of his or her own need, or does it seem to arise out of an authentic desire to help?

Can the leader laugh at himself or herself? Leaders who can laugh at themselves may be ones who do not take themselves so seriously that they want to bend others to their own will. Leaders who can freely admit their own foibles and shortcomings are less likely to demand perfection (even less, total obedience) from followers.

☐ If a Client Gets Involved With a Group or "Cult," How Should the Counselor Respond?

Lifton (1981) suggests that restraint should be exercised by mental health counselors while coercion should be challenged either by the spiritual group or by those opposed to that group. If a parent or friend coerces someone to leave a group, sometimes it solidifies that person's attachment to the group. At the very least, it undermines the person's autonomy and integrity. If the person is a minor and is physically or psychologically prevented from seeing those legally authorized for their care, criminal charges may be lodged against the group. In that case, the law enforcement, not the counselor, takes the lead in any event. The counselor has an important, but supportive, role.

On the other side of the coin, the counselor can critique coercive elements of any spiritual or religious group with which a client may be involved. It is important to note that a *critique* is not a *criticism*. Criticism is a judgment, maybe even a pre-judgment, about a group or affiliation with a view or deprecation or denunciation. Often a group is denounced for a single reason.

A critique is another matter. A critique is a systematic, methodical, good faith (non-malicious) interpretation of a group or affiliation. If not objective, it is at least balanced.

Carloyn Wah, a New Jersey lawyer concentrating in child custody and visitation, has written a brace of articles that specifically address the role of mental health counselors and religious affiliation. These articles also offer excellent clues about how counselors can analyze religious affiliations in the light of children's best interest. In her article titled "The Role of the Mental Health Care Professional in Evaluating a Minor's Capacity to Select Religious Affiliation" (1998), she reviews the traditional custody arrangement of religion follows custody to the emerging standard with an emphasis upon the child's own decision-making capacity. The hallowed best interest of the child standard is little help when a dispute about religious upbringing arises between the custodial and non-custodial parent. After all, how can one rule about which religious or spiritual tradition is better?

A case directly on point helps. In **Khalsa v. Khalsa** (1988), a trial court in New Mexico ordered the non-custodial parent to restrict Sikh religious activities during visitations. The children were six and two years old at the time of separation and had been raised in a Sikh environment. After separation, the father, remaining active in the faith, wished for the children to maintain their Sikh religious and cultural identities and filed for sole custody.

In reversing the previous decision, the appeals court decided along traditional legal lines and required that any justification that prohibits religious restrictions in visitations must be specifically, factually, and convincingly demonstrated. The court required the trial court to consider these tests, which can be very helpful and applicable for counselors in unpacking the religious affiliation of children:

1. Whether there is detailed, factual evidence that conflicting beliefs or practices (of the parents) pose substantial physical or emotional harm.
2. Whether restricting the religious interaction between the parent and child is likely to relieve this tension.
3. Whether such restrictions are narrowly tailored to minimize interference with the parent's religious freedom.
4. A fourth test, following the third, is the author's suggestion, stemming from a recent legal trend recognizing a limited right of children to determine their own religious or spiritual lives. This trend is evidenced in such legal regimes as the U.N. Convention on the Rights of the Child (Bullis, 1991b). We examine this test below.

The bottom line is: speculation should play no part in religious or spiritual factors in custody determinations. In fact, the American Psychological Association disallows a psychologist from making custody recommendations when he or she sees one of the parents with or without the children (Wah, 1998, p. 234). The same is true for evaluating a minor's religious or spiritual choice in religious affiliation. While there is no question that parents and guardians have control over much of their children's lives, including their religious and spiritual lives, counselors are not parents and their role in acting as expert witnesses must be circumspect.

☐ Counselors as Expert Witnesses in Cases Involving Religious Affiliation

It is no secret that in more complicated custody cases, specifically where sexual abuse or harm stemming from religious or spiritual affiliation is alleged, that counselors are often asked to testify as expert witnesses, write evaluations, or otherwise serve to help the court to make custody decisions. Moreover, counselors are also asked by parents to evaluate their children's religious affiliation. Wah (1998) suggests objective tests and corroborative witnesses as two principle means by which counselors can evaluate the present, imminent, or possible future harm. She recommends objective tests, available to counselors, that help evaluate the child's self-esteem, hopefulness, educational functioning, anxiety and coping skills, and critical thinking and moral judgment.

We addressed the role of expert witnesses at some length in chapter three. Some key points bear emphasis here, especially as they relate to the issue of religious affiliation in child custody claims. Shuman (1997) asserting that the "current wave of litigation (including the *Daubert* case we discussed earlier) reflects a shift towards greater restrictiveness . . . " (p. 558). Thus, counselors who testify as experts about children may look forward to increased scrutiny of their credentials. As the courts become more accustomed to social science experts, they also may become more demanding of credentials specific to both their general field of expertise and the specific issue about which they testify. Shuman goes on to write that when "courts face mental health professionals' pure clinical inference to explain a child's delayed reporting of abuse based on the expert's theories derived from treating abused children that do not purport to rely on scientific research, courts generally only scrutinize the expert's qualifications, not the expert's methods and procedures and whether there are good grounds to support them" (pp. 562–563). Thus, Shuman speaks to a trend that courts may apply to child custody cases as well.

Shuman's insights can also be applied to custody assessments when religious or spiritual behaviors are at issue. The following are general suggestions that the counselor may wish to take into consideration whether they are serving as expert witnesses in a custody or removal dispute, whether the counselor is asked to make an assessment for the courts or social services, or whether the counselor is asked to opine in a private counseling session about a child's situation by a custodial parent, a concerned parent, or a parent hoping for custody.

1. *Does the one asking for the assessment have an agenda, or is he or she a relatively disinterested party?* A judge, for example, will be an objective party. He or she will not have a point of view. However, others may not be so sanguine as to the results of your inquiries or your opinions.

   A prescription for the natural tendency to "please the one who pays you" might be to imagine that you will have to defend both the content of your opinions and your credentials for presenting them in court. You will have to defend these in the form a cross-examination—a form of pain sometimes likened to a tooth extraction. Even if you will not have to undergo such an ordeal, imagining that you will have to defend your opinions against close scrutiny might place one on special notice to form opinions with the utmost professional skill and care.

2. *Be ready to defend your role as an "expert."* We addressed this issue in chapter three and will not rehearse it again. Suffice it to say that you will need to represent your credentials accurately. *Accurately* is the operative term. Neither puff your credentials as the other side will discover it, nor humble yourself as your credentials will help the judge and jury assess your credibility. If there is any inaccuracy in your presentation of credentials, they are likely to be exposed.

3. *What "evidence" do you have to form your opinions?* This is the crux of your testimony. Your opinions will be challenged in two ways: 1) on the methodology you used to reach your conclusions, and 2) on how reasonably and well you have tied your conclusion to your data. You can be sure that the opposing attorney will point out, pointedly, that other conclusions might be reached with the same data. Realizing that the social sciences are not the hard sciences, data is still necessary to support conclusions. Conclusions based solely upon twenty years in the field or some theory are likely to be less credible than a variety of tools and clinical observations.

4. Specifically in cases where the spiritual or religious upbringing of the child is at issue, the following items seem likely to present a credible job done of collecting relevant data:

   a. Several interviews in person with the child, preferably alone.

   b. Interviews with the child's religious or spiritual leaders.

   c. Cite visits to the place of worship, during worship or other activities. Such a visit might have obviated the *Harris* case, to be described later in the chapter, where the danger of snake handling during a worship service was at issue in the child's well being. If the counselor sees the worship service and related activities, they can make an eyewitness account. This accomplishes two things. First, it increases the credibility of the data used to reach the conclusion. Going to see an event is more verified than taking someone else's word for it. Second, it allows the counselor to personally view the child in the context of the issue of conflict.

   d. An examination of the child's self-image by psychological testing. It may be a good idea to have such tests independently scored and interpreted. This independence further insulates the expert from charges of bias or favoritism.

5. Be ready to relate and to explain any compromising information. How much you are being paid. If you are being paid, you have joined the ranks of a "hired gun." Be ready to state your fee in court as well as any other compromising information that is at all relevant to your credibility. Any such material is grist for the other side's mill.

Wah (1998) also describes the law's tolerance for "cults" and (as she describes it) minority religions. For example, it is unlikely that child abuse or neglect statutes will only sometimes prevail against parents who raise their child in unconventional or minority religious or spiritual environment. Such was the ruling of the Minnesota Supreme appeals court where Department of Social Services [DSS] officers wanted to remove children from a home because their parents refused to allow the children to take standardized norm reference examinations.

The parents objected on religious grounds (*Matter of Welfare of T. K. and W.K.*, 1991). In overturning DSS, the appeals court ruled that the state constitution made guarantees even stronger than those of the federal constitution and that, once a sincere religious belief has been established (see Chapter 1) the state has to prove that its compelling interest cannot be achieved by any less drastic means (than, for example, removing children from an otherwise fit home).

The above case also demonstrates an aspect of law sometimes overlooked by those unaccustomed to the intricacies of jurisprudence. That is, state law can offer more religious protections than federal law. It is important that counselors recognize that each state has its own constitution and its own varying degrees of religious freedoms and freedoms of conscience (as in the Minnesota case). State law cannot give less protections than the federal constitution, but it can give more.

While the state is limited in limiting vague possibilities of future harm, the state need not hesitate to protect a child from immanent or present harm such as are afforded by child abuse or neglect statutes. However, the state cannot deprive parents of their children because parents believe things that are unusual or do not comport with social norms. Thus, a court cannot remove a child from his or her home because of parents' adherence to holistic medicine, vegetarianism, or communal living (Wah, 1999, p. 122).

In terms of child custody arrangements, spiritual and moral issues can play important and legally recognizable considerations. These have been, and continue to be, important aspects of judges' considerations. However, as in almost everything else in the law, even these are not absolute.

In *In re Marriage of Gould* (1984) the Supreme Court of Wisconsin overruled both its lowers courts and disallowed a child's removal from her mother who was living, unmarried, with a man for several years. After initially living with her mother, the child was removed to her father after he filed a petition for the removal. The lower courts, recognizing that spiritual and moral environment was an important and lawful criterion to determine custody, among others, the trial court ordered a "moralsocial" study. Indeed, one of the express items in that state's custody determinations is: "The child's adjustment to the home, school, religion, and community" (Wisc. Stats, 1981–82, §767.24(2)).

That study, conducted by a social worker, concluded no harm was done to the child by living with mom, but that harm, in the form of conflicted values, may arise in adolescence. The child was removed.

In reversing the two courts' decisions to remove the child, the Wisconsin did not quarrel with spiritual or moral assessments made to determine the best interests of the child. It did quarrel with the legal conclusion that the child's removal was necessary for the child's best interest.

The state Supreme Court found that the test for a modification for custody arrangements is different from the initial custody determination. The "best interest" is the initial determination and the "necessary for the best interests" is the test for a "modification" of that initial custody determination. This might seem like legal nit–picking, but when we consider the additional trauma that might incur to the child after being with one parent for a time and then having to pull up stakes and move elsewhere and bond with another set of circumstances, it makes more sense.

Even potentially dangerous religious activity must be closely scrutinized for its actual, demonstrable danger. In *Harris v. Harris* (1977), a mother lost custody because her church believed in snake handling as a religious practice, such as is noted in Mark 16:17–18:

> He who believes and is baptized will be saved, but he who does not believe will be condemned. And these signs will accompany those who believe: in my name they will cast out demons; they will speak in new tongues; they will pick up serpents, and if they drink any deadly thing, it will not hurt them; they will lay their hands on the sick, and they will recover. (Revised Standard Version)

The Mississippi Supreme Court dug deeper into the facts of a *seemingly* open-and-shut case and found that the mother was not qualified to handle snakes by the church and had no intentions of doing so, and the child was never in the vicinity of the snakes themselves. Thus, the court eschewed a facile approach to finding the immediacy and relevancy of the danger posed to determine the actual and likely threat. Counselors, when asked to make judgments and evaluations on child or adult religious practices, should be equally penetrating in their pursuit of the relevant facts.

Are there specific statutes that protect citizens, especially children, from harmful religious or spiritual practices? The criminal and civil law has an impressive array of ordinances, statutes, and negligence laws designed to protect children. These are well known among counselor, including child abuse statutes, that we need not rehearse again here.

Another species of legislation, however, deserves our specific intention. These are criminal statutes that are written deliberately to address the specific kinds of harm most associated with religious or spiritual abuse. Illinois has promulgated a pair of statutes that criminalize what is called ritual or ritualized abuse. We recite these statutes in their entirety for two reasons: 1) criminal statutes, by their very nature, sanctions extremely specific behaviors (if the statute does not actually state a prohibition, it is unlikely that a defendant will be convicted under it) and 2) criminal behaviors are clear what is permitted as well.

These themes are noted in the following statute. This statute has immediate relevance for us as this statute is specifically aimed at "ritualized" behavior.

Ritual Mutilation (Chapter 5/12-32 § 12–32 West Supp. 1999)

(a) *A person commits the offense of ritual mutilation, when he or she mutilates, dismembers or tortures another person as part of a ceremony, rite, initiation, observance, performance or practice, and the victim did not consent or under such circumstances that the defendant knew or should have known that the victim was unable to render effective consent.*

(b) *Sentence. Ritual mutilation is a Class 2 felony.*

(c) *The offense ritual does not include the practice of male circumcision or a ceremony, rite, initiation, observance, or performance related thereto.*

As ever, there are important points to consider in this statute. First, it addresses informed consent, in fact, it uses the term effective consent. This statute does not specifically apply to children, who cannot give consent in any case. Even an adult cannot give effective consent without specific knowledge about the outcome, procedure, and any side effects. Thus, as we have noted in an earlier chapter, a yes does not necessarily mean the requirements of an informed consent have been satisfied.

Second, the concept of scienter, also mentioned in an earlier chapter has once again appeared. The operative, statutory words "the defendant knew or should have known" are what scienter is all about. In the context of this statute, consent to "mutilation" is voided if the defendant has scienter that such consent is invalid.

Third, the statute is fairly clear in what is prohibits and fairly clear in what it allows. Part "(c)" seems to allow for the traditional and ancient Jewish rite of circumcision, known as the *Brit Milah*. This rite, carried out by the *mohel*, is the religious rite of circumcision where the male foreskin is cut off and offered to God. Currently, some adherents offer a corresponding female rite, obviously without the circumcision, but with blessings, songs, and readings called a "Brit Ha-Bat" (Frankel & Teutsch, 1992).

This exception is an excellent illustration of legislatures trying to head off a constitutional challenge. Clearly, a brit or bris is not the kind of act the statute was trying to prohibit, but the broad language in part (a) would likely cover such acts. In that event, counselors who participate in such "mutilations" or counsel those who do, might fall into the criminal activity. Counselors need to know what religious and ceremonial acts are exempted from criminal statutes, as in the one above.

The Illinois Ritualized Abuse of a Child statute (5/12-33 § 12-33, West's Supp. 1999) is even more detailed:

(a) A person is guilty of ritualized abuse of a child when he or she commits any of the following acts with, upon, or in the presence of a child as part of a ceremony, rite or any similar observance:

(1) actually or in simulation, tortures, mutilates, or sacrifices any warm-blooded animal or human being;

(2) forces ingestion, injection, or other application of any narcotic, drug, hallucinogen or anaesthetic for the purpose of dulling sensitivity, cognition, recollection of, or resistence to any criminal activity;

(3) forces ingestion, or external application, of human or animal urine, feces, flesh, blood, bones, body secretions, nonprescription drugs or chemical compounds;

(4) involves a child in a mock, unauthorized or unlawful marriage ceremony with another person or representation of any force or deity, followed by sexual contact with the child;

(5) places a living child into a coffin or open grave containing a human corpse or remains;

(6) threatens death or serious harm to a child, his or her parents, family, pets, or friends that instills a well-founded fear in the child that the threat will be carried out; or

(7) unlawfully dissects, mutilates, or incinerates a human corpse.

(b) The provisions of this Section shall not be construed to apply to:

(1) lawful agriculture, animal husbandry, food preparation, or wild game hunting and fishing practices and specifically the branding or identification of livestock;

(2) the lawful medical practice of male circumcision or any ceremony related to male circumcision;

(3) any state or federally approved, licensed, or funded research project; or

(4) the ingestion of animal flesh or blood in the performance of a religious service or ceremony;

(c) Ritualized abuse of a child is a Class 1 felony for a first offense. A second or subsequent conviction for ritualized abuse of a child is a Class X felony for which the offender may be sentenced to a term of natural life imprisonment.

For the purposes of this book, there are three items to be discussed in this statute. First, among the exemptions are a broad religious exemption for ceremonies and the narrow exemption for male circumcision, as we have discussed earlier. Without such exemption, this statute, covering the wide array of actions as it does, would likely be held unconstitutional.

Second, this statute is a good example of the wide variety of behaviors legislators consider to be connected to the ritualized abuse of children. Counselors working with either perpetrators or victims of child ritual abuse should be well-versed in their state's law concerning this kind of abuse. Many states will not have such explicit statutes. Some states may pass them in the future.

Third, this statute is different species of statute from other child abuse laws. While the purpose, of course, is to prevent child abuse, the specific kinds of rituals associated here do not require any mens rea or guilty intention to fall under this statute. This is a rare, but not unknown, avenue of criminal law. Under statutes that require no *mens rea*, the defense that the alleged perpetrator did not mean (intend) to harm the child is irrelevant. The very fact that he or she conducted the prohibited ritual act with the child is sufficient for conviction. Thus, this statute should be considered a major new development in child abuse and in "cultic" legislation.

Legal Consequences for Counselors and the Issue of Prosecutorial Immunity

What are possible legal consequences if a counselor tries to extricate a client (or anyone else) from a religious group against their will?

Counselors who get involved in trying to convince, coerce, or otherwise extricate a client from a religious group against their will must be prepared for the legal consequence. The first preparation is to know what the legal consequences are.

Prosecutorial immunity is the avoidance of civil or criminal liability or guilt arising from their part in the judicial process. Counselors, usually as part of Department of Social Services or Child Protective Services, or other agency who aids the district attorney's office in investigating abuse. Thus, the counselor can be sued for being part of an investigation within their regular job duties. The law allows that, in the prosecutorial process, people make good faith mistakes. Prosecutorial immunities shield those involved in the investigation and prosecution of defendants from such mistakes. For example, the caseworkers assisted in expanding the investigation from beyond abuse into the murder of one child and in the interviewing of child and adult witnesses.

Simply put, the legal consequences are mixed. For the counselor's perspective, they are basically negative. After all, any court appearance is not a happy one. The best that can happen is that the case will be dismissed, as it was in *Kerr v. Lyford* (1999). Eugene and Geneva Kerr's civil rights were violated when they were arrested and jailed in the rape, kidnapping, and murder of Kelly Wilson. Among those the Kerrs sued were case workers and employees of the Texas Department of Human Services in federal court. The district court dismissed the case on grounds of immunity. The federal court of appeals affirmed that decision.

The Kerr's children were committed to foster care. Once there, the children told graphic stories of devil worship, blood, knives, and the dismemberment of babies by their parents and grandparents. Originally, the investigation and prosecution was initially conducted by the County District Attorney's office. After investigating the alleged crime scene, they found three potential sites that had allegedly incriminating evidence such as a shovel with blood residue on it, a red shed mentioned by the children, with some evidence of recent washing, and a circular clearing also mentioned by the children. There was evidence, as well, that some of these statements were offered "spontaneously and voluntarily," but others were related from vigorous and coercive questioning. Later, the Texas Attorney General's Office took over the prosecution because it declared that the former investigation was "botched."

A botched prosecution doesn't mean a successful lawsuit for malicious prosecution—or, as in the instant case against the caseworkers, malicious prosecution, civil conspiracy, false arrest, seizure, and imprisonment. Such suits would require that the case workers investigated the plaintiffs without probable cause and with malice. The plaintiffs, among other things, would have to prove that the government intended to violate their rights. The court of appeals ruled that the evidence, some of which was mentioned in the previous paragraphs, was enough to establish probable cause.

Thus, counselors who work for government agencies should be cognizant of the case in which they are asked to investigate. They should take an affirmative and proactive role in ensuring that the investigatory procedures comport to constitutional standards.

The handling of witnesses is particularly important in this respect. In the *Kerr* case, and in many other cases of ritual abuse, the battle of the experts often comes down to whether or not the investigators elicited testimony, particularly from children, in an unbiased, uncoached, and unaided manner. Even subtle inflections of voice can be construed as helping the young, impressionable witness remember facts most helpful for the prosecution. Often, such helpful testimony is thrown out and the entire case is in put in jeopardy.

A story, of which I am personally aware, is a clear indication of the perfect response for a witness to make when asked if the prosecution (or defense) is asked about their "coaching." In a Virginia child dispute case, a defense attorney asked the child if the commonwealth's attorney's office had told the child about what to say in court.

> "Yes," answered the child.
> The commonwealth's attorney tensed. The judge leaned forward.
> "And what did the attorney tell you to say," the defense counsel asked with anticipation.
> "She said always to tell the truth," replied the little girl.

One could almost hear the sigh of relief from the commonwealth's attorney. This is an example of instant credibility. Any other response, particularly a response from the little girl that hinted the commonwealth's attorney tried to steer the child's testimony in any one particular direction, that she should use any particular words, or even to omit some facts, would be damaging, or even fatal to the case. In the worst-case scenario, it might rise to the level of suborning **perjury**.

By now, it should be clear to counselors that they should in no way coach a potential witness. Helping a client remember an event for therapeutic purposes is an entirely different matter than helping a witness remember facts for the purposes of testimony. When a client becomes a witness, the manner in he or she remembered testimony will be placed at issue. More than one case has been sunk because a therapist or counselor has "tainted"the witnesses' recollection by helping them remember facts.

The previous story of the little girl witness is both illustrative and instructive. Not only did the commonwealth's attorney not coach the child, but she only affirmed that the child tell only what she knew—just tell the truth. The commonwealth's attorney was thus seen as taking no active role in any way pressuring or persuading the child to say nothing except what the girl herself knew. In that same way, any attempt by a counselor to impose any change or direction to the client's memory will probably damage the client's testimony.

Counselor's need to understand the difference between what makes for good therapy and a good witness. There are two different standards. It may be that *therapeutically*, a client should dig deeply into real or even imagined memories to address issues of hurt, past abuse, uncertainty, grief, and damaged self-esteem. In this way, the counselor is not the judge of the veracity of client memories, but the guide through those *feelings* that memories elicit.

A witness has a completely different standard. In court, a witness needs credibility. Credibility is inversely proportional to the amount of help received in remembering the events in question. The less prompting, the more credibility. Counselors who help their clients therapeutically can compromise them jurisprudentially.

So, what is the counselor to do? There are two suggestions: First, counselors should make their priority the health and well-being of their clients. That is their job. Their job is not to make their clients better witnesses.

The second suggestion follows from the first. If the counselor knows that litigation is pending or likely to arise from the memories of their clients, he or she should have a talk with the attorney handling the case. After receiving permission from the client to do so, the counselor can confer with the attorney about how the counselor is conducting the interventions with the client. This puts the attorney on notice as to how the other side might challenge the client's testimony.

Conferring with the attorney does nothing to change the therapeutic role of the coun- selor, nor does it jeopardize the rightful value of the counselor's judgment. It simply separates the roles of attorney and counselor and offers each insight into the demands of each other's jobs.

☐ Vicarious Liability and "Deprogrammers:" Relevance for Counselors

Vicarious liability or *respondeat superior*, are ever-present elements in the equation of counseling with spiritual or alternative interventions as we have seen. We discussed vicarious liability in Chapter 3. This goes double when the counselor involves him or herself in religious groups. As we have noted earlier, the counselor may become responsible for the acts of an employee or the counselor may get his or her employee liable if they are the employee and commit bad acts.

The case of *Scott v. Ross* (1998) serves to illustrate how the legal doctrine of vicarious liability can apply to a group dedicated to deprogramming someone in a religious group. Plaintiff Scott, an 18-year-old, along with his two siblings (both minors), joined a religious organization, despite the will of their mother. She wanted to get them out, so she contacted someone connected with the deprogramming organization, a defendant in the case. The contact person referred Scott's mother to Ross. Ross and three other defendants allegedly abducted Scott for five days. After such time, he faked acceptance of the deprogrammer's position, they apparently let down their guard, and he escaped.

Scott sued in federal court under the legal theories of deprivation of his civil rights, negligence, and outrage. So, while it was Ross (with three other defendants) who actually conducted the deprogramming, the plaintiff's mother found Scott through the deprogramming organization. In Washington, the state where this action was brought, the **principal** (the deprogramming organization) would be held liable if the agent (allegedly Mr. Ross and others, *if* they) acted on behalf of the principal and within the scope of their employment. The deprogramming organization was sued as the principle. In other words, the deprogramming organization was being sued for being in on the referral of the deprogrammers.

The trial court (district court) found the defendants liable for the civil rights violations and negligence and awarded Scott $875,000 in compensatory damages and $4 million in punitive damages (one defendant settled before trial). The jury allocated 10% of the negligence liability and $1 million of the punitive damages against the deprogramming organization. The defendants appealed, claiming, among other things, that the district court misconstrued Washington State agency law and that the evidence was insufficient to impose liability. The appeals court affirmed the lower court's judgment.

This case demonstrates significant legal issues when a counselor works on behalf of others to take someone from a religious organization of their choice. First, to go back to square one, there would be no case at all if Scott wanted to return to his family. He did not. So, the first issue yields the first lesson—and that is know the dynamics in which you enter. The counselor needs to know, fully and explicitly, if and to what degree the deprogramee wants or is open to being rescued. On a related issue, the mother's minor children did not sue. They could not because, as minors, they were under the legal control of their mother.

Second, state law of **agency** and principles of vicarious liability apply. Even the federal court applied state law. As we learned in the Preface, each state law might be different. This is another reason why counselors need to know the law of the state in which they practice.

Third, deprogrammers have a number of different causes of action that can be lodged against them. The ones cited in this case are only illustrations. If counselors chose to conduct this work, they must at least know some possible legal consequences. Additionally, as we have seen, not conducting the actual deprogramming is no protection against liability. As this case demonstrates, the deprogramming organization was assessed over a million dollars for just referring the matter to another.

☐ Vicarious Liability Against Social Services and Other Government Agencies

Another case points out that vicarious liability can be assessed against counselors who work for government agencies such as a county social service agency or child protective services who become involved in extricating someone from a religious group. What can be true for private citizens and organizations can also be true for governments. Specifically, this case addresses the "conflict between the legitimate role of the state in protecting children from abusive parents, and the rights of children and parents to be free from arbitrary and undue government interference" (*Wallis v. Young*, 1999).

Two children and their parents, Bill and Becky Wallis, sued the City of Escondido, California, and its Social Service Agency and Child Protective Services after the children, then aged two and five, were taken from their parents under police custody, placed in a county institution, later taken to a hospital for anal and vaginal examinations, and not returned to their parents for two and one-half months. This action was commenced upon the statement by Becky Wallis' sister, an institutionalized mental patient (diagnosed with dissociative disorder and multiple personality disorder), who told her therapist a story about child sacrifice connected to Satanic witchcraft within this family. The patient had previously made a child abuse report against the Wallis' which, upon investigation, was found to be without merit.

Once the sister made the second report to a therapist (a mandatory reporter), the county investigated. There was factual unclarity about who in the Child Protective Services (CPS) office or the district attorney's office authorized the order to pick up and take custody of the children, which the city police executed. The police testified that they relied upon representations from "someone at CPS" that a pick-up order was issued. After that, they testified that their job was to locate the children and enforce the law. The officers took it solely upon verbal authority that a lawful order was issued. As it turned out, no pick up order was ever issued by a court or anyone else.

The Wallises sued in federal court, alleging violation of their constitutional rights, including the rights to be free from arbitrary and unreasonable search, undue invasions of their privacy, as well as numerous state claims. CPS and the County Social Services settled out of court. Then the district court dismissed the other counts on grounds the City has either qualified or absolute immunity in summary judgment. However, the court of appeals reversed.

The appeals court found that there were sufficient questions of fact to preclude summary judgment. Briefly stated, the court concluded that a jury could reasonably conclude that the government employees acted in a way, either by procedure or policy, that may have compromised the Wallis' rights.

This case yields one central lesson and a few corollary lessons. For the counselor who may be involved in similar proceedings, the central lesson is about reliance—wise or unwise trust placed upon the representations and judgments of others can mean the difference between a suit against you or your department and a legally sufficient disposition.

The following comments are intended to initiate questions and discussions about normal procedure. Over time, practice can become far less rigorous than policy would dictate. These comments do not criticize operating procedure, but are designed to check assumptions about routine practice and procedure with the goal of greater safety. This safety, of course, is particularly important where the care and welfare of children are concerned.

1. Reliance upon usual procedure. Make sure that the proper procedures are in place and followed when obtaining a custody order. This may sound obvious to seasoned professionals and the author makes no suggestions that those involved were negligent or even unwise. But the fact is a material mistake was made, a mistake with serious consequences. It was more a matter of reliance. Government officials placed reliance upon second- and third-hand information, or unreliable information.

   In the crush of caseloads, most professionals find ways of saving time and energy. This case revealed that government officials relied upon each other's verbal representations that (a) a pick up order should be issued, (b) a pick-up order was signed, and (c) a pick-up order was issued. Each point of decision was assumed to have been properly and thoroughly investigated and executed.

   This case cannot be divorced from its Satanic-ritual context. The sense of urgency and extreme expediency may have played a role in this case.

2. Reliance upon the statements of an abuse reporter. While there is no question that U.S. public policy favors the wide latitude in reporting suspected cases of abuse, the reliance on any single report should keep the privacy rights and due process rights of the one being reported upon keenly in mind. In other words, counselors should balance the foreseeable harm to the child against the chance that constitutional rights of the suspected perpetrator might be harmed.

As previously noted, the law immunizing reporters requires that the report be made in *good faith*. Good faith means the lack of malicious intent. A malicious report of child abuse is the total absence of evidence to that effect and the will to get back at someone. Having an evil ulterior motivate for reporting child abuse is a sure way to eviscerate good faith. Without good faith, the exemption from civil and criminal liability is eliminated. So, the reporter may be subject, for example, to charges of defamation.

While the author is no friend of armchair quarterbacks, the *Wallis* case offers insights into factors that might be considered to fall into the categories of legal, if not ethical, *bad faith* reporting. Examining a reporter's motives for making such an allegation is not beyond the professional responsibilities of those determining the validity of the report. Does the reporter have anything to gain by making the report? Does the reporter have any obvious impairments in judgment? Is any prior relationship between the reporter and the reportee suggestive of further investigation? *Wallis* is particularly poignant on this point.

These factors do not have to unduly slow the pace of an impending abuse investigation, nor to harm the interests of the child. However, the *Wallis* decision is one from which to learn the impact of such decisions.

The following questions may help focus relevant issues:

1. *What, exactly, is the counselor's role?* The first and perhaps most important role a counselor can play relative to a client involved with a religious group—even a worrisome group—is to act with the same diligence and exercise the same independent judgement as one would in any other therapeutic or difficult situation. Why should this area be any different?

   The author hopes that one of the lessons learned from this study of law and ethics is that, while legal and ethical regimes might be new and challenging learning, the skills and wisdom gained from clinical practice and training are also invaluable in addressing the challenges of these interventions. Many of the same skills the counselor has already honed keep the counselor in good stead in these issues as well. Where it is necessary to confront or complement the world view of the client or student, let the wisdom of practice and the practice of law and ethics be the guides.

2. *What is asked of the counselor?* Be clear and specific about what is the role the counselor is asked to play. Where the role is unclear or questionable, the counselor can raise those issues at that time. The sooner the counselor raises ethical or legal issues in the process, the easier it will be either to decline further involvement or to limit the role played. Once the counselor jumps both feet into a counseling or consulting situation, the harder it is to extricate themselves from involvement. Then, of course, the counselor must take steps so as not to give rise to abandonment of the client claims.

3. *Who requests the counselor intervene?* The counselor must uncover who the *real* client is. On its face, this might seem a ridiculous question. But in therapeutic relations, as well as in life, things may not be as they appear. These issues can be discerned with a conscientious analysis through the "ethical ecology." What motivates the client to seek therapy is a starting question? The motivation may come within or it may come from a parent or friend that is really pulling the strings. Certainly, the one motivating our Mr. Taylor in the case study above for receiving the attentions of programmers was not he, himself. It is doubtful that he would ever become a satisfied customer of those attentions. Suits may follow.

4. *What are operative ethical principles?* Fairness, self-determination, and objectivity for a start. Fairness is how equitable a process is. In law, fairness is often expressed in term of due process. Due process (both substantive and procedural) refers to how consistently law and legal processes are applied to defendants under similar circumstances. As noted earlier, *Miranda* warnings must be given to all criminal defendants who fit certain criteria. Similarly, all things being equal, shouldn't a person who joins one religious affiliation be treated with the same dignity as one who joins a religious group that one does not approve?

   The issue of fairness and self-determination must not be content-based, but based upon the process by which an adherent is treated. It may be helpful to reconstruct this case along the *process* versus *content* methodology. Eliminating the content of the religious affiliation, was the process for either analyzing the alleged harm of the group or for extracting the young man fair? Did it further his self-determination or dignity? Once again, the process is emphasized here because the author believes that courts are less likely to depend upon characterizations of the "cult" by either party, but more likely to depend upon the practice of the affiliation.

An analysis of the process for evaluating the group on *process* over *content* would center on the following questions.

1. What was the evidence of harm to the young man?
2. If harm is alleged, what is the nature of the harm?
3. What is the seriousness of the harm?
4. What is the evidence of this harm? Is the harm known only by hearsay? Or does the parent or guardian have direct, personal evidence of that harm?
5. If the harm is hearsay? How credible or reliable is the source?

An analysis of the process for extricating the adherent may flow from these questions:

1. Who asks for the extraction or intervention? What is their relationship to the member? Is this relationship a legal one (that is, is the relationship a parent to a minor child or an adult child?)

2. Is the manner of extraction or "deprogramming" consistent with state and federal law? Or is it kidnapping or unlawful imprisonment by another name?
3. Is the adherent a party to these deliberations? Were they consulted? Is this done with their informed consent?
4. If the adherent's "deprogramming" is decided upon is extricating the least invasive or restrictive means of accomplishing it? This least restrictive means test comes right out of constitutional tests for the restriction of religious activities to conform to constitutional requirements. We apply it here as an ethical concept.

The "least restrictive means" tests urges the parties not to take the "bull in a china shop" approach to achieving their ends. Even if parents want their minor child out of a religious affiliation, does it require kidnapping them—with the attendant risk of them simply running away again or exacerbating the rift already between them? Are there less draconian approaches, like having a trusted friend intercede on the parents' behalf? Coming home for a short, but temporary visit? Asking for a neutral third party to intercede?

Of course, as mentioned earlier, a parent usually should and must exercise control over their minor children and the counselor should exercise fair judgment in treating their clients. Self-determination, just like the First Amendment, is a strong, but not an absolute value. Self-determination is limited by parental control of minors and public and personal safety.

The same is true for objectivity. No one is completely objective. Without perfect objectivity, there is always the danger of conflict of interest. The cures for conflict of interest are either disclosure or divestiture. A counselor may disclose sympathy or antipathy for an affiliation of their client. Disclosure is a way of giving the client the necessary information to make decisions about their own treatment. As the bias intensifies, the cure harshens. If a counselor's actions or ideologies are intense and intractable, divesting (referring) the client may be necessary.

Stated in yet another way, objectivity is a key ingredient in the legal and ethical practice of spiritual and complementary counseling. Objectivity need not mean that the counselor eschews any religious or spiritual belief. It does mean, however, that the counselor produces legally cognizable evidence for his or her conclusions. If the counselor pronounces that the religious affiliation is dangerous, harmful or beneficial, it should be based upon evidence. Taken from Wah (1998, 1999) as well the learnings from the cases and comments in this chapter, 4 points to remember about evidence are important. Again, we speak not here of what evidence is necessary or excludable in law courts, but for counselors to act upon harm.

First, the evidence of harm should be testable. Testability mean some evidence of immanent harm. Proof of past harm may be important—always taking care not to prejudge a person only from their past.

Second, threats may also qualify, if they seem immanent and credible. Physical evidence of harm, the implements of alleged harm, or any other objects that affirm testimony may be helpful in making an accurate determination.

Third, corroborative witnesses are also helpful. If independent witnesses acknowledge events and facts that the counselor has come to believe, they provide an objective source of verification.

Fourth, first-hand knowledge of events and facts provide objectifiable evidence of facts upon which to draw conclusions. Personally witnessing a home environment, actual harm done, and ritual implements, or anything else that can verify the testimony can be helpful.

☐ Conclusion

This chapter and the following one are really extensions of Chapter 5—the ethics chapter. One of the consequences of a diverse society is a diverse ethical and cultural outlook on religious and spiritual behaviors. What one person may call a "cult" another person might call a "religion" or "spiritual group." After all, one of the foundations of the United States is religious liberty. This chapter discussed the legal and ethical role of counselors with clients who are involved with such groups who some may deem threatening or dangerous. Counselors and their agencies might face legal consequences when they act on behalf of clients or their families.

This chapter offers guidance in how counselors might assess religious activity for therapeutic purposes. Such assessment values process over content. Assessments based upon the content of a religious group run into serious constitutional difficulties as we have noted throughout this book.

This chapter also outlined some of the legal consequences for counselors and their agencies when acting as counselors, "deprogrammers," "rescuers," or expert witnesses regarding such groups. These consequences can involve both civil and criminal sanctions. Additionally, statutes are illustrated that criminalize certain "ritual" child abuse and mutilations.

☐ Legal/Ethical Exercises and Audits

1. What has been your own experience with religious groups or organizations? Do you find them supportive, comforting, coercive, inclusive, exclusive? By what specific criteria do you make such assessments?
2. How would you react if a client wanted you to "save" or "rescue" a family member of theirs from a religious group?
3. What do you think should be the requirements for an "expert witnes" to be allowed to testify on the dangerousness of any religious group? Would these criteria be the same as for an expert witness in a child custody case in which a parent's religious group were an issue?
4. Should parents have unlimited rights to raise their children in any religious group they choose? What might some of the limits be, if any?
5. Do you agree that specific criminal statutes be promulgated for "ritual abuse" or "ritual mutilation"? Why or why not? If yes, how might you effect such a policy decision?
6. If you were one of the counselors involved in the Kerr v. Lyford case, how might you have handled things differently?
7. How might the legal doctrine of *respondeat superior* or vicarious liability apply in a social services department, school, or private agency when a client's therapeutic issue involves religious group, "deprogramming," or related issues. If you were a supervisor of a counselor intervening in the Kerr case, how might you ensure that such problems would not arise?

The "Cultural Defense," Liability in School Counseling, and Vicarious Liability for Social Work Schools

☐ Objectives

1. To acquaint the reader with a minority, but growing, body of legal doctrine that has direct relevance to clients and counselors—the "cultural defense".
2. To apply the "cultural defense" to another legal issue raised in a diverse cultural milieu, that is, female genital mutilation.
3. To explore the connection of "cultural defenses" to a well-known defense, named the "battered women's defense."
4. To further explore how particularly school counselors might legally and ethically determine how to strike the balance between being culturally and spiritually sensitive to students and staff and to abide by their professional, policy, and legal mandates. This balance is illustrated both by the cases of female genital mutilation, whistle blowing, personal and public prayer, public moments of silence, the distribution of religiously or spiritually based literature, and the Equal Access Act.
5. To describe specifically how counseling educators and schools can be held liable for the harm done by their students under the legal doctrine of vicarious liability.

This final chapter addresses issues particularly significant to counselors who conduct multi-cultural practices, school counselors, and counselor educators. Chapter 7 ties in several issues of the law and counseling in spiritual and complementary therapies. These issues include spiritual and religious diversity, counseling liability under *respondeat superior* and vicarious liability, criminal sanctions for abuse related to spiritual and cultural acts, and the dilemmas of school prayer and religious and spiritual diversity addressed by school counselors.

This final chapter addresses three significant issues arising from spiritual and complementary counseling especially as it applies to minors, school counselors, and counseling supervisors. These issues arise from an increasingly culturally and spiritually diverse population. This diversity, of course, expresses itself in school and in counseling situations in which minors and students are involved.

These issues include the "cultural defense" as it applies to serious felonies and in female genital mutilation. In a society where different cultures express themselves, values and laws will almost inevitably clash. These clashes have deeply rooted religious and spiritual components; ritual mutilation is no exception. Of course, U.S. law has something to say about such activity. Counselors need to understand some of the ethical and legal issues involved in these clashes as they may directly apply to their practices.

Chapter seven also addresses some prevalent aspects of culturally diverse spiritualities and their attendant counseling implications in the public schools. As noted earlier, public schools are some of the most hotly contested areas of public life where religion, spirituality and alternative lifestyles and ideas are expressed. In some ways, as we have already seen, it is a public forum to express those ideas, beliefs, or practices. In some other ways, schools have a heightened duty to be both neutral in religious expression and to protect the health and well-being of students—most of whom are minors. In this culturally and religiously charged mix, school counselors (and private counselors who address such issues) must have a broad knowledge of the main legal principles inherent in such work. This chapter discusses school defamation, "moments of silence," and school prayer, school policies for the distribution of religiously or spiritually oriented literature and the Equal Access Act and school counselors.

Finally, a convergence of two legal doctrines we have discussed will combine in our third main topic of this chapter. We have discussed vicarious liability and respondeat superior. We have also discussed the many civil claims that can be lodged against counselors for using spiritual and complementary interventions. These legal streams combine to make a mighty, but often unforeseen, river of potential liability. That is, what is the potential for a claim against a counseling school for the liability of its students in training programs. Both medical schools and theological schools are struggling to address this very issue. Counseling programs would do well to do the same.

In an increasingly diverse society, behaviors from other cultures are increasingly visible and prevalent in counseling clients. Other works have addressed the how to in culturally sensitive counseling practices and we will not rehearse those issues here. However, this chapter addresses the legal implications of those issues: the "cultural defense" and cultural diversity in schools and other public settings and the vicarious liability of colleges and universities who have counseling positions where student interns work in the field.

☐ Case Study: Second-Degree Murder or Mitigating Cultural Circumstances?

Helen Wu was a native of the People's Republic of China. She later emigrated to the United States when Gary Wu, the man who later married her, suggested marriage and having children. Mr. Wu, also a native of the People's Republic, had emigrated some years earlier. At that time Ms. Wu did not marry Mr. Wu, but bore his child. She returned to the People's Republic and subsequently married Mr. Wu when she re-emigrated into the United States.

After the Wu's married, their son told his mother, Mrs. Wu, disturbing news: (a) that Mr. Wu mistreated him, and (b) that Mr. Wu carried on a romantic relationship with another woman. Distressed, Mrs. Wu took the cord off a set of blinds and strangled her young son to death. She was charged with second-degree murder. At trial, the defense counsel asked the judge to instruct the jury that they could take into consideration her cultural background. The defense argued that her actions would be treated leniently, if not excused, in her former country. As it was, she was sentenced to 15 years to life in prison.

She based her appeal to the California Court of Appeals on the theory that the trial court's ruling was **reversible error**. Reversible error means that the judge found some error grievous enough to have the conviction overturned. The legal concepts of premeditation and deliberation were necessary elements of her conviction. That is, the state had to prove that Mrs. Wu planned to murder her son with malice aforethought. Mrs. Wu argued that her cultural background was significant in determining her state of mind when she slew her son. She argued that the trial judge should have instructed the jury that they could consider her cultural background to determine whether or not she had the requisite state of mind to be convicted of second degree murder. She argued that in her country of origin (China), her son would be considered an outcast and socially perish because of the father's actions.

This defense is known as a cultural defense and has been raised in cases as wide ranging as child abuse, murder, and female genital mutilation. This question can be posed in many ways, depending upon a person's point of view. If you favor the defense, you might ask whether someone brought up and inculcated in one set of cultural values should be held accountable for the values of another culture. If you do not favor the defense, you might ask why a defendant should be allowed to plead to a lesser offense or be excused from crimes because he or she was born in another country. Either way, this issue places cultural sensitivity at direct loggerheads with the protection of children, self-determination, and equal treatment under the law.

So, when is it murder and when is it mitigating circumstances? The California Court of Appeals ruled that the defendant's cultural background could be relevant in showing whether or not the defendant had the necessary state of mind to sustain her conviction. The court found that a jury might properly conclude that, because of her cultural background, her outrage at her husband's infidelity and abuse might have so shocked her that she could not be charged with second-degree murder. She might be charged with a lesser crime—perhaps voluntary manslaughter (Gallin, 1994).

☐ The Relevance to the Spiritual and Complementary Counselor

Why do counselors need to know this emerging area of law? Counselors who use spiritual and complementary interventions need to know about the varieties of the cultural defense for two reasons. The first reason is that such counselors, often quite sensitive to cultural diversity (as spirituality is culturally diverse) and have clients who are culturally diverse. Their clients may present issues where their actions, while quite acceptable in their own cultures, can be illegal under U.S. federal or state law. The counselor should recognize if and when their clients may become criminal defendants and when their cultural outlook may prevent them from understanding the forensic nature of their actions.

A second reason is that counselors, particularly those who employ spiritual or complementary counseling, may be subpoenaed or become expert witnesses in cases addressing cultural, spiritual or religious diversity. They should know the anatomy and physiology of such a defense before they seek to become surgeons. The next section describes the expert testimony of the psychologists in the *Wu* case.

The third reason is that spiritual or religious practices of their clients themselves may pose the threat of criminal sanctions for either the client or the counselor. Just because an act, done by the counselor or client, is spiritual or religious in nature, does not mean that it has unbridled protection. We have beat that dead horse pretty well in the introduction and chapter one. However, this also means that a spiritual or religious *defense* is not always countenanced by courts.

It is well for us to recall **U.S. v. Meyers** (1996) that we met in the introduction. The criminal defendant was convicted of a drug related charge and defended himself by saying that his use of marijuana was motivated by a religious or spiritual practice and belief. He appealed on a religious argument for constitutional protection.

The U.S. Court of Appeals for the 10th Circuit did not agree and upheld his conviction. The court said that defendant's beliefs were more properly characterized as a philosophy or, perhaps, a way of life. These two terms do not reach the constitutional status for religious or spiritual protection.

Besides the importance of this case for its religious analysis, under this case shows how a case can rise and fall on how judges characterize facts of the case. Here, the subtle difference between "a way of life" and a "religion" meant the difference between innocense and a criminal conviction. We now turn to the "cultural defense" itself.

☐ The "Cultural Defense"

The "cultural defense" is a defense, based upon a person's culture, that mitigates or excuses their otherwise criminal act. Of course, the "cultural defense" can include religious and spiritual activities and beliefs. The "cultural defense" is different in one important way from that of a defense based upon a religious or spiritual defense or a defense based (as we have seen) upon the Religious Freedom Restoration Act (RFRA). The principle difference is that the cultural defense, to the best of this author's knowledge, is not statutory. Where state and federal constitutions and statutes, such as the *RFRA*, protect religious and spiritual activities, the "cultural defense" is accepted or rejected by judges and juries on a case-by-case basis.

The cultural defense, while not denying doing the deed, the defendant denies the *mens rea* to be convicted. In United States' jurisprudence, this translates to the defense of diminished capacity. A person has a diminished capacity when their mental status disqualifies them for a charge consistent with their behavior. Perhaps the most widely known diminished capacity is "the heat of passion" defense. This defense is raised in domestic quarrels, such as when one spouse discovers their other spouse in bed with a third party and shoots them. The heat of passion defense will, no doubt, be raised in those circumstances because of the shock and disorientation accompanying such a sudden disclosure. This defense, however, cannot be raised if upon a discovery of the infidelity, the discovering spouse leaves, gets in a cab, drives to a friends house, asks the friend to borrow a gun, commiserates with the friend over cappuccino, returns, and shoots the spouse's lover. Courts would find that the discovering spouse had plenty of time to get over the initial shock and that the "heat of passion" had decreased to an internal temperature of icy revenge.

Alternatively, those favoring the cultural defense often rest their assertions upon the ethical mandates of cultural sensitivity and diversity. An interesting example of entering into how cultural sensitivity can illuminate, if not excuse, behavior comes from the *Wu* case itself.

Volpp (1994) describes the expert testimony of Professor Juris Draguns, expert in cross-cultural psychology, who described for the court the dynamics between Mrs. Wu and her son. This professor likened Mrs. Wu's relationship to her son with the dynamic of parent-child suicide by American mothers in Chicago during the 1920's. He explained how these mothers did not yet regard their infants as possessing their own separate identities and lives. The mothers, motivated by love and pity, struck down their children to save them suffering as they, themselves, had suffered. Thus, the mothers seemed genuinely mazed that society condemned them.

While the above-cited cases militate in favor or a "cultural defense," the next section mitigates against it. This juxtaposition is important to note. The "cultural defense," to date, enjoys limited currency in the law. To suggest that this defense is a legal trend would be overstating the case. The far stronger and more consistent position of U.S. jurisprudence is the welfare of children, as the next section demonstrates.

☐ The Cultural Defense and Child Custody

A form of the cultural defense can be applied in child custody cases. A state judge in Chicago awarded custody of an African-American child, known as Baby T., back to his biological mother after a white couple had cared for Baby T. since he was 8 days old. The biological mother was a former cocaine addict. Baby T. was three years old at the time of the custody decision. The state Department of Children and Family Services (DCFS) initially awarded custody to the white couple, who were an appellate judge and the longest-tenured city alderman.

In reversing the initial decision, the state judge, who is white, said that DCFS gave short shrift to the racial background of Baby T., saying "Unless the position of the department is that there is no such thing as African-American culture, this issue deserves more attention than to check a box that says not applicable." Upon winning the adoption dispute, Baby T.'s mother said that she is now drug-free, had found religion, and said, "When God is for you, he's greater than the weight of the world against you" (Race helps mother win custody, 1999).

It should go without saying, at this point in the book, that counselors who use complementary and spiritual therapies are very likely to run into such cultural and racial issues. After all, it is very difficult to strictly separate the "spiritual" and "cultural." A focus on race or culture, as well as "spiritual" may often play an important role in the counseling session or policy debate. This case shows that the cultural defense is not just used in the forensic venue, but many other areas of personal and public counseling and health as well. The next section addresses the cultural defense in a forensic venue.

☐ Female Genital Mutilation and the "Cultural Defense"

The cultural defense is also a putative argument in female genital mutilation (FGM). FGM, known as "sunna" in some countries, is a procedure whereby either the hood of the clitoris is removed, or the entire clitoris is removed, or the clitoris and either the labia minora or the labia majora is removed as well. Estimates report that 80 million girls worldwide undergo FGM, particularly in Somalia, Djibouti, the non-Moslem parts of Sudan, and in parts of Mali, Nigeria, Egypt, and Ethiopia (Kellner, 1993).

This procedure, generally, has received no official recognition from Moslem officials. Most commentators believe the surgery is a cultural, not specifically a religious exercise (Lancaster, 1998).

The "cultural defense" should this procedure occur, would most likely fail. The parents or the person performing it, would most likely fall under the purview of some part of that state's child abuse law.

Some states have enacted legislation particular to FGM. Such a state is Illinois whose statute is replicated below:

Female genital mutilation (Chapter 5/12-34 § 12-34, West Cum Supp. 1999)

(a) Except as otherwise permitted in subsection (b), whoever knowingly circumcises, excises, or infibulates, in whole or in part, the labia majora, labia minora, or clitoris of another commits the offense of female genital mutilation. Consent to the procedure by a minor on whom it is performed or by the parent or guardian is not a defense to a violation of this Section.

(b) A surgical procedure is not a violation of subsection (a) if the procedure:

　(1) is necessary to the health of the person on whom it is performed and is performed by a physician licensed to practice medicine in all of its branches; or

　(2) is preformed on a person who is in labor or who has just given birth and is performed for medical purposes connected with that labor or birth by a physician licensed to practice medicine in all of its branches.

(c) Sentence. Female genital mutilation is a Class X felony.

As ever, there are a couple of comments this statute necessitates. First, this statute offers a classic example of informed consent in a criminal statute. In this instance, the issue is not whether the consent was an informed one. It is an issue of relevance. It states expressly that, even if the minor or their parent or guardian gives such consent, it is no defense to charges under this statute. Thus, in this rather rare instance, even parental/custodial informed consent is irrelevant. Even the best intentioned parents or guardians in the world cannot consent to this procedure. Even if the culture in which the parents, guardians, or child were raised values or requires this procedure, it is no defense under this stature.

Second, it is worth highlighting who is charged under this statute. While it may seem fair to charge the parents or guardian if they consent to this procedure, it is the one who actually performs the procedure that is charged. This has its drawbacks and its advantages. The drawbacks can be that the parents, set upon conducting this procedure, might attempt to procure another person to perform the procedure if their first choice is charged. Not charging the parent or guardian might enable forum shopping for another person to do the procedure. Forum shopping means trying out various jurisdictions for the one legally conducive for your purposes.

The advantages are that if the parents were charged, convicted, and jailed, the children would be deprived of their parents and become wards of the state. An additional advantage of this statute is to discourage a class of specialized persons who conduct this procedure for profit or otherwise.

As stated earlier, the cultural defense pits ethical and legal notions against one another. On one hand the ethical values of self-determination, autonomy, and privacy militate towards allowing for at least some kind of culturally sensitive forbearance or leeway in adjudicating such issues. It is hard to see what the future holds for the cultural defense and how it will spread into other jurisdictions and its capacity to set precedent.

The author cannot make such predictions, but can assert some conditions that may impact the strength of this defense. These include the extent to which states may statutorily allow the cultural defense. (The author is unaware of any at this writing) and the extent to which juries will intentionally not find guilt because of a cultural defense. This jury determination is also known as **jury nullification**. This is the intentional refusal by a jury to either acquit or to convict based upon the jury's own sense of fairness, even though there is legally enough doubt to acquit or enough guilt to convict.

Parents or guardians may vigorously argue in favor of such culturally oriented tatoos, scarring, piercing, or other physical transformations. These may be appalling to some, but maybe not to others—particularly where religion or spiritual concerns are at stake. For example, a parent or guardian may vigorously compelling assertions as to why their daughter should endure FGM. While not the opinion of this author, arguing another's point of view is a practice well-developed skill among lawyers. Those assertions may include: that they want to return to their native country and this is acceptable, even mandatory practice there, that FGM is a religious obligation and it is sinful or shameful not to have it done, or that American culture sexualizes children much too early and FGM protects children from premature sexual experiences.

On the other hand, and these seem to predominate in the FGM statute above, children ought not be subject to such a painful, involuntary procedure, particularly there are no medial benefits and where there are future emotional and social detriments. These detriments can be diminished sexual pleasure and health, emotional scarring from the trauma involved and secrecy involved in the procedure, and social and cultural isolation from having undergone such a procedure. It seems clear that a person's sexual self-image would be marred by cutting out a very organ of sexual pleasure. It also seems clear that sexuality in those who have undergone FGM would seem socially, spiritually, and physically quite different—in body, mind, and spirit. Clearly, the statute suggests that any benefits of FGM in the cultural mind of the parents are far outweighed by the harm.

FGM is not on the top ten list of problems associated with diverse religion and spirituality faced by counselors. However, FGM can be seen as another case study for cases of spiritual or religious clashes in counseling. Caught between two opposing cultural norms and expectations, how are counselors to address them? The following are suggestions to help counselors articulate and think through some of the issues.

Employ the duty test as described in Chapter 4. As indicated in that chapter, these steps are: 1) identity the relevant and requisite duties, 2) prioritize those duties, 3) determine who owes the duty, and 4) determine to whom the duty is owed.

It seems clear, for example, that school counselors owe a duty of loyalty and obedience to school system or to the system or institution for which they work. A paycheck implies such obedience and loyalty. The exact nature of what that obedience is may vary. Below is a list of the likely suspects. They are not necessarily listed in descending order of importance, but obeying state and federal laws and institutional policies are obviously serious considerations.

1. *Obey applicable state and federal law.* This would be the duties of the first order. A counselor should be well acquainted with any law governing their practice or professional life. This is the function of this book. This book also encourages counselors to attend training sessions, in-service training, and other educational opportunities that responsibly address the legal issues surrounding culturally sensitive child welfare issues, child abuse laws, and the laws surrounding religion and the public schools.
2. *Obey policies and procedures in place at the institution.* The school or other institution probably has rules that specify procedures in many situations encountered by counselors. It is important to know and understand all those rules.

Should a counselor disagree or have questions involving a procedure, the time to question or to clarify that procedure is before a crisis occurs, not in the midst of one.

Where no policy is in place take three steps: imagine scenarios not addressed by the policy, suggest actions to superiors, and get some kind of action plan in writing, even if it is just an outline.

3. *Obey the ethical requirements of the profession in which you are licensed.* All licensing agencies have codes of ethics or codes of conduct. They are public documents. Counselors should read them, understand them and keep up with any changes in them.

4. *Obey the requirements of the certifications under which you employ your interventions.* For example, if you are a certified hypnotherapist or a biofeedback practitioner, you may well have duties associated with using those interventions instituted by the training organization.

5. *Obey higher duties only as a last resort and only after fully considering the consequences.* A current joke is that "The ten commandments are commandments—not suggestions!" This is a suggestion, arising out of the venerable but risky "whistleblowing" tradition. Sometimes federal and state laws do not serve the highest ends of justice. The same is true for codes of ethics. In such cases, as we know, employees are sometimes asked to conduct themselves in a manner that may or may not be lawful, but still place others in imminent danger. It not beyond likelihood that counselors, working either in the public or private section, may have opportunity to consider the application of a whistleblowing situation—either for themselves or a coworker.

Some of the intricacies of whistleblowing are found in *Walters v. Maricopa County* (1999). The plaintiff brought a wrongful termination action against his employer for allegedly firing him for disclosing information damaging to the county. His version of the story is that he told his employers that he was using estimated figures to prepare a budget to remedy potential environmental hazards.

These estimated figures found their way into a prospectus in county bonds—contrary to fraud and security statutes. He told his supervisors that it was illegal for the figures to be used. Later, he was fired. He fought the termination in court and the court dismissed his suit saying that his exclusive remedy was in the state's whistleblower act. Because the plaintiff did not follow the remedy prescribed by the Act that a public employee may make a complaint to the personnel board if they feel they have been fired as a reprisal for disclosing information.

The Arizona Court of Appeals reversed and remanded holding that the Act was permissive, not mandatory. The employee *could* make the complaint, but it was not a requirement. Thus the plaintiff was not precluded from taking his claim to state courts even thought he did not make a complaint to an administrative board.

Of course, it is always very tricky to determine the highest end of justice. While many courageous and determined people have blown the whistle for our greater good, such action can also be a misapplied notion of "I am right and the rest of the world is wrong." Such an attitude helps no one. A balanced approach might be characterized by the following:

1. Get legal advice.
2. Make sure of your facts.
3. Search your own motives.
4. Are there collateral gains?
5. Explore administrative remedies.

6. Count the costs. Sometimes the costs of an action should not be nit-picked to death. Sometimes they should be considered at length! This may be one of those times. Once you blow the whistle, its too late for second thoughts.

It probably will happen that conflicts arise between two important ethical traditions. For example, the practice of confidentiality and client welfare have been fertile ground for placing counselors between keeping client confidences and protecting their health and safety. These conflicts, in the judgment of this author, have largely been resolved in that counselors now routinely place clients on notice as to the limits of confidentiality. Yet, other conflicts may arise and should not be ignored.

First, let employment supervisors know when conflicts arise. Everyone in the situation is likely to act wisest when not in crisis. Under deadlines and the press of an emergency is not the moment for the most careful consideration.

Second, make written plans for contingencies. If a conflict exists and is discussed with supervisors, memorialize the resulting plans in writing. In the heat of crises or in the passage of time, memories are likely to fade.

Third, if a conflict persists, particularly between two legislative mandates, make the conflict known in writing. Sometimes in other legal areas, the state attorney general issues advisory opinions. These advisory opinions are designed to avoid future conflicts before they develop into a full-fledged court conflict. State licensing boards, for example, may issue such advisory opinions to clarify rules and procedures, particularly when they conflict with other state law or school board regulations.

Illustrating these concepts is the *Tribulak* case discussed in Chapter 3. In that case, a licensed counselor in a private, religious counseling clinic sued the clinic in federal court because, among other things, his supervisors wanted him to pray more. His employer required that he also include more Biblical references in his counseling. The clinic restricted his marital case load because Tribulak was having marital difficulties. He felt it was inappropriate and quit. In affirming the district court's ruling, the U.S. Circuit Court decided that he did not have a righteous suit for religious or sexual discrimination. The court concluded that Tribulak did not prove that his lack of prayer in counseling was consistent with his religious beliefs and that his counseling restrictions were discriminating. However, this case does give us an example of a counseling employee who was not asked to use *less* spiritual or alternative interventions, but more. Either way, counselors need to know both the rules of law, codes of ethics, and to apply their own independent judgment toward their clients.

As a means of fully considering these issues and consequences, it may be helpful to employ ethical ecology discussed in Chapter 5. As noted earlier, this involves examining the players in a given situation and their motivations or drives.

☐ Cultural Diversity, Spirituality and Complementary Counseling in Schools and other Public Settings

We have addressed school issues already in chapters as examples of criminal and civil law as well as related to "cultic" or to religious affiliation and religious freedom in schools. We will not retravel old territory.

Yet, there are particular issues involved in counseling students, minors, and others where the rule of "in loco parentis" may apply. This venerable and persistent legal doctrine sets forth the responsibilities of school officials to act, in limited ways, as temporary parents for the minors under their charge. An illustration may help.

A minor was arrested for bringing a knife longer than 2.5 inches to school. This high school student was convicted in juvenile court and ordered home on probation. At trial, the student motioned to suppress the knife because it was unlawfully seized contrary to the 4th amendment's prohibition against unlawful searches and seizures.

Her person was searched and the knife was seized pursuant to a school policy with a criteria neutral on its face. On the day the student was searched, the assistant principal determined that all students who were more than 30 minutes late for school and who entered the attendance hall without requisite passes would be searched. Students and their parents were given written notice about the policy and it was redistributed regularly.

Interestingly, this was a case of first impression for the California court of appeals. This means that this kind of issue has not been decided by a court of that jurisdiction or higher before in that state. So, the court relied upon the precedent from federal law and cases from other states to make its decision.

It held that the random metal detection-type searches, if conducted without suspicion attached to the individual herself, are legal (do not violate the Fourth Amendment). It conducted a "balancing test" and placed the interest of the government for safe schools on one side and the interest of the individual against unwarranted intrusion on the other side. The scale tipped in the balance of safety (*In re Latasha W.*, 1998). This tipping is often necessary to keep guns out of the school.

Interestingly, a citizen on the street would not usually be subject to such random searches. There are not police outside on street corners "randomly" searching citizens for illegal firearms. Schools are places where the courts suffer individual invasions of privacy for the substantial government policy for the safety of minors. After all, the government forces them to be in school in the first place.

Because the government requires minors to be in school, it has a higher duty to protect them. This means that freedoms are sometimes curtailed relative to the general population. The following issues arise from this convergence of constitution claims.

☐ Praying or Meditating with Students

The legal position of a school counselor is different from that of the private counselor, practice in their private offices. If a student asks their personal, private counselor to pray with them, the claims upon the private counselor are largely private claims. The licensing codes of ethics are public, but probably do not prohibit a private counselor from praying with a private client, mostly for 1st amendment reasons. The professional agencies (APA, NASW, ACA, etc.) probably also eschew such regulations, also because of First Amendment reasons.

The equations in the ethical ecology change when a school counselor is asked to pray or meditate, particularly on school property during work time. The players are different—with much more public claims upon the school counselor. These claims will ultimately make the decision different from that of a private counselor. The money paying the salary is public money. The property upon which the school counselor acts is public property. The regulations under which the school counselor acts are public regulations, not those of a private office or agency. In fact, it may be argued that there is no private act when a school counselor is working. Everything a school counselor does "on the job" is a public act, subject to public scrutiny.

Nor are fine distinctions likely to make much of a difference. In this case, whether a school counselor "prays" with a student or "meditates" with a student, or whether the counselor prays with a student or for a student in his or her presence, is probably a distinction without a difference. Precious few theologically or psychologically lay people are going to know the differences between prayer or meditation practices—or care. If the counselor is conducting any exercise whereby an image is evoked, a mythological, spiritual, or name is evoked, or anything close, it is likely to be termed by some as a prayer. If a school counselor wants to stand on such a distinction, he or she may end up spending some time at deposition or trial explaining it. If it seems like the litigation surrounding school prayer has a chilling effect upon exercises pertaining to meditation, it's probably true.

It may be prudent to avoid the term meditation altogether. If the counselor wants to run a class on relaxation or concentration, name it so. Narrowly construe the name of the procedure to reflect its stated purpose. In any event, the counselor needs to have a clear and unambiguous (and constitutional) purpose for any such exercises.

A similar ecology can be drawn in making the distinctions between praying with and student and paying for a student. Bullis (1996) reported that, while 83.5% of clinical social work respondents reported professional comfort in praying privately for clients, only 37.1% of respondents reported professional comfort in praying "with" a client. Personal comfort with such prayer reflects this disparity with 70.5% comfortable in praying for a client and 24.5% comfortable in praying with a client. (See Appendix C).

It is unlikely that school officials, parents, or the general public will know or care to distinguish whether a school counselor prays with or for a student. If a counselor does so during work time and/or school property, it is likely to cause political and constitutional problems. The ethical ecology equation must include the purposes and concerns of parents and the constitutional concerns of school officials and those likely to prosecute suits against the school system.

☐ Defamation and School Counselors

We have discussed the general statutes for defamation (libel and slander) in Chapter 3. We place defamation here again because school counselors have particular occasion to discuss students with teachers and other school administrators. School counselors regularly assess students. Unfortunately, there is also regular occasion to commit slander. This section focuses upon slander because that is the form of defamation most likely to be inadvertently committed by school and other institutional counselors. As ever, we first examine a statute and California's (Civil Code §46) does nicely:

> Slander is a false and unprivileged publication, orally uttered, and also communications by radio or any mechanical or other means which:
>
> 1. Charges any person with crime, or with having been indicted, convicted, or punished for crime;
> 2. Imputes in him [or her] the present existence of an infectious, contagious, or loathsome disease;
> 3. Tends directly to injure him in respect to his office, profession, trade or business, either by imputing to him general disqualification in those respects which the office or other occupation peculiarly requires, or by imputing something with reference to his office, profession, trade, or business that has a natural tendency to lessen its profits;
> 4. Imputes to him impotence or a want to chastity; or
> 5. Which, by natural consequence, causes actual damage.

Slander and libel (defamation) are often referred to as damage to one's reputation, particularly as it relates to one's specific profession. For example, the current author is, among other things, an ordained Presbyterian minister. Now if someone published the notion that a layperson was an atheist or agnostic, it may not rise to defamation. But to announce (publish) the notion that the present author is an atheist may lead to a defamation case. Why?

The reason is that defamation addresses a specific publication's impact upon specific careers and lifestyles. Accusations that a minister is an atheist can have more dire consequences for a minister than for a, say, medical doctor or psychologist. Thus, one must examine the specific situations and persons involved to ascertain the threat of defamation.

How can this apply to counselors who discuss, assess, or otherwise clarify or confer with students on religious or spiritual matters? Slanderous comments can be easily generated as the variety of alternative spiritual, social, and political groups and ideologies apper in schools.

Some contemporary Wicca debates were noted in Chapter 1. If a student proclaims that he or she follows witchcraft or shamanism or other earth religions, is it conceivable that conflicts and expressions of opinions may be expressed? Such comments may rise to the level of slander if they harm the reputation or opinion of others in the school.

The old joke was that school systems could be sued as easily as it would be to conceal a tape recorder in the teacher's lounge. It's only a joke if you are not the one sued. The fact is that many inadvertent comments stemming from a student's religious or spiritual behavior may rise to the level of slander. Off-hand comments that a student's beliefs are crazy, stupid, or other derogatory term—even subtle ways of denigrating a student's religion—may be construed as slander. It doesn't matter why the potential slanders were made. It only matters that they were communicated—published, as the statute says.

But the statute mentions profits or business—how do these apply to students? School counselors play a significant role in the development of young people: They can make recommendations or not to teachers, and can aid in college admission—or not. What a counselor says or does not say to other school officials (e.g., teachers, administrators, guidance counselors) or even other students can make an appreciable difference in the students academic career.

The argument might well be made that school counselors must speak with and evaluate their students. Of course, that is where the California Code's term of privilege plays an important legal role. The Civil Code (§46) sanctions false and unprivileged publications. The next section in the California Civil Code (§47) reads:

> A privileged publication of broadcast is one made:
> (a) In the proper discharge of an official duty.
> (b) In any
>   (1) legislative proceeding,
>   (2) judicial proceeding,
>   (3) in any other official proceeding authorized by law ...

Nothing should be included in a file that does not have clear relevance to a student. Unverified, extraneous, or irrelevant material should be avoided. A test for any included material might be 1) would you want to explain in court any material you wrote and 2) could you verify or defend any included data or opinion?

☐ Counselors and Moments of Silence

One of the hottest issues in public education today is school prayer. Most in-school prayer, led by school officials, during regular school activities would probably be held unconstitutional. In 1992, the U.S. Supreme Court extended its constitutional prohibition of compulsory classroom prayer to clergy-led prayers at out-of-school gatherings such as graduations. The U.S. Court of Appeals for the **5th Circuit** (Texas, Louisiana, and Mississippi) ruled that such prayers are constitutional if they are "nonsectarian and nonproselytizing." The **11th Circuit** (Alabama, Florida, and Georgia) permits student-led prayer, but requires the prayer as a matter of free speech—so long as it is student initiated (Deibel, 1999). These issues are legally fluid and will take the clearer light of future decisions by the U.S. Supreme Court to settle them.

While predetermined prayers by teachers are less frequent (largely because of constitutional challenges), moments of silence are more common. While no means universal, these provisions and the attendant public comment and scrutiny may cause some concern, questions, or educating moments for school counselors. The Illinois period of silence (§105 ILCS 20/1, 1998) is an illustration:

> In each public school classroom the teacher in charge may observe a brief period of silence with the participation of all the pupils therein assembled at the opening of every school day. This period shall not be conducted as a religious exercise but shall be an opportunity for silent prayer or for silent reflection on the anticipated activities of the day. (§1)

School prayer laws are among the single most frequently litigated aspects of the First Amendment. These laws try to walk labyrinthine lines between the rights of parents to have values or religious or spiritual activities in school and those who find that any or some religiously or spiritually motivated activities are either discriminatory or antagonistic to their own views. It would be easy for a school counselor to get caught in the middle. However, knowing how courts interpret these laws can be of great help how counselors can articulate their own position or the position of their school district.

The Distribution of Religiously or Spiritually-Based Literature

Similarly, school counselors may get questions and have to field concerns about the distribution of spiritual or religious material on or near school grounds. Again, counselors are not the spokesperson of the courts or the school's legal counsel, but the rationale for their decisions on such matters may help them articulate the legal and ethical positions taken by either side.

In *Peck v. Upshur County Board of Education* (1998) the **4th Circuit** Court of Appeals had to decide whether it was permissible for a local West Virginian minister to make available (not distribute) at a predetermined date and predetermined location. The school board agreed, if certain guidelines were followed, and were promptly sued. The guidelines included that the tables where the literature were distributed be located in places where students normally congregate so that the students would not feel watched. The source for the Bibles could not be identified, no school employee was to be involved in the process of availability, and no person was to stand by the tables encouraging students to take one. Additionally, while the district court allowed the availability to continue, it did require that a disclaimer be placed on the site of distribution that the school district neither sponsored nor endorsed the availability of the literature (Duff, Dubberly, Turner, White, Boykin, LLC, 1998).

The Court of Appeals had to decide whether the school district was a neutral forum for the availability of literature. Clearly, the school board decided to open the school to outside groups to make their literature available. In the law, this is called an open forum. The Court had to decide if the school board was neutral and unbiased in its provisions for an open forum. The Court found that, given the rules promulgated by the school board and the procedures for implementing them, the school board was committed not only to creating an open forum, but making it fair and unbiased.

In reaching its decision, the Court likened the rules governing the school's open forum to the federal law known as the Equal Access Act (EAA). Applying only to secondary schools, the EAA allows religiously based groups to meet in schools which also allows non-curriculum groups to meet there as well. The Court found that, so long as the school board in the *Peck* case allowed non-religious free speech, it must provide religious free speech on an equal basis. This federal law is the subject of the next section.

☐ The Equal Access Act and School Counselors

The Equal Access Act (EAA) was promulgated in 1984 and was designed to guarantee the right of ideological groups to have equal access to meeting places in schools just as non-ideological groups, such as the Spanish Club or the Chess Club, have. Senator Denton, one of the Act's author's, said that "secondary school students engaging in religious speech have the same rights to associate together and to speak as do students who wish to meet to discuss chess, politics, or philosophy" (130 Cong. Rec. at 19,216 (1984)).

The EAA states in part:

> It shall be unlawful for any public secondary school which receives Federal financial assistance and which has a limited open forum to deny equal access or a fair opportunity to, or discriminate against, any students who wish to conduct a meeting within that limited open forum on the basis of the religious, political, philosophical, or other content of the speech at such meetings. (20 U.S.C. §§4071-4071(a))

As one might expect, this statute has given rise to litigation. In *Hsu v. Roslyn Union Free School District* (1996) students wishing to form an after-school Bible Club successfully negotiated an agreement with the school, on all but one point. The sticking point was the Club's insistence that the Bible Club's officers be exclusively Christians. The school refused Club recognition on the grounds that this condition violated school policy prohibiting any kind of discrimination on the basis of any protected class, including religion.

The U.S. Court of Appeals for the 2nd **Circuit** ruled that the Club's provision for Christian officers was essential to the expressed content of the Club and for its intended and expressed purpose and identity. The Club's provision did not violate the EAA because such a provision would not draw the school into the establishment of religion or undermine the school's efforts to discourage discrimination.

The rationale and subsequent court decisions of the EAA are significant for school counselors because they offer insights into how such counselors may approach religious or spiritual issues with their clients and students. This statute and case offer an indication that the First Amendment is not the much touted "wall" separating church and state. It is more like a porous membrane. The First Amendment does not obligate government to ignore or to dissuade religious or spiritual free speech. To reiterate concepts noted in the introduction and chapter one, the First amendment only prohibits the establishment of any one religion or undermining the free exercise of religion.

It seems clear that religion and spirituality will be a continuing hot topic in secondary schools. Counselors cannot expect to be free from discussing religion and spirituality with students. Counselors, at the very least, should encourage a more than superficial look at religious groups who ask to use school facilities or to form groups that use school facilities. The *Hsu* case encourages school officials and school counselors to look at the role of the group, its stated purposes and how it is formed, and officer qualifications, membership qualifications (if any).

Additionally, the counselor could educate and engage both administration and students on such issues that are likely to arise. It probably is not the case where the counselor will be seen as the initiator of such discussions, it seems clear that student raise these issues on their own. School counselors, for from avoiding such issues, should and can (constitutionally acceptable) discuss religious and spiritual questions as they arise from the students.

☐ The Equal Access Act and Gay-Lesbian School Clubs

The Equal Access Act and the First Amendment are not only applicable to cultural and religious-spiritual issues, but to sexual orientation issues as well. In *Colin v. Orange Unified School District* (2000), students sued to **enjoin** the school district disallowing their application to form a student-run, in-school Gay–Straight Alliance Club. The U.S. District Court for the Central District of California granted the plaintiff's suit for a preliminary junction. The school district was enjoined from refusing the students' application to form the club. The students won their suit.

In the court's determination was based upon a number of considerations stemming both from the Equal Access Act and the First Amendment's guarantee of free speech. Again, one of the requirements of the Act is to be that there should be no discrimination against whom should be allowed to use school facilities for the purpose in forming clubs. That is, the content or message of the group should not be used to unfairly deny a club's access to school grounds. The school district allowed other groups access to form clubs including: the Asian Club, the Black Student Union, the Christian Club, and Koinonia (for Catholic students). The court concluded that the school district did not exactly allow for equal access when it disallowed the Gay–Straight Alliance Club.

The court also noted that the school district had already established a "limited open forum" at the high school in allowing the above-mentioned, non-curricular clubs on school grounds. To now disallow the Gay-Straight Alliance Club access was an decision based upon the Club's message. That decision was content-based and, thus, violative of the Act. As we have already noted, school counselors and school officials must be careful not to offend either the First Amendment or the Equal Access Act when determining which groups it will or will not allow on school grounds. Denying the local Wiccanor pagan group while allowing other religious groups places the burden upon the school to show a non-content, non-discriminatory reason why.

☐ Schools and Mandatory Student Fees

Another issue brought forth by students in educational institutions is the mandatory student activity fees used to found some extra-curricular groups, but not others. This issue is another significant concern to college and university counselors because it is a countervailing trend in law limiting mandatory student resources for ideological groups. Counselors need to be aware that groups, including religious and spiritual groups, cannot receive favorable school treatment just as they cannot receive unfavorable treatment. Counselors, knowing the rationale of such cases as the following, can better raise the level of religious or spiritual discussion on campus, can better explain the policy of the school administration, and can better help articulate individual student's religious or spiritual concerns.

Student plaintiffs complained that their mandatory student fee to the University of Wisconsin-Madison (UW) was funding political and ideological activities. Some of the groups funded were: International Socialist Organization, Students of National Organization for Women, the Madison Treaty Rights Support Group, and UW Greens. The plaintiffs argued that to fund these groups, with specific ideological stands, is to prejudice only some voices in the free speech chorus. Religious or spiritual groups, hypothetically, could either have been on the receiving end of UW's largess or on the complaining side.

For their part, the University argued that these groups had a free speech right to be heard on campus. The Court, while agreeing with the notion that these groups have a free speech right, noted that is not the issue. The issue was a three part test to determine whether these groups, and not others, should have their free speech funded by a fee that all UW students must pay. In fact, some wags call this process not free speech but fee speech. This three part test asks:

1. Is the challenged activity germane to the Regents' asserted interest (the Regents is the governing body of the University)
2. Is the compelled fee justified by the vital policy interest?
3. Does using compelled fees to fund a private organization which engages in political/ideological activities significantly burden free speech.

The Court concluded that the University failed to sustain its burden on any of the three tests. The University claimed that these groups were part of the educational process and promotes diverse opinions on campus. The Court ruled, however, that a broad educational defense cannot excuse the discriminatory effect of the UW's policy. Second, UW asserted that it is part of students' education to help run the school through funding decisions. The Court was unimpressed noting that the decision for most UW students is that they must fund groups to which they are opposed, or they cannot get a diploma. Third, the Court found that funding the groups deeply burdens the objecting student's own freedom of speech. The funded groups use the money to garner public support and attract adherents (Garrett, 1999).

In chapter one, we examined *individual* expression of religious or spiritual constitutional questions. We, here, turn to religious questions in institutional settings. The rights are the same, but the context is different.

☐ Vicarious Liability of Counseling Schools and Programs

In Chapter 3, we discussed the legal concept of vicarious liability. It is within easy intellectual reach to see how employers may be liable for the misdeeds of their employees. This final section addresses the vital issue as to the liability of schools for their students on field education, or practicum programs. By whatever designation, schools that offer degrees in social services or counseling offer a practice program whereby students get hands on experience. This section addresses the hypotheticals whereby students who engage in spiritual or complementary counseling are sued and schools are named defendants as well. This is an issue of major concern to supervisors and for educational institutions, as well as it should be.

We specify and narrow our inquiry to the kinds of liability suits likely to occur in complementary and spiritual interventions. As we have discussed vicarious liability, scope of employment and other such issues previously we need not rehearse them again.

As we have previously seen, legal analogies are often useful in considering trends and preventative actions as we do here. Both social work schools and graduate medical education have been the subjects of such inquiries. Gelman and Wardell (1988), after surveying the kinds of suits likely at social work schools, suggest that school must be continually aware of the student's changing environment and the growing demand for accountabilities. Perhaps a preliminary preventative strategy for students and their supervisors is the ethical ecology exercise described in Chapter 5.

Getting to know the legal, social, religious, and spiritual ground upon which the student is working in field education may serve two purposes: 1) to acquaint the student and supervisor about the players (both major and minor) the student is likely to encounter; this exercise may make the student aware of less conspicuous players who will, nonetheless, be important players, and 2) acknowledge the motivations and drives of those players. This is particularly true for the less conspicuous players. It may be that unnamed or unspoken expectations are current at the field work placement. Examining each and every player's motivations and expectations, can immunize the school and the student from being blind sided. Such expectations might well be memorialized and clearly articulated in field work agreements.

In a follow up article by Gelman (1990), he examines field work agreements and suggests, for example, that one agency not borrow agreements in an effort towards efficiency and that responsibilities be clearly defined. Given the discussion of this book, it comes as no surprise that a private, religiously based social service agency might take a different view of such interventions as clarifying religious or spiritual goals, prayer, meditation or other interventions than a publicly funded counseling department or agency. Even private agencies, no matter what type of licensed counselors might have individual preferences and expectations, particularly regarding using spiritual or complementary interventions. These expectations should be disclosed, reviewed, and articulated in field work agreements. Simply placing the light of day upon exactly what interventions are or are not acceptable can go along way clearing up any confusion in this respect. Of course, this clarity should also be communicated clearly to the client as well. We have discussed the necessity for such disclosures in prior chapters.

Gelman and Wardell (1988) also point out that if school in any way warrant or guarantee that their students are competent in some areas, the schools may be forced to face up to that promise in court. This means that the advertisement or recommendation of students for specific field placements may be warrants of competence as it were. This is another reason that each, individual student's fitness must match the demands of their field placement.

In discussing graduate medical education and the liability for medical school residents, Reuter (1994) prompts us once again about the necessity of coming to terms with the issue of "scope of employment" issue that we had struggled with in Chapter 5. The analogy between medical and counselor education is a close one. He rightly reminds us that in affiliation agreements (between hospital and medical school) and other documents, courts may well determine who intends to have how much control over the resident's work. This is a crucial point.

Counseling programs will want to determine to what extent they or the field education placement agency or institution will control the work of the student. Such questions are certainly relevant:

1. Who has responsibility for day-to-day supervision and discipline?
2. How often and to what degree does the school or field placement assign clients, work hours, method(s) of intervention, or discipline?
3. How much say does the student have in choosing his or her placement or supervisor? Correspondingly how much say does the site supervisor have in choosing a student? How much influence does the school have in placing a given student at a given site?
4. How much influence does the accrediting body of the school or the field site have in determining the criterion of who gets place where?

Some final cases help put some specificity upon this section. Again we sometimes seek law by analogy. How free can a supervisor be to render an opinion of a psychology student to the Board of Examiners without fear of losing a libel suit. (Notice I said losing a libel suit. There can be no surefire way to immunize anyone from suing anyone, we only can try to minimize liability.) It seems that, so long as the comments are clearly relevant to the professional inquiry and made without malice, they may be fairly free to do so. A psychology intern filed charge of libel against his supervisor under these conditions and the trial court summarily dismissed the suit, and a Georgia appeals court affirmed saying that unless malice is shown such supervisors have conditional immunity (*Cohen v. Hartlage*, 1986).

☐ Conclusion

This chapter further explored the role of cultural and spiritual diversity that can impact counselors. This diversity is illustrated by the unfortunate and distressing phenomena of female genital mutilation (FGM) and the controversial defense known as the "cultural defense." Many states have already criminalized FGM. The "cultural defense" poses the ethical and legal issue of whether criminal acts in the United States ought to be mitigated because such acts are not sanctioned in the perpetrators country of origin or cultural milieu. How should counselors intervene where their clients act out of a religious, spiritual, or cultural frame of reference that is antithetical or even criminal in this country?

School counselors are in the front line trenches of spiritual, religious, and cultural controversies. This chapter addressed a wide range of spiritually and religiously charged issues that are unresolved even after several Supreme Court rulings. In fact, many of these issues are so specifically fact driven that they may well have to be resolved on a case-by-case basis should they wind up in court. This chapter has addressed some of these prominant examples including school prayer (or moments of silence), defamation, and the Equal Access Act. Moreover, this chapter offered several suggestions as to how counselors might begin to understand legal and ethical issues surrounding these issues.

☐ Legal/Ethical Exercises and Audits

1. Do you now, or have you ever had a client who raised the issue of a "cultural defense" in any of its varieties, to explain raising a child or any other conduct otherwise considered illegal or unethical? What was your response? What are your limitations

as to such conduct defended by religious, spiritual or cultural considerations? Do you have any?

Are there behaviors that you think are wrong or punishable even though they are culturally, religiously, or spiritually accepted or encouraged in another culture?

Would you explain your reactions to a client? Only if asked? How about a child or elder abuse situation?

2. Religious and spiritual issues are as lively on campus as they are in society—and equally ambivalent as well. Does your school have policies in place to determine what behavior, symbols, or literature is allowed on school grounds? Is there a process by which students can appeal or explain any decisions requiring them to change their practices, clothing, or what they distribute?

3. What is your defamation vulnerability quotient? How closely do you hold evaluations, reports and client confidences? Put another way, what would your peers say about how you keep confidences?

How are the systems designed to maintain confidences in your office or agency working? Is there an ethic of confidentiality supported by supervisors? Are there systems by which employee evaluations and client records maintained confidential?

4. You are supervising students in a counseling program. Do you know the limits and the extent to which you are responsible for their clients? How closely do you have to monitor them? Have you worked out any arrangements for such supervision with your administration and the training site?

CHAPTER

A Brief Afterword

This might be the shortest chapter ever written. A very brief afterward may be necessary to review and reconnect with the original intention of this book—to remind us that there is a forest in all these legal and ethical trees.

This book is in no way intended to dissuade anyone from practicing their spiritual or complementary counseling practice. Elements of law and spirituality should deepen and strengthen this practice. Certainly, the law and ethics makes demands on counselors. But those demands exist already. This book only sheds light on them. Shedding light on issues should never be construed as an impediment. It should be a challenge and an opportunity to better serve clients, the public and the professions under which we practice.

In fact, this book's sole purpose is to help make that practice safe, honorable, creative, productive—in other words—sacred.

A

How to Find the Law

This Appendix is a short guide on strategies for finding legal materials for the non-lawyer. Legal citation is unlike social science citation; however, you may want to explore the law first hand. Where to look is just as important as how to look.

☐ Where to Look for Statutes and Case Law

1. The quickest way to locate statutes and case law is to have a lawyer find them for you. You may have an attorney friend who can locate the relevant statutes say, on the clergy-penitent privilege or the spiritual exemption for prosecution for child abuse. The lawyer can also offer related case law to help interpret the statutes.

   It may be that the use of your lawyer friend's legal library is your best bet. If that's the case, the legal assistant in your friend's office can probably provide the necessary guidance. It is important to specify what statute you need. For example, if you are a licensed counselor, psychologist, or clinical social worker, you can locate the statutes codifying those professions' codes of ethics. In that case, you should tell the legal assistant or secretary that you are looking for, say, the statute regulating clinical social workers and their codes of conduct or codes of ethics. It is important to realize that the words clinical social workers (or whatever clinical designation), code of ethics, or ethics amount to keywords to look up in the indexes.

2. College or university libraries often have those legal materials that are particular to their jurisdictions. Thus, a state university in New York will often have all the statute books for New York, their books containing state court decisions, and the regional reporter containing the most important cases decided in New York state courts. Similarly, college or university libraries might well stock current state statute volumes and corresponding indexes.

   It is a good idea to become fast friends with the research librarians. They can be of enormous help in pointing out the extent of the collection, what the collection contains, and the location of volumes. See the glossary for a more detailed description of **regional reporters**.

3. The next best way is to go to a law library in a law school. Such libraries, obviously, has extensive law collections from all jurisdictions and a legal research librarian who can help. If the librarian has the time (an appointment may help) he or she can direct you to the right stacks and give you enough guidance at least to get you started.

☐ How to Look for Law

1. If you wish to find a statute from scratch, find the state statute section and get the index for that state. Look up the general title or the general topic of the law in which you are interested in the index. This may require some persistence. An index is only as useful as its specificity and clarity. For example, if you want to see the therapeutic exploitation statutes discussed in Chapter 2, sometimes the index will list them under exploitation, therapeutic or therapeutic exploitation or even some other designation. You might need to look up the general heading of counselor or mental health to find these statutes.

   In this respect, looking up specific statutes from keywords in the indexes sometimes requires the patience of Job. It is often necessary to look under a variety of related terms in order to find the statute citation.

2. When the needed statute is located, a citation number and perhaps a volume name is given. Armed with this information, turn to the statute volumes themselves. If a name or title of the volume is given along with the numerical citation, look for the titled volumes, then look under the sequential numerical citation. Usually, the first set of numbers refers to the volume number. A fuller description of this process follows.

3. If you know the statute citation number, from this book, or another source, you can go right to the statute volumes. The statute volumes themselves will be located alongside the indexes. The first set of numbers generally refers to the volume number, chapter, or title of the statute volume. Larger states not only have many numbers of volumes, but have specific titles for their statutes. For example, in Chapter 7, we examined the California "slander" statute with a citation of Civil Code §46. Thus, to find this citation, three pieces of information are necessary. First, you need to remember that you need to look under the California statute. Second, you need to find the volumes titled "Civil Code" on their bindings. Third, you need to find the right section number, in this case §46.

4. We're not finished yet. Statutes change. To keep up with statutory amendments, periodic, but regularly published softbound supplements are issued that can be slipped into the backs of the hardbound volumes. It is much less expensive to provide supplements than to replace numerous hardbound volumes when statutes change. Because these supplements slide into a back pocket in the volumes, they are commonly called "pocket parts." Thus, when we cited the Illinois Ritual Mutilation statute in chapter (Chapter 5/12–32 § 12–32 West Supp. 1999) we should note that the "West Supp. 1999" designation means that the West Publishing Company published the supplement in 1999. This is the most recent supplement as of this writing.

5. Finally, most statute books are not simply lists of statutes. Most have annotations to the statutes. These provide such useful information as some legislative history and date of passage. Additionally, the case annotations at the end of the statute will carry short synopses and citations of cases interpreting the statutes. This is a relatively easy way to find cases that have been decided under the statute. These case notes are very brief case synopses, but offer the citations and the essence of the decision.

☐ Computerized Legal Research

Computerized legal research and citation is a whole new avenue for legal research. Two major computerized systems or data bases, Lexis/Nexis and Westlaw, are widely used by legal professionals. Because this book is not designed for legal professionals, discussion of them will be limited. If you have access, however, to law schools or to attorneys they may be willing or able to help you conduct legal research on their computers. Computerized legal research is much more efficient than the traditional method of pouring over cases bound in books. However, as one might expect, it is more expensive.

Another method is the free legal data bases that are on the Internet. Of course you need to pay an Internet fee to service providers. Access to some legal material for every state and some federal material is possible. As those who have done searches on the Internet know well, the search requires patience, perseverance and the right keywords. This work can't help too much with the patience and the perseverance parts, but it can with the keywords. These steps may help increase the efficiency of a legal search on the free data bases.

1. *Have a clear idea for what you are looking.* Browsing is fun in bookstores but can be a real time-waster in legal research. If you do not have a clear idea of exactly what you want to know, it will probably be hard for the research librarian to help much. Not that you must have the precise legal terminology for what you want to know, but some idea of the information sought is necessary. Don't begin the search until you have a good idea, at least for yourself. For example, if you want to find out whether or not your state has cases exempting "spiritual healing" from child abuse convictions, you might not have all the right words.

    Additionally, you'll need to know whether you want to find a statute or case law. If it doesn't matter, then the search can be more general and will probably be more lengthy.

2. *Have a clear idea under what jurisdiction you are looking.* The more specific the jurisdiction, the more specific keywords you can enter, such as federal law, federal statutes, Iowa law or other such keywords. In any case, the more specific you can be about jurisdiction, the more efficient your search can be. It goes without saying that even once you have reached the webpage for your state or federal law or other legal site, you will need to point and click through some avenues and choices before you reach what you want.

    It seems likely and reasonable that counselors will be most interested in the state law where they practice and/or are licensed. Should a counselor want to move to another state, research in that jurisdiction is also important. Still, in all questions of law, it is important to check both state and federal statutes and case law.

3. *Have a clear idea of why you are looking.* Determining *why* you are looking for a case or statute can determine how deeply you need to explore the law. For example, if you just want to have the counselor confidentiality statute for your state on file, it is sufficient to just copy the statute (looking, of course, for the pocket part as well).

    If you want to find out if a client's admission about future, possible ritual abuse from are confidential or require disclosure, deeper study may be warranted. You might well even consider speaking to an attorney to get the question answered.

4. *Know when to engage legal counsel.* Self-help legal research may be fine for general, nonlitigated questions. But the more serious and specific the question, the more you need legal counsel. The money spent for a half-hour or hour consultation is money well spent. It is good to remember that some legal questions can yield serious consequences for you, your clients, and your career. A trip the lawyer's office can be viewed as professional preventative medicine. It is good to remember that it is not the place for the counselor to opine to clients on legal matters. It also bears repeating that the insights and information in this book are not legal advice either.

☐ A Note on Citations

Enormous amounts of information are available simply from the citations. They can tell what level of court decided the case. They can tell the jurisdiction of the court—that is, whether it was a state or federal case—even in what state the court resided.

Additionally, the citations specifically locate the statute or the case from the volumes upon volumes in any law library.

Let's look at a couple of examples from this book. In Chapter 1 we cited:

State v. Speed, 90 Wash. App. 1047, Wash. App. LEXIS 705 (1998).

First things first. The first of the case names is the plaintiff, or if the case is on appeal, it is the name of the one bringing the appeal. In this case the state brought this appeal. The second name is the one who must defend. "90" is the volume number of the set of law books and "1047" is the page number of the case. "Wash. App." means three things: 1) it is a state, not a federal case, 2) it was decided in the State of Washington, and 3) it was an appellate court that decided the case. Generally speaking if the case was decided by the highest state court, the designation would be simply the state abbreviation such as "Wash."

This case is also registered in a computerized system of legal research called "LEXIS." As mentioned earlier, there are other computerized systems, but this is the one used in this instance. As previously stated, Wash. App." means an appellate court in that state. Then comes the company name (in this case, LEXIS) followed by the company-assigned number of the case. The page numbers on computerized searches are differently organized than on the traditional methods, as you will note in the citation of this case in the reference section of this volume. Obviously, there are no "volume" numbers in a computerized system. Finally, the year of the decision is in parentheses.

Another citation, also from Chapter 1, puts a slight twist in legal citation. The citation is:

Hester v. Barnett, 723 S.W.2d 544 (Mo. Ct. App. 1987).

This citation, also from a state court, cites to the regional reporter, not the state reporter's system. Regional reporters include major cases from a number of states within a geographical region. For example the case above is cited to the Southwestern regional reporter (S.W. in the citation), which includes Arizona, New Mexico, Nevada, and Missouri. There are several regional reporters, published by West Publishing Company, including Northeastern, Southern, Southeastern, Northwestern, and Pacific. The regional reporters are an efficient and more economical way to report the most important appellate cases from a number of different states without having to subscribe to each state's reporter system. The "2d" means that this regional reporter is in its second edition. The volume and number designations are in the same locations as in the Washington state reporter—first the volume number then the page number.

An example of a citation including both the state reporters and the regional reporters is found in Chapter 2:

People v. Steinberg, 79 N.Y.2d 673, 595 N.E.2d 845, 584 N.Y.S.2d 770 (1992).

The middle cite (595 N.E.2d 845) is the regional citation for the Northeastern reporter in the second edition. The regional cite is flanked by two New York state law reporters (N.Y. second series, and the N.Y. supplement, second series)

Let's examine now some federal citations. First, a famous one—the citation for the controversial Miranda warning:

Miranda v. Arizona, 384 U.S. 537, 16 S.Ct. 1138, 41 L.Ed. 256 (1966).

This citation immediately tells the reader that this is a Supreme Court decision. The last citation (L.Ed.) is the lawyer's edition and the "S.Ct." stands for the Supreme Court. These two later reporters publish the cases relatively quickly. The official U.S. government cite is the first citation, but cases are reported at later dates. Of course, the year of the decision is posted at the end of the citation.

So what of the lower two federal courts? The intermediate court, as mentioned earlier are the Circuit Courts of Appeal. Their citation abbreviation is "F." for federal. A single "F." cite means that volume is from the 1st edition (earlier cases). Most cases in our lifetime within the past 20 years have been under the second edition cited as "F.2d" and in the late 1990s a third edition was instituted, in the 1990s noted as "F.3d".

The lowest or trial court in the federal system is the district court. Those courts are designated as "F.Supp." In the parentheses for the federal district court is the specific jurisdiction of the court and the date of decision; for example, "E.D. Va., 1999" means that this decision was made by the Eastern district court of Virginia and decided in the year 1999.

Glossary of Legal Terms and Abbreviations

Affirm: A "higher" court's agreement with and assent to a "lower" court's previous opinion. See reverse, overturn, and remand.

Agency: The legal doctrines and principals of agents and principals.

Agent: An employee; someone who works for a principal (employer) and who is controlled or works to the benefit of that principal. See principal.

Appeal: To request a higher court to review the ruling of a lower court.

Appellate court: "Upper" level of court to whom "lower" courts. Also, called court of appeals.

Beyond the pleadings: refers to the offering of evidence beyond merely pleading it. Saying it is true requires some proof.

Bonafide: Term used to connote good faith, authenticity, or no malice.

Cause of action: The terms of art and related principles that are the legal bases for a law suit.

Certiorari or "cert.": Traditionally, a writ issued by a superior court to order a review of an inferior court's decision. Now it usually refers to notice that the U.S. Supreme Court has granted a review of a lower court's ruling—in citations, such as in this book, that notice is designated "cert." If the request for a review is denied, the citation is "cert. den'd."

Civil law: The brand of law addressing private claims by private parties. See Criminal law.

Computerized legal research: Two of the major firms provide on-line, in-depth, complete legal research. As it happens the writer used Lexis research engine; thus, a LEXIS citation is given along with the traditional West Publication cites in the Reference section.

Criminal law: The brand of law addressing public claims by public and private parties. See Civil law.

Defendant: The one who must defend themselves in court. The same term is used in both civil and criminal courts. See plaintiff.

Deposition: A "question and answer" session where a witness for one side is asked questions by lawyers from the other side. These answers are sworn statements and can (and often are) used to impeach the credibility (See Glossary) of witness later at trial.

Dicta: Comment, made by judges in the course of a written legal decision, that does not bear directly upon the decision itself.

Discovery: The collecting of legally relevant data, information, witnesses, records, or other "evidence" in preparation for a trial or litigation.

Due Diligence: The attention and inquiry to satisfy the legal standard in the oversight of an agency, corporation or other legal entity. Although often applied to the oversight of a Board of Trustees or a Board of Directors in the oversight of their businesses, one might use the ethical analogy to the oversight of a supervisor to an employee counselor.

Due Process: Rights afforded by law ensuring fair treatment under the law. These include arrest processes, investigative techniques, and trial procedures. The *Miranda* warning is an illustration of due process rights.

Duty: The legal obligation to do something or not to do something. If that legal obligation is not discharged, liability or guilt may attach.

Duty Determination: Author's term for the identification and prioritization of duties and/or obligations. This determination includes identifying who owes the duty and to whom the duty is owed.

Enjoin: To legally forbid. Often a judge will issue an injunction to stop some action. If instruction is disobeyed, a contempt of court may be filed.

Ethical claim: Author's term for an ethical allegation or assertion.

Ethical ecology: Author's term for the environment, including the players, constituents and motivations, in which ethical decisions are made and executed.

Expert witness: Allowed in both federal and state courts, such experts help judges and juries understand technical aspects of a case. Both sides of a case will call expert witnesses if they are helpful. A judge must rule that they are so qualified, however.

Federal circuit courts: The mid-range of federal jurisdiction. These 13 circuits are appellate courts which review federal district court cases under appeal. The geographic distribution of the circuits are described, by their numerical designations:

1st Circuit: Maine, New Hampshire, Massachusetts and Puerto Rico
2nd Circuit: Vermont, New York, and Connecticut
3rd Circuit: Pennsylvania, New Jersey and Delaware
4th Circuit: West Virginia, Virginia, Maryland, North and South Carolina
5th Circuit: Mississippi, Louisiana, and Texas
6th Circuit: Michigan, Ohio, Kentucky and Tennessee
7th Circuit: Wisconsin, Indiana and Illinois
8th Circuit: Arkansas, Missouri, Iowa, Nebraska, Minnesota, North and South Dakota
9th Circuit: California, Nevada, Idaho, Montana, Oregon, Washington State, Alaska and Hawaii

10th Circuit: Kansas, Oklahoma, Colorado, New Mexico, Utah and Wyoming
11th Circuit: Alabama, Georgia and Florida

The specialized systems known as Washington "DC" and "federal" circuits round out the 13 federal circuits.

Federal District Courts: These are the federal "trial level" courts. Naturally, these courts are more numerous than the higher, circuit courts. For example, while the 4th circuit court sits only in Richmond, Virginia, the federal district court has two courthouses, one in the western (Roanoke) and one in the eastern part of the state (Richmond).

Felony: Serious charge in a criminal case.

Forensics (forensic): Concerned with legal proceedings or argument.

Foreseeability: The legal doctrine that an event could or should have been predicted; thus, avoided. Such prediction and avoidance is sometimes an element of negligence. See "scienter"

Guilty: Legal determination of wrongdoing in a criminal case. See liability.

Immunity: Legal amnesty.

Impeach the credibility: To uncover errors, inconsistencies, or downright falsehoods in a witness' testimony. This scores points for the one who uncovers such impeachments (See "deposition"). In the worst case, such falsehoods can rise to the level of perjury (See this Glossary).

Indictment: A criminal is "indicted" when a grand jury (or similar body) rules that enough evidence has been shown that the accused has committed the crime. A grand jury is used for more serious crimes like felonies.

Informal consent: An agreement and assent that is both voluntary and knowing.

Interalia: "among other things."

Jurisdiction: Power of court to hear a case.

Jurisprudence: The art and science of law.

Jury nullification: Where a jury refuses to renders a verdict consistent with the evidence. Where it nullifies an acquittal where there is sufficient evidence because the jury thinks it is unjust to do so. Conversely, a jury that find a defendant guilty where there is sufficient evidence to acquit, "nullifies" the "correct" verdict.

Intent or intentionality: A legal requirement for most (not all) determination of guilt or liability. In the criminal law this amounts to the *mens rea*. Legal intent does not mean that a defendant will each and every consequence to be guilty or liable. For example, a drunk driver can be charged with vehicular homicide if they kill someone else on the road, when they had no intent to do so. The law might impute a legal intent to cause harm when a person is so reckless as to drink and drive. See strict liability.

Legislative (or statutory) history: The documents of policy and procedure that describe the rationale, origin and purposes behind a statute as well as its subsequent enactments. This history offers judges a clearer way to understand why the statute was enacted so that judges may more clearly interpret that statute.

Liability: The determination of "guilt" in a civil action. See guilt.

Litigants: Parties to a lawsuit—known mostly as the plaintiffs or defendants.

Malpractice: Professional negligence. See negligence.

Mens actus: The "guilty act" necessary to be convicted under most criminal statutes.

Mens rea: The "guilty mind" (i.e., intent) usually necessary to be convicted under most criminal statutes.

Misdemeanor: A lesser degree of criminal charges. For example, some states consider misdemeanor theft to be less that $500. Over that amount is a felony.

Modus operandi: The "means of operation;" that is, how a criminal does their job. A bank robber will have pretty much a set pattern of how he or she most efficiently or effectively (so to speak) accomplishes the task.

Negligence: Wrongdoing in a civil action. Negligence will be determined to the extent that actions or inaction falls below the standard of care. Professional negligence is called "malpractice."

Overrule or overturn: A higher court's decision to alter, to vacate, or to otherwise disagree with a lower court's ruling. When a previous decision is overruled, that decision, or that part of the decision, is vacated.

Perjury: Basically to lie under oath. Specifically, to make material, relevant, intentional statements under oath. This is a felony.

Plaintiff: Usually the one who brings the action.

Precedence: The legal doctrine that requires subsequent cases to be decided in accordance with the rulings of previous cases of greater power or jurisdiction.

Principal: In agency law, a principal is the one who controls the agent.

Privileged communication: The communications between parties that cannot be discovered in court. This privilege exists mainly between clergy and penitent, husband and wife, and lawyer and client. It may exist between other parties as well as defined in statute or case law.

Probable cause: Elements necessary to believe that an infraction has been committed. Such elements are taken from the surrounding totality of circumstances—and does have limitations. For example, search warrant cannot be arbitrarily granted, but must have some reasonable cause to believe that the search will yield evidence of a crime.

Regional reporters: A series of case law reporters that gather the most important decisions from a cluster of states in sets of volumes. For example, the New York State regional reporter is called "Northeastern"—with either the 1st or 2nd editions. The other state decisions in the Northeastern reporter are: Atlantic, Southern, Southeastern, Pacific, and Northwestern.

reh'g den'd: abbreviation for "rehearing denied." In the subsequent history (See this Glossary) this is a determination that a higher court or the same level court will not rehear the case or an issue in the case.

Remand: Once a higher court has reversed or overturned a lower court's decision, the case may be sent back, or remanded, also for a new trial or further proceedings.

Respondeat superior: "Let the master answer" for the wrongdoing of employees.

Reverse: When an appellate court "reverses" a lower court's decision, it sets the decision aside, it voids it. The appellate court can "reverse" a decision in whole or in part. When a court reverses, the case is often sent back to the trial court for other actions "consistent with the ruling" of the higher court. See remand.

Reversible Error: An error at trial that may invalidate the decision.

Scienter: "To know or should have known." This legal maxim has great importance in tort law or in negligence claims. If a defendant "knew or had reason to know" that the events were going to take place, he or she had a legal obligation to avoid it. Thus, liability may attach. See Foreseeability.

Section: Part of a statute. The abbreviation for one section is "§", for two or more sections the abbreviation is "§§".

Settle: When those involved in a legal conflict resolve their differences before a judicial decision is rendered. As a technical matter, a "settlement" can occur seconds before a civil jury or judge renders a decision. Most settlements occur, however, before going to trial.

Standard of care: The legal threshold for determining the level of responsibility.

Standard of proof: The legal threshold for determining guilt or liability. In criminal cases the standard is a very high one—"beyond a reasonable doubt." For civil cases it is either the higher standard of "clear and convincing evidence" or the lower standard of "preponderance of the evidence."

Stare decisis: "Stable decision." The legal doctrine that emphasizes legal consistency. See precedence.

State reporters: Each state will have its own, unique system of reporting their court rulings. They can run into dozens of volumes in a series. In this work we have used other abbreviations for state court reporters:

N.Y.S.2d = New York State Supplement, second edition

Strict liability: A civil law principle that, under certain circumstances, a defendant will not have the usual defense that "it was not their fault." These circumstances include where a public carrier (like an aircraft) does something that it is not supposed to do. The plaintiff, without knowing the exact cause, can assert that the plane should not have crashed. The defendant is held "strictly" at fault.

Subpoena: A court order to appear as a witness, to answer questions in a deposition (See this Glossary) or for other legal proceedings. A subpoena is a court order and to refuse it means one may be in contempt of court (See this Glossary).

Subsequent history: Whether or not the case went to appeal and what happened there. Was it reversed, overturned, or affirmed? This is also colloquially known as "Shepardizing" after the name of the company who specializes in the data used for such research.

Summary judgment: A judge's determination that a case does not have the legal sufficiency for further review by a jury or otherwise; thus, the case is dismissed as a matter of law.

Third-party liability: Liability that attaches to a party not in the closest connection to the plaintiff. The "third party" will be a defendant. The first and second parties will be, say, the counselor and the client. That is the "normal" direction of liability. Extending this liability to third parties means that the counselor may be liable to, for example, the parent or a friend of a client.

Tort tortious: A term for a civil case, often a negligence claim. This term means "twisted;" that is, it tries to rectify "twisted" acts.

Trier of fact: The statutory entity that determines the truth of claims and decides guilt or liability-either a judge or a jury.

Unpublished decision: A decision not in general reporters; it has limited precedence value.

Verdict: A jury's decision—either "guilty" or "not guilty." A civil court will either hold a defendant either "liable" or "not liable." Appellate courts do not have "verdicts," they decide to "affirm, "reverse" etc. See glossary for these terms.

Vicarious liability: Liability imposed upon an employer arising from the wrongdoing of an employee. See respondeat superior.

TABLE 5. Practitioners' Reports of Professional Ethics and Personal Comfort with the Use of Religious or Spiritual Interventions in Practice

Interventions	% Reporting Professionally Ethical	% Reporting Personally Comfortable
Explore Client's Religious Background	94.7% ($n = 108$)	97.3% ($n = 110$)
Explore Client's Spiritual Background	99.1% ($n = 112$)	96.4% ($n = 108$)
Use or Recommend Religious Books	55.0% ($n = 60$)	41.3% ($n = 45$)
Use or Recommend Spiritual Books	88.6% ($n = 101$)	83.3% ($n = 95$)
Teach Spiritual Meditation to Clients	71.8% ($n = 74$)	36.7% ($n = 40$)
Meditate Spiritually with Clients	45.1% ($n = 46$)	19.3% ($n = 21$)
Pray Privately *for* Client	83.5% ($n = 91$)	70.5% ($n = 79$)
Pray *with* Client in Session	37.1% ($n = 39$)	24.5% ($n = 27$)
Use Religious Language or metaphors	66.4% ($n = 71$)	54.1% ($n = 59$)
Use Spiritual Language Metaphors	88.4% ($n = 99$)	81.6% ($n = 93$)
Touch Client for "healing" Purposes	13.5% ($n = 14$)	10.9% ($n = 12$)
Read scripture with Client	32.4% ($n = 35$)	21.4% ($n = 24$)
Recommend Participation in Religious Programs (Sunday School, religious education)	72.1% ($n = 80$)	65.5% ($n = 74$)
Recommend Participation in Spiritual Programs (Meditation groups, 12-step programs, men's/women's groups)	95.4% ($n = 104$)	91.8% ($n = 101$)
Help Clients Clarify Religious Values	78.2% ($n = 86$)	72.3% ($n = 81$)
Help Clients Clarify Spiritual Values	95.6% ($n = 108$)	94.7% ($n = 107$)
Refer Clients to Religious Counselors	90.0% ($n = 99$)	87.3% ($n = 96$)
Refer Clients to Spiritual Counselors	85.2% ($n = 92$)	80.9% ($n = 89$)
Help Clients Develop Ritual as a Clinical Intervention (House blessings, visiting graves of relatives, etc.)	90.9% ($n = 100$)	86.5% ($n = 96$)
Participate in Client's Rituals as a Clinical Inervention	57.1% ($n = 60$)	38.0% ($n = 41$)
Explore Religious elements in Dreams	82.6% ($n = 90$)	61.5% ($n = 67$)
Explore spiritual Elements in Dreams	93.6% ($n = 103$)	82.6% ($n = 90$)
Recommend Religious/Spiritual Forgiveness, Penance, or Amends	65.1% ($n = 71$)	57.7% ($n = 64$)
Perform Exorcism	5.7% ($n = 6$)	3.6% ($n = 4$)
Share Your Own Religious/Spiritual Beliefs or Views	60.9% ($n = 67$)	60.2% ($n = 68$)

D
APPENDIX

Resources for Mediatherapy

In suggesting these mediatherapy resources the author makes two disclaimers: 1) that all of the these films may not be suitable for all types of clients or suitable for younger viewers at all, and 2) that this list is not complete or exhaustive. It is up to the counselor to ascertain the suitability and appropriateness of these materials for individual clients. They do, however, present counselor-wide applicability and an opportunity for the counselor to illustrate and to apply religious and spiritual themes and ideas with clients.

☐ Suggested Readings

Besides the books cited in this work, the following are fairly general books that might be helpful to the practitioner. This list in not exhaustive, but offers the counselor some suggestions for bibliotherapy.

Abbey, E. (1977). *The Journey Home*. New York: Plume.
Ali-Shah, O. (N.d.). *Sufism for Today*. New York: Alif.
Baggley, J. (1995). *Doors of Perception*. Crestwood. NY: St. Vladimir's Seminary Press.
Barks, C. (Tr.). (1995). *The Essential Rumi*. San Francisco: HarperCollins.
Belitz, C., & Lundstrom, M. (1997). *The Power of Flow*. New York: Harmony Books.
Bhattacharya, D., & Archer, W. G. (1969). *Love Songs of Vidyapati*. New York: Grove Press.
Blakney, R. (Ed.) (1941). *Meister Eckhart*. New York: Harper Torchbooks.
Brown, J. (1990). *The Spiritual Legacy of the American Indian*. Crossroad, New York.
Charters, A. (Ed.) (1992). *The Portable Beat Reader*. New York: Penguin Books.
Cleary, T. (1995). *Zen Essence*. Shambhala, Boston.
Cohen, L. (1993). *Stranger Music: Selected Poems and Songs*. New York: Vintage Books.
Conway, D. J. (1995). *By Oak, Ash & Thorn: Modern Celtic Shamanism*. Llewellyn, St. Paul, MN.
Dagyab Rinpoche (1995). *Buddhist Symbols in Tibetan Culture*. Wisdom Publications, Boston.
Fischer-Schreiber, I. (1996). *The Shambhala Dictionary of Taoism*. Shambhala, Boston.
French, R. (Tr.) (1993). *The Way of the Pilgrim*. Pasadena, CA: Hope.
Ginsberg, A. (1961). *Kaddish and Other Poems*. San Francisco: City Lights.
Ginsberg, A. (1986). *White Shroud: Poems 1980–1985*. New York: Harper & Row.
Goldsmith, J. (1956). *The Art of Meditation*. New York: HarperCollins.
Goldsmith, J. (1986). *Practicing the presence*. HarperCollings, San Francisco.
Halifax, J. (Ed.) (1979). *Shamanic Voices*. New York: Dutton.
Hahn, T. N. (1995). *Living Buddha, Living Christ*. New York: Riverhead Books.
Harrison, J. (1996). *After Ikkyu*. Boston: Shamhhala.

Harrison, J. (1998). *The Shape of the Journey: New and Collected Poems*. Port Townsend, WA: Copper Canyon Press.

Hoffman, E. (1989). *The way of Splendor: Jewish Mysticism and Modern Psychology*. Northvale, NJ: Aronson.

Jung, C. G. (1965). *Memories, Dreams, Reflections*. New York: Vintage.

Kadloubovsky, E., & Palmer, G. (Tr.) (1995). *Unseen Warfare*. Crestwood, NY: St. Vladimir's Seminary Press.

Kadloubovsky, E., & Palmer, G. (Tr.) (n.d.) *Early Fathers from the Philokalia*. London: Faber & Faber.

Kaplan, A. (1988). *Meditation and Kabbalah*. Northvale, NJ: Aronson.

Kerouac, J. (1994). *The Scripture of the Golden Eternity*. San Francisco: City Lights.

Kovacs, M. (Tr.). (1989). *The Epic of Gilgamesh*. Stanford, CA: Stanford University.

Kushner, L. (1977). *Honey from the Rock*. New York: Harper & Row.

Masters, R. & Houston, J. (1972). *Mind Games: Guide to Inner Space*. New York: Dell.

Merton, T. (1961). *Selected Poems of Thomas Merton*. New York: New Directions.

Merton, T. (1965). *The Way of Chuang Tzu*. New York: New Directions.

Mitchell, S. (Ed.) (1989). *The Selected Poetry of Rainer Maria Rilke*. New York: Vintage International.

Naranjo, C. & Ornstein, R. (1971). *On the Psychology of Meditation*. New York: Viking Press.

Narayan, R. K. (1988). *The Ramayana*. Penguin, New York.

Neihardt, J. (1932). *Black Elk Speaks*. New York: Pocket Books.

Patchen, K. (1957). *Selected Poems*. New York: New Directions.

Rawson, P. (1978). *The Art of Tantra*. New York: Thames & Hudson.

Reps, P., & Sensaki, N. (1994). *Zen Flesh, Zen Bones*. Boston: Shambhala.

Rothenberg, J. (Ed. & Comp.). *Shaking the Pumpkin*. Garden City, New York: Doubleday.

Schure, E. (1961). *The Great Initiates*. New York: Harper & Row.

Smith, J. (Ed.). (1998). *Breath Sweeps Mind: A First Guide to Meditation Practice*. New York: Riverhead Books.

Snyder, G. (1978). *Myths & Texts*. New York: New Directions.

Starhawk. (1988). *Dreaming in the Dark: Magic, Sex and Politics*. Boston: Beacon Press.

Thoman, D. (1946). *Collected Poems*. New York: New Directions.

Woldstein, D., & Kramer, S. (1983). *Inanna: Queen of Heaven and Earth*. Philadelphia: Harper & Row.

Test Questions: Chapter by Chapter

☐ Preface

1. How would you describe your level of fear or concern over legal consequences in your counseling practice? If you are a student, what is your level of concern over legal issues on becoming a counselor? What resources or seminars have you attended that address such issues? What questions are still pending for you?
2. Have you located and read the newest version of the state statute under which you are licensed or intend to be licensed? List three reasons for doing so.
3. What behaviors, therapies, or interventions do you now use (or intend to use) that might be considered alternative, complementary, or spiritual in nature? How did you get acquainted with such therapies? Do you have formal training in them? Have you taken seminars? What books have you read?
4. Considering the case of *Spratt v. County of Kent,* do you think that the plaintiff Spratt was within his legal and ethical bounds to practice his treatment by spiritual means? Why or why not? What behaviors might he have changed to make his legal case side in his favor?
5. In reviewing the DSM-IV code V62.89, Religious or Spiritual Problem, what specific issues or presenting problems might also be included in this diagnosis? What are some such issues that you might have come across in your training or practice? Were these resolved? How?
6. After reviewing the criteria for a protected religious belief enunciated by the district court, what spiritual or religious beliefs or practice might not fall into the protected sphere? Why or why not? Do the think that the district court's criteria is too inclusive or too exclusive?
7. Are there therapies and interventions that are not listed by the Advisory Panel in the section on the NIH classification? Should past life regression, exorcism, tarot readings, or channeling be included?

☐ Chapter 1

1. What is the location of the courts (federal and state) which have your practice under their jurisdiction. If you were to appeal a decision from each jurisdiction, in which city would that court be found?

2. Did you agree or disagree with the Supreme Court ruling in *Employment Division, Department of Human Resources v. Smith*? Why or why not? Under the same facts as in the case would the Religious Freedom Restoration Act make a difference in the outcome? Why or why not?
3. Do you agree with the decision in the magic rock case (*Cowan v. Strafford School District*)? Why or why not? If you were the school counselor for this school, how would you address this issue if the following clients presented themselves at your door: (a) an irate parent, offended by the rock and letter, (b) a student who liked the rock idea, (c) the teacher who came to you for guidance, (d) an administrator who sought your help?
4. What behaviors, therapies, or interventions *might* subject counselor to the statute mentioned in the *Marks v. Rosenburg* case? What arguments might a counselor use in an inquiry from the local district attorney's office?
5. After the reviewing the facts and decision in the *In re Pleasant Glade Assembly of God* case, answer the following questions. If a client, a religious person who believed in demons, asked you to cast out demons from his or her person, car, or house? What legal or ethical consequences might you consider? How might your licensing boards feel about it? How do you, personally, feel about it?

☐ Chapter 2

1. After reading the *People v. Cardenas* case, do you think the women there did nor did not give their consent to the defendant's treatments? Why or why not? Are there other instances where adults might not be in positions to truly give consent to a counselor's interventions?
2. Have you ever had a client where you had to persuade the client to do something, such as take his or her medication, get a medically needed operation, etc? What is the difference, as you see it, between therapeutic persuasion and coercion or duress? Is there a difference?
3. Consider the Therapeutic Deception or Exploitation statute. What are some of the stresses under which a counselor might be susceptible to having sex with a client? What are some treatments, interventions, or dynamics in conducting *complementary* counseling that might evoke sexual feelings either on the part of the client or the counselor? How might a counselor guard against acting on such feelings? How might a counselor use such feelings on the part of the client toward therapeutic (and legal and ethical) ends?
4. In reviewing the *Farley v. Henderson* case, discuss the questions that follow that case in the text. Then discuss: what, if any, claims do you make about the interventions, methodologies, or therapies that you use? Can you substantiate them? Is such substantiation necessary for the clients?
5. Review the North Carolina statute criminalizing "phrenology, palmistry, clairvoyance," etc. Also review the *People v. Sanchez* case. Under what circumstances might aspects of some complementary or spiritual counseling run afoul of the North Carolina statute? Might a counselor use the imagery, stories, and parables of the various world religions in counseling discussions, as well as say, imagery of the tarot or astrology, that might not run afoul of such a statute? Does the state in which you practice have such a statute?
6. What is your policy about touching clients? Do you hug them? Never? Occasionally? How about holding hands?

7. After reading the section on informed consents and the consent form for visualizations in Chapter 5, answer these questions: Do you obtain informed consents before you proceed with any interventions or specific therapies? Some? Any? What are some legal consequences if you get such consent and if you don't?

8. How would you respond if a client asked if or how hallucinogens might enhance his or her spiritual, telepathic, or psychic strengths. What might be some legal consequences for discussing the use of hallucinogens? How about encouraging their use? How about suggesting where the client might get some?

9. Child abuse can be both a public policy issue and counseling issue. What if a client literally "spared the rod and spoiled the child" out of a religious belief? Would you need to report him or her to child protective authorities? Are you a mandatory or permissive reporter? Would you treat them differently from those who lose control of their anger and hit their children?

10. You are a school counselor. The guidance counselor, principal, or teacher at your school asks for advice on a student. The student claims to be a satanist. She or he wears an upside-down cross, carries around and talks with other students about Anton Levay's *Satanic Bible* (1969), and writes class essays on the benefits of devil worship. What is your response to these people? What are the legal consequences, if any, for doing nothing? What are the legal consequences for doing whatever it is you are thinking?

☐ Chapter 3

1. Reconsidering the case of **Spratt v. County of Kent** from another point of view, how do the facts of the case comport to the four traditional elements for a civil action? What arguments could you make to make the religious discrimination more persuasive? What are the things you would do differently to help your case?

2. After reviewing the discussion on both *scienter* and informed consent, think of a situation where you now might ask for an informed consent. Now with the Consent Form for Visualization available for additional guidance, answer the five questions following the discussion of *scienter*. These five questions are to be considered in the context of an intervention of the reader's choice.

3. After reading the sections on "standard of care" and the three suggestions following them, describe specifically how you know that your practice or future practice meets the standards of care for your profession. How can you objectively know that you meet the standard of care for each and every one of your specific interventions or therapies—especially if they are complementary or spiritual in nature?

4. Has such a standard of care been objectified for *any* of the complementary or spiritual interventions you use? Who sets them? How are they set? Who is to say you have or have not met the standards?

5. This is an experiential exercise regarding defamation (libel and slander). After reading the appropriate section, just listen in the lunchroom, at the water cooler, or other setting where the conversation turns to bosses, clients, or other coworkers. Are there potentially slanderous statements made there? Conduct this exercise over a two-week period to test how much slander goes on, even inadvertently.

6. Re-examine the 7 questions directly following the discussion of the *Slover* case. How might you take steps to avoid publishing opinions as opposed to statements of fact? Are there interventions used by your staff that might seem unprofessional by a licensing board?

7. As you peruse the Internet and your e-mails, are there potentially defamatory statements being made there? What is the nature of such defamatory remarks? If you were the subject of such remarks, how might you respond?

8. How would you describe the legal differences between hurt feelings and the intentional infliction of emotional distress?

9. How can counselors be sure that they are not misrepresenting any aspect of their practice, such as credentials, licensure, efficacy of therapies or interventions, or billing information? How much explaining or consent is legally needed to ensure clients have a complete and fair understanding of the counselor and his or her methods of treatment?

10. Does your practice have a trademark or a trade name? How do you know that others have not already registered it? How can you protect your own trademarks or trade names?

11. After reviewing both the sexual harassment and the vicarious liability and *respondeat superior*, imagine you are the owner or director of a counseling agency or department. How might mistakes by your employees make your agency and department vulnerable to such suits? What specific policies and procedures would you initiate to avoid your employees making your agency or department vulnerable?

☐ Chapter 4

1. How are counselors like and unlike other professionals who may offer spiritual or complementary treatment? Midwives? Chiropractors? Hypnotherapists? Pastoral counselors? Acupuncturists?

2. What are some of the exemptions to licensure that, for example, the North Carolina statute allows? Find your own state's licensing statute (using the procedure in the appendix) and list the exemptions for your own state. Are there any *components* in your practice that may be exempted in your state?

3. What are the ethical restrictions and requirements for any of the private licensing agencies (APA, NASW, etc.) to which you may belong? If you can, find out their standards for ethical violations, due process during those hearings and standards for sanctions. What are some of the "due process" considerations embodied in those standards? Are there *other* due process considerations that should be embodied there?

4. What might be some specific examples of some complementary therapies or spiritual therapies that should be exempted from licensure or limitation? What legal or ethical arguments would you use to make your case?

5. How would you make a legal argument to have your complementary or spiritual therapy or intervention covered by insurance? What provisions in the insurance policy might apply? What supporting evidence might you gather to support your claim?

6. Again you are the director or manager of a private counseling agency or social service department. What specific areas of oversight and control would you use to make sure that none of your employees runs afoul of insurance reimbursement rules?

7. Consider your own insurance. What are the maximum allowable limits of your coverage? Does that favorably compare to other similarly situated counselors? What are the exemptions of your coverage? Are you covered to defend against a hearing before a state licensing board or agency?

☐ **Chapter 5**

1. How would you describe the cosmology under which you practice? How does it compare/contrast with your colleagues? How does your cosmology compare/contrast with those of your (a) professors, (b) state licensing board, (c) state legislature?
2. Where would you place yourself and your cosmology/ideology between the "scientific" and "spiritual" categories noted in this chapter? Have your changed your ideas since college or graduate school?
3. What information about your cosmology/ideology might you disclose? Under what circumstances might you disclose such information? What "cues" from your clients might you look for in to inform your decision to disclose?
4. Make your own ethical ecology on an issue pertinent to your practice. Who are the actors or components? What are their attitudes, drives or motivations surrounding this issue? How would you rank the relative weight of each of the players in the decision process? What new information is revealed here? How does the exercise clarify your thinking on this issue?
5. Conduct the duty determination model on an ethical instance in your practice. What are the duties involved? How would you rank them? Why? Who owes the duty and to whom is the duty owed? Do these parties change? How? Under what circumstances?
6. What are some, if any, of the ethical norms that you think need to be changed in (a) your licensing board, (b) your state legislature, or (c) your private licensing association? What are some of the ways that you might effect such change, specific to complementary or spiritual therapies?
7. Take the part of the beleaguered school counselor. Do you agree with the current balance of religion in the public schools? What is that balance in your state? Are there specific limitations on spiritual support, discussion, or counseling enumerated for school counselors in your state?
8. Recount some of the ways in which a school counselor may or may not run afoul of state or federal law in their counseling duties? How might a counselor effectively argue to defend him or herself?
9. Examine the illustrations of duties noted in this chapter. Under "client self-determination," how would you operationally differentiate between *coercing* and *encouraging* a client to (a) take his or her prescription medication, (b) continue treatment, (c) clarify his or her values, (d) remember and relate his or her dreams to you, (d) learn a meditation/relaxation exercise, (e) pay his or her bill?
10. How do you know that you are or are not covered by your state's privileged communication statute or mandatory child abuse/elder abuse reporting statute?

☐ **Chapter 6**

1. How do you define a cult or religious sect? What are the operational, clinical characteristics that you would use to determine the difference between a religious group and a recognized religion? How would you describe how a court might determine whether one group's activities or behavior might or might not be constitutionally protected?
2. How might you describe the clinical criteria you use to determine if a client's involvement is helpful or harmful to that client?

3. How would you address a parent or another family member of a client who wanted you to either rescue the client from a religious group or to testify in court as to the danger posed by that group? How would you intervene with a client who had a friend/relative involved with a religious group over which the client was very fearful or anxious?
4. Do you have any religious or spiritually-driven child abuse statutes similar to the ritual mutilation or ritual abuse statutes noted in this chapter? Do counselors have any obligations under these (your state's) statute?
5. Does your agency or department enjoy "prosecutorial immunity"? What are the limitations and rights under your state's statute?

☐ **Chapter 7**

1. Should Helen Wu have been allowed any mitigating circumstances in her sentence? Why or why not? If you were a expert psychiatric witness for the defense how might you testify? If you were a expert psychiatric witness for the prosecution how might you testify?
2. What are some crosscultural religious, spiritual or complementary counseling situations you have encountered in your practice? How have such situations differed from the norms of the dominant culture(s)? How have such situations influenced how you treated the client?
3. The following two questions use the illustration of female circumcision to examine the role of the counselor in spiritual or complementary cross cultural situations, one might substitute another situation in its stead.
   a. You are a school counselor and a student admits that her mother is going to have her circumcised, how might you respond? What is your reasoning for your decision? Answer the same question as if you were counseling a teacher who asked for advice on this same student?
   b. Suppose you are a counselor with a mother as a client who wants to circumcise her daughter. What is your treatment like?
4. Again we illustrate public policy toward spiritual or complementary treatments through the example of the school counselor. A religious or spiritual group wants you to be their advisor. Would you or wouldn't you? Why? Suppose the following groups ask you to be their faculty or staff advisor: (a) Wiccans, (b) Evangelical Christians, (c) A "dungeons and dragons" club, (d) A "Harry Potter" group? Is there any constitutional or legal difference between being an advisor to each of these groups?
5. How might the Equal Access Act apply to a Moslem student group who wished to meet for Friday prayers in the school counselor's office, versus the local chapter of the parapsychological student group who wants to have a business meeting after school on Tuesday? Are there any statutory differences between the two groups and what they want to do on school property? Are there any facts that would make a legal difference in the outcomes?

References

Ackerman, E. (1999, January 19). Millennial madness, Jerusalem jitters. *U.S. News and World Report*, pp. 32–33.

Adams, F. (n.d.). *The genuine works of Hippocrates*. New York: Wm. Wood.

Akin, P. (1999, June 23). Priestess challenges decision on Wicca. *Richmond Times-Dispatch*, p. B1.

Allegro, J. (1970). *The sacred mushroom and the cross*. Doubleday, New York.

American Psychiatric Association (1994). *Diagnostic and statistical manual of mental disorders* (4th ed.) Washington, DC:

Associated Press, (1997, March 5). Exorcist to pay patient $2.4 million. *Richmond Times-Dispatch*, p. A9.

Associated Press. (1999a, February 10). Teen witch sues school over pentagram ban. *Richmond Times-Dispatch*, p. A2.

Associated Press, (1999b, May 22) Judge: School district violated religious rights. *Washington Post*, p. A12.

Associated Press, (1999c, June 8). Pope praises Copernicus. *Richmond Times-Dispatch*, p. A4.

Associated Press, (1999d, July 3). Judge reverses Wicca ruling. *Richmond Times-Dispatch*. p. B1.

Associated Press, (1999f, September 28) Physician convicted of fraud. *Richmond Times-Dispatch*, p. B1.

Associated Press, (1999g, December 17) Orthopedic surgeon gets two years for aloe shots. *Richmond Times-Dispatch*, p. B4.

Associated Press, (1999h, December 22). Study: Doctors ill-inform patients. *Richmond Times-Dispatch*, p. A14.

Associated Press, (1999h, 25 March). Wicca follower wins case. *Richmond Times-Dispatch*, p. A3.

Associated Press, (2000a, March 31). Ex-doctor enters plea of guilty in aloe case. *Richmond Times-Dispatch*, p. B4.

Associated Press, (2000c, August 30). Ban on pot use continued. *Richmond Times-Dispatch*, p. A8.

Baba Ram Dass, (1971). *Be here now*. Kingsport, TN: Lama Foundation.

Barnhart, H. (1995). The Barnhart concise dictionary of etymology. HarperCollins, New York.

Bartal v. Brower, 993 P.2d 629 (Kan. 1999).

Blackowiak v. Kemp, 546 N.W.2d 1 (1996).

Block v. Gomez, 201 Wis. 2d 789, 549 N.W.2d 783 (Ct. App. 1996).

Book jacket returns can include costly mistakes. (1999, November 14). *Richmond Times-Dispatch*, p. G5.

Borawick v. Shay. 68 F.3rd 597, (2d Cir. 1996), *cert. den'd*. 116 S. Ct. 1869, 134 L.Ed.2d 966 (1996).

Borrego v. Agency for Health Care Administration, 675 S.2d 666 (Fla. App. Dist.1 1996).

Braddock, C., Edwards, K., Hasenberg, N., Laidley, T., & Levinson, W. (1999, December 22). Informed decision making in outpatient parctice. *Journal of the American Medical Association*, Vol. 282, No. 24, 2313–2320.

Braden, G. (2000). *The Isaiah effect*. New York: Harmony Books.

Brown v. Board of Education, 347 U.S. 483, 74 S.Ct. 686, 98 L.Ed. 873 (1954).

Budapest, Z. (1979). *The holy book of women's mysteries* (Parts 1 & 2). Los Angeles, CA: Susan B. Anthony Coven #1.

Budwin v. American Psychological Association, Cal. App. LEXIS 912, 24 Cal.App.4th 875, 29 Cal. Rptr.2d 453 (Cal.App. 3 Dist.1994).

Bullis, R. (1990a). Child abuse reporting requirements: Liabilities and immunities for clergy, *Journal of Pastoral Care, 44*(3), 244–248.

Bullis, R. (1990b). Swallowing the scroll: Legal implications of the recent Supreme Court peyote cases. *Journal of Psychoactive Drugs, 22*(3), 325–332.

Bullis, R. (1990c). When confessional walls have ears: the changing clergy privileged communications law. *Pastoral Psychology, 39*(2), 75–84.

Bullis, R. (1991a). The spiritual healing "defense" in criminal prosecutions for crimes against children. *Child Welfare, 70*(5), 541–555.

Bullis, R. (1991b). The UN Convention on the rights of the child. *Child and Adolescent Social Work Journal, 8*(3), 239–250.

Bullis, R. (1992). *Law and the management of counseling agency or practice.* Washington, DC: American Counseling Association.

Bullis, R. (1995). *Clinical social worker sexual misconduct and the ethics of dual relationships.* Chicago: Nelson-Hall.

Bullis, R. (1996). *Spirituality in social work practice.* Washington, DC: Taylor & Francis.

Bullis, R., & Mazur, C. (1993). *Legal issues in religious counseling.* Louisville, KY: Westminster/John Knox Press.

Campbell v. Cauthron, 623 F.2d 503 (1980).

Castenada, C. (1972). *Journey to Ixtlan.* Auckland, New Zealand: Penguin.

Charell v. Gonzalez, 660 N.Y.S.2d 665, 173 Misc.2d 227 (1997).

Cohen, M. (1996). Holistic health care: Including alternative and complementary medicine in in insurance and regulatory schemes. *Arizona Law Review, 38*, 83–164.

Cohen, M. (1998). *Complementary and alternative medicine.* Baltimore: John's Hopkins University.

Cohen v. Hartlage, Ga. App. LEXIS 2047, 179 Ga.App 847, 348 S.E.2d 331 (Ga.App. 1986).

Colin v. Orange Unified School District, CV 99-1461 (USDC, 2000).

Cowan v. Strafford School District, U.S. App. LEXIS 6804, 140 F.3d 1153 (8th Cir. 1998) (Unpublished), *reh'd den'd.* U.S. App. LEXIS 10106 (1998).

Cunningham v. Agency for Health Care Administration, 677 So.2d 61 (Fla.App. 1 Dist.(1996).

Daubert v. Merrell Dow Pharmaceuticals, Inc., 509 U.S. 579 (1993).

Doe v. Redeemer Lutheran Church, 555 N.W.2d 325 (Ct. App. Minn., 1996).

Doore, G. (Ed.) (1988). *Shaman's path.* Boston: Shambhala.

Deibel, M. (1999, November 16) Justices plunge into another prayer struggle. *Richmond Times-Dispatch,* p. A2.

Doctor fined for selling drugs over the internet (2000, April 1). *Richmond Times-Dispatch,* p. A2

Duff Dubberly, Turner, White, Baykin, LLC, (1998). *Bible distribution in the public schools* [On-line]. Available: www.lawoffice.com.

Ehrenwald, J. (Ed.) (1991). *The history of psychotherapy.* Northvale, NJ: Jason Aronson.

Eisel v. Board of Education of Montgomery County, 597 A.2d 447 (Md. 1991).

Eisenstadt v. Baird, 405 U.S. 438, 92 S.Ct. 1029, 31 L.Ed.2d 349 (1972).

Employment Division, Department of Human Resources v. Smith, 494 U.S. 872 (1990).

Fake doctor (2000, 27 July). Richmond Times-Dispatch, A2.

Farley v. Henderson, U.S. App. LEXIS 20790, 883 F.2d; 709 (9th Cir. 1989)

Farmer, R. (1999, April 25). Cliques' pursuits—not dress key, some say. *Richmond Times-Dispatch,* p. A12.

Feasby, C. (1997). Determining standard of care in alternative contexts, *5 Health L.J.* 45.

Federal Rules of Evidence. (1993) West St. Paul, MN.

Ferguson v. People, Colo LEXIS 152, 824 P.2d 803 (Colo. 1992), *reh'g den'd.* Colo. LEXIS 159 (1992).

Frank, J. (1973). *Persuasion and healing.* New York: Schocken.

Frankel, E. & Teutsch, B. (1992). *The encyclopedia of Jewish symbols.* Northvale, NJ: Aronson.

Frye v. U.S. 293 F. 1013 (DC, Cir. 1923).

Gallin, A. (1994, May). The cultural defense: Undermining the policies against domestic violence. *Boston College Law Review,* 723–745.

Garrett, F. (1999). *Mandatory student activity fees used to support student organizations which engage in political or ideological activity violate the First Amendment rights of objecting students* [On-line]. Available: www.lawoffice.com.

Gelman, S. (1990). The crafting of fieldwork training agreements. *Journal of Social Work Education, Winter*(1), 65–75.

Gelman, S., & Wardell, P. (1988). Who's responsible? The field liability dilemma. *Journal of Social Work Education, Winter*(1), 70–78.

Griswold v. Connecticut, 381 U.S. 479, 85 S.Ct. 1678, 14 L.Ed.2d 510 (1965).

Gross v. Allen, 22 Cal. App. 4th 354 (1994).

Halifax, J. (Ed.) (1979). *Shamanic voices*. New York: Dutton.

Harris v. Harris, Miss. LEXIS 2391, 343 So.2d 762 (Miss. 1977).

Hester v. Barnett, 723 S.W. 2d 544 (Mo. Ct. App. 1987).

Hollywood Clinic, (2000, 27 July). Associated Press.

Hostetler, A. (1999, March 18). Medical role for pot is seen. *Richmond Times-Dispatch*, p. A1.

Hsu v. Roslyn Union Free School District, U.S. App. LEXIS 11294, 85 F.3d 839, (2d Cir. 1996).

Huxley, A. (1954). *The doors of perception*. New York: Harper & Row.

Huxley, F. (1974). *The way of the sacred*. New York: Doubleday.

Iazzo v. Department of Professional Regulation, 638 So.2d 583 (Fla.App.1 Dist. 1994).

In re Bartha, 63 Cal.App.3d 584, Cal. App. LEXIS 2040; 134 Cal. Rptr. 39 (Cal. Ct. Appeals, 1976).

In re Guess, 327 N.C. 46, 393 S.E.2d 833 (N.C. 1990).

In re Latasha W., 60 Cal.App.4th 1524, 70 Cal.Rptr.2d 886 (Cal.App. Dist.2, 1998)

In re Marriage of Gould, Wisc. LEXIS 2286, 116 Wis.2d 493, 342 N.W.2d 426, (1984).

In re Murtha, 115 N.J. Super. 380, 279 A.2d 889, *certification den'd*, 59 N.J. 239, 281 A.2d 278 (1971).

In re Pleasant Glade Assembly of God Rev. Lloyd McCuchen, Rod Linzay, and Holly Linzay, Tex. App. LEXIS 1998 6567, 991 S.W.2d 85 (1998), *original proceeding stayed*, Tex. App. LEXIS 219 (1999).

Jackson, S. (1997, June 27). Alternative medicine: Not so alternative anymore (pp. 1–4). *Business Week* [On-line]. Available: www.businessweek.com.

Jaffee v. Redmond, 518 U.S. 1 (1996).

Jeffries v. Kansas Department of Social & Rehab. Serv., 946 F. Supp. 1556 (D. Kansas, 1996).

Jewison, N. (1971). *Fiddler on the Roof* [Film].

Kafatos, M., & Nadeau, R. (1990). *The conscious universe*. New York: Springer-Verlag.

Kakar, S. (1982). *Shamans, mystics and doctors*. Boston: Beacon Press.

Kalweit, H. (1988). *Dreamtime & inner space*. Boston: Shambhala.

Karasek v. Lajoie, N.Y. LEXIS 1837, 92 N.Y.2d 171, 699 N.W.2d 889, 677 Ny.Y.S.2d 265, (1998).

Karpel, C. (Ed.). (1975). *The rite of exorcism*. New York: Berkeley Medallion.

Khalsa v. Khalsa, 751 P.2d 715 (N.M. Ct. App. 1988).

Kingrey, J. (1999, 20 March) Alternative medicine challenge fails. Seattle Times.

Kellner, N. (1993). Under the knife: Female genital mutilation as child abuse. *Journal of Juvenile Law, 14*, 118–132.

Kelley v. Texas State Bd. of Medical Examiners, 467 S.W.2d 539 (Tx. Ct. Civil Appeals, 1971).

Kelly v. Marcantonio, U.S. App. LEXIS 18396, 187 F.3d 192 (1st Cir. 1999).

Kelly v. Marcantonio, 678 A.2d 873 (R.I. 1996).

Kerr v. Lyford, U.S. App. LEXIS 7194, 171 F.3d 330 (5th Cir. 1999).

Kleiner, C. (2000, March 13). A push becomes a shove. *U.S. News & World Report*, 49–50.

Koerner, B. (1999, December 6). For heroin addicts, a bizarre remedy. *U.S. News & World Report*, p. 82.

Kotler, J. (1999, June 22). Indian medicine men ply trade in city. *Richmond Time-Dispatch*, p. A4.

Krajewski-Jaime, E. (1991). Folk-healing among Mexican-American families as a consideration in the delivery of child welfare and child health care services. *Child Welfare, 60*(2), 157–167.

Krassner, M. (1986, June). Effective features of therapy from the healer's perspective: a study of curanderismo. *Smith College Studies in Social Work*, 157–183.

Kumho Tire Co., Ltd. v. Carmichael, 526 U.S. 137, 119 S.Ct. 1167, 143 L.Ed.2d 238 (1999).

Laird, J. (1984). Sorcers, shamans, and social workers: The use of ritual in social work practice. *Social Work*, March–April, 123–129.

Lambert v. Yellowsley, 272 U.S. 581, 42 S.Ct. 210, 71 L.Ed. 422 (1926).

Lancaster, J. (1988, June 21). Village gives up painful ritual. *Washington Post*, p. A19.

LaVey, A. (1969). The Satanic Bible. Avon, N.Y.

Lein, J. (1999). Recovered memories: Context and controversy. *Social Work, 44*(5), 481–484.

Lightman v. Flaum, 687 N.Y.S.2d 562 (Sup. 1999).

Lifton, R. (1981). Cult formation. *Harvard Mental Health Newsletter, 7*(8) [On-line]. Available: "Carol Giamalvo's Cult Information and Recovery" http://member.oal.com/_ht_a/carol2180/cult form.

LLN v. Clauder, 203 Wis.2d 570, 552 N.W.2d 879, Wisc.App. LEXIS 937 (Wisc.App. 1996).

Loving v. Virginia, 388 U.S. 1, 87 S. Ct. 1817, 18 L. Ed. 2d 1010 (1967).

Magleby v. State, 564 P.2d 1109 (Utah, 1977).

Majebe v. North Carolina Board of Medical Examiners, 106 N.C. App. 253, 416 S.E.2d 404 (1992).

Makris v. Bureau of Professions & Occupations Affairs, 599 A.2d 279 (Pa.Cmnwith. 1991).

Masters, R., & Houston, J. (1966). *The Varieties of psychedelic experience*. Delta, New York.

Matter of welfare of T.K. and W.K., 475 N.W.2d 88 (Minn. Ct. App. 1991).

Matthies v. Mastromonaco, 310 N. J. Super,. 572 (1998).

Marks v. Estate of Hartgerink, Iowa Sup. LEXIS 50, 528 N.W.2d 539 (1995).

Marks v. City of Roseburg, Ore. App. LEXIS 4865, 65 Ore. App. 102, 670 P.2d 201 (1984).

Meyers, C. (1997). Expanding *Tarasoff*: Protecting patients and the public by keeping subsequent caregivers informed. *Journal of Psychiatry & Law*, Fall, 365–375.

Miranda v. Arizona, 384 U.S. 436, 86 S. Ct. 1602, 16 L. Ed. 2d 694 (1966).

Mulrine, A. (1999, March 1). So you want to be a teenage witch? *U.S. News & World Report*, p. 70.

Nally v. Grace Community Church, 157 Cal. App. 3d 912, 204 Cal, Rptr. 303 (1984), appeal after remand, 194 Cal. App. 3d 1147, 240 Cal. Rptr. 215, (1987), rev'd, 47 Cal. App. 3d 278, 763 P.2d 948, 253 Cal. Rptr. 97 (1988), cert denied, 490 U.S. 1007 (1989).

NASW News. (2000, September). *Agency restricts internet counseling*, p. 12.

Neuberger, C. (1999, April 3). Judge upholds midwifery law; charges stand. *Richmond Times-Dispatch*, p. B1.

New Revised Standard Version, Harper Collins Study Bible (1989). New York.

Newyear v. Church Ins. Co., U.S. App. LEXIS 23250, 155 F.3d 1041 (1998).

New York Times News Service (2000, April 5). Who's reading your e-mail? *Richmond Times-Dispatch*, pp. A1, A3.

Neuzer v. Korn, 127 D.L.R. (4th) 577. (This is a decision by the Supreme Court of Canada.)

Nicholson, S. (1987). *Shamanism*. Wheaton, IL: Theosophical Publishing House.

Pakula, A. (1976). *All the Presidents Men* [Film].

Peck v. Upshur County Board of Education, 155 F.3d 274 (4th Cir. 1998).

People v. Ashley, N.Y. App. Div. LEXIS 6590, 172 N.Y.S. 282, 184 A.D. 520 (1918).

People v. Cardenas, Cal. App. LEXIS 13, 21 Cal. App.4th 927, 26 Cal. Rptr. 2d 567 (2d Dist. 1994) (Certified for partial publication).

People v. Clayton, 704 N.E.2d 919 (Ill. App. 2 Dist. 1998).

People v. Kelly, 17 Cal.3d 24, 549 P.2d 1240, 130 Cal. Rprt. 144 (1976).

People v. Malcolm, N.Y. Misc. LEXIS 1096, 154 N.Y.S.919, 90 Misc. 517 (1915).

People v. Sanchez, 84 N.Y.S.2d 440, 643 N.E.2d 509, 618 N.Y.S.2d 887 (1994).

People v. Steinberg, N.Y. LEXIS 1590, 79 N.Y.2d 673, 595 N.E.2d 845, 584 N.Y.S.2d 770 (1992).

People v. Tychankski, 78 N.Y.2d 909, 577 N.E.2d 1046, 573 N.Y.S.2d 454 (1991).

Pinkus v. MacMahon, 29 A.2d 885 (S.Ct. N.J., 1943)

Plessy v. Ferguson, 163 U.S. 537, 16 S.Ct. 1138, 41 L.Ed. 256 (1896).

Puharich, A. (1974). *The sacred mushroom*. New York: Doubleday.

Race helps mother win custody. (1999, March 9). *Washington Post*, p. A6.

Radhakrishna, S. (Tr.). (1950). *The Dhammapada*. Oxford Press, Oxford.

Ramona v. Ramona, (Super Ct., Napa Co., No. 61898) (2d App. Div.) Pet. For rev. den'd., Cal. LEXIS (1996).

Ramona v. Superior Court, Cal. App. LEXIS 658, 57 Cal. App.4th 107, 66 Cal. Rptr.2d 766 (Ct. App. 2d Dist. 1997).

Ravenwolf, S. (2000). Teen Witch. Llewellyn Publications, St. Paul, MN.

Reuter, S. (1994). Professional liability in postgraduate medical education. *Journal of Legal Medicine*, *15*, 485–531.

Reutkmeier v. Nolte, 179 Iowa 342, 161 N.W. 290 (1917).

Rivers v. Rivers, 511 So.2d 30 (La. App. 1987).

Roe v. Wade, 410 U.S. 113, 93 S.Ct. 705, 35 L.Ed.2d 147 (1973).

Rowinski, J. & K. (1999). *L.L. Bean Outdoor Photography Handbook*. The Lyons Press, New York.

Sabastier v. State, 504 So.2d 45, (Fla. App. 4 Dist. 1987).

Sale, D. (1999). Overview of legislative development concerning alternative health care in the United States [On-line]. Available: www.healthy.net/public/legal-lg/regulationsfetzer.

Sanville, J. (1975). Therapists in competition and cooperation with exorcists: The spirit world clinically revisited. *Clinical Social Work Journal*, *3*(4), 286–297.

Scheffler v. Archdiocese, No 952180 Minn. Ct. App. (1997).

Scott v. Ross, U.S. App. LEXIS 6889, 140 F.3d 1275 (9th Cir. 1998), reh'd den'd. U.S. App. LEXIS 20804, 151 F.3d 1247 (9th Cir. 1998).

Self-Realization Fellowship Church v. Ananda Church of Self-Realization, 59 F.3d 902, U.S. App. LEXIS 16433 (9th Cir. 1995).

Shuman, D. (1997). What we permit mental health professionals to say about the "The best interests of the child"? An essay on common sense, *Daubert*, and the rules of evidence. *Family Law Quarterly*, *31*(3), 551–569.

Slover v. State Board of Clinical Social Workers, 144 Or.App. 565, 927 P.2d 1098 (1996).

Spielberg, S. (1993) (Dr.) Schlinder's List [Film].

Spiritual Psychic Science Church of Truth v. City of Azuza, Cal. LEXIS 318, 39 Cal. 3d 501, 703 P.2d 1119, 217 Cal. Rptr. 225 (1985).

Spratt v. County of Kent, 621 F. Supp. 594, 1985. U.S. Dist. LEXIS 13988 (1985)

State v. Blake, 695 P.2d 336 (Hawaii App. 1985).

State v. Eichman, 155 Wis.2d 552, 456 N.W.2d 143 (Wis. 1990).

State v. Miranda, 56 Conn. App. 298, 742 A. 2d 1276 (Conn.App. 2000).

State v. Motherwell, 114 Wash. 2d 353, 788 P. 2d 1066 (Wash. 1990).

State v. Ohrtman, 466 N.W.2d 1 (Minn. App. 1991).

State v. Speed, Wash. App. LEXIS 705, 90 Wash. App. 1047, (Wash. App. 1998) (Unpublished), *rev. den'd*. Wash. LEXIS 884, 136 Wash. 2d. 1025, 969 P. 2d. 1065 (Wash. 1998).

Tarasoff v. Regents of University of California, 17 Cal.3d 425, 551 P.2d 334, 131 Cal. Rptr. 14 (1976).

Taylor v. Gilmartin, U.S. App. LEXIS 16963, 686 F.2d 1346 (10th Cir. 1982); *cert. den'd*. 103 S.Ct. 788 (1983).

Tilton v. Marshall, 925 S.W.2d 672 (1996).

Tribulak v. Minirth-Meier-Rice Clinic, No. 95-4008 (8th Cir., 1996) (unpublished).

Trear v. Sills, 82 Cal.Rptr.2d 281 (Cal. App. 4 Dist. 1999).

Tuma v. Board of Nursing, Ida. LEXIS 413, 100 Idaho 74, 593 P2d 711 (Ida. 1979).

Tuman v. Genesis Associates, 894 F. Supp. 183 (E.D. Pa., 1995).

Turner v. Department of Professional Regulation, State of Florida, Fla. App. LEXIS 101, 591 So.2d 1136 (Fla. App. 1992).

Underhill, E. (1915). *Practical mysticism*. New York: Dutton.

U.S. v. Brown, 95-1616 (8th Cir. 1995) (Unpublished).

U.S. v. Hartz, U.S. App. LEXIS 24036, (4th Cir. 1995) (Unpublished).

U.S. v. Meyers, 95 F. 3d 1475 (10th Cir. 1996).

U.S. v. Trammel, 445 U.S. 51 (1980).

Villoldo, A., & Krippner, S. (1987). *Healing states*. New York: Fireside.

Volpp, L. (1994). (Mis)Identifying culture: Asian women and the "cultural defense." *Harvard Women's Law Journal*, *17*, 57–101.

Voss, R. et al. (1999). Tribal and shamanic-based social work practice: A Lakota perspective. *Social Work*, *44*(3), 228–241.

Wah, C. (1998). "Evaluating a minor's capacity to select religious affiliation." *Journal of Family Law,* 12(4), 229–246.

Wah, C. (1999). "Religion and minors: evaluating potential benefits and potential harms." *American Journal of Family Law,* 13(2), 115–132.

Wall Street Journal, (2000, February 1). *Employee virtue rules can't be applied just to women, court says,* p. A1.

Wallis v. Young. U.S. App. LEXIS 21950, 193 F.3d 1054, (1999).

Walters v. Maricopa County, 990 P.2d 677 (Ariz.App.Div. 1 1999).

Washington Physicians Serv. Assn. v. Gregoire, (9th Cir. 1998).

Washington Physicians Serv. Assn. v. Gregoir, 967 F. Supp. 424 (W.D. Wash. 1997).

Wren, C. (2000, January 2). Coalition counters war on drugs. *Richmond Times-Dispatch,* p. A2.

Zakhartchenko v. Weinberger, N.Y. Misc. LEXIS 473, 159 Misc.2d 411, 605 N.Y.S.2d 205 (Sup. Ct. 1993).

Ziske v. Luskin, N.Y. Misc. LEXIS 2773, 524 N.Y.S.2d 145, 138 Misc.2d 38 (Sup. Ct. 1987).

INDEX

A

Alternative medicine, defined, xvi–xvii, 19
    defined by National Institute of Health, xvi
Analogies (legal)
    between counseling and medical
        practice, xv
    between early criminal cases, 11–13
    between midwives and counselors (see also
        licensure, 80–81
Assumption of the risk (See also Civil
    defenses), 71–72
Astrology
    cases, 11–13

B

Bio-psycho-social-spiritual model, ix, 100–109

C

Child abuse, 149–150
    good (bad) faith reporting, 129
    religious exemptions for, 151
    reporting statutes, 128–129
    Ritual abuse, statute, 151–152
Civil law, defined (see Glossary also), 6–7
Civil law actions 15, 47–48, 51
    conspiracy, 50–51
    constitutional claim, 48–62
    defamation (libel and slander), 55–61
    employment case on religious
        discrimination, 2–3, 7–8
    equal protection claim, 48–50
    intentional infliction of emotional distress,
        61–62
    scienter (in civil law), 51–52
Civil defenses
    Assumption of the risk, 71–72
    religious exemptions to child abuse and
        medical malpractice (See also child
        abuse), 31–33

statutes of limitations, 42–43, 72–74
    "Unsound mind" civil defense, 74
respondeat superior, 65–68, 123, 137,
    155–156, 176–178
standard of care, 53–54
vicarious liability, 65–68, 123, 137, 155–156,
    176–178
Coercion, 19–20
    and religious affiliation, 137
    case, 18–19, 137–139
Code of Federal Regulations,
Codes of ethics
    National Association of Social Workers,
        106, 113
Complementary counseling, defined, xvi
Confidentiality, 169
    and school counselors, 99–100, 121, 124–125
    and privileged communications, 125
Consciousness
    and cosmologies, 110–111
Consent, cases 19–20
    informed (see informed consent), 2–3
Conspiracy (See also Civil law actions),
Constitutional definitions 110–111
    religion, xv
Cosmologies (See also ethical ecologies and
        cosmologies), 103–110
    and consciousness, 110–111
Criminal law, defined (see Glossary also), 17
    early counseling cases, 11–13, 36–37
Criminal charges (See also criminal
        "defenses", 36–37
    Aggravated sexual assault, 20–22
    Child abuse (See also entry "child abuse",
        31–33
    Fraud, 22–24, 74, 92–94
    Peyote, marijuana and other hallucinogens,
        8, 29–31
    Practicing medicine without a license,
        27–28
    Ritual Mutilation, statute, 151